2023

Bob Steele on the Radio

The Life of Connecticut's Beloved Broadcaster

PAUL HENSLER

Paul Hensler
5/2021

McFarland & Company, Inc., Publishers

Jefferson, North Carolina

LIBRARY OF CONGRESS CATALOGUING-IN-PUBLICATION DATA

Library of Congress Cataloging-in-Publication Data
Names: Hensler, Paul, 1956– author.
Title: Bob Steele on the radio : the life of Connecticut's beloved broadcaster /
  Paul Hensler.
Description: Jefferson, North Carolina : McFarland & Company, Inc., Publishers,
  2019. | Includes bibliographical references and index.
Identifiers: LCCN 2019029380 | ISBN 9781476679327 (paperback : acid free
  paper) ∞ | ISBN 9781476637495 (ebook)
Subjects: LCSH: Steele, Bob, 1911–2002. | Radio broadcasters—United States—
  Connecticut—Biography. | WTIC (Radio station : Hartford, Conn.)
Classification: LCC PN1991.4.S74 H46 2019 | DDC 791.4402/8092 [B]—dc23
LC record available at https://lccn.loc.gov/2019029380

BRITISH LIBRARY CATALOGUING DATA ARE AVAILABLE

ISBN (print) 978-1-4766-7932-7
ISBN (ebook) 978-1-4766-3749-5

Front cover photograph of Bob Steele © 1944 from the Steele family collection

Printed in the United States of America

McFarland & Company, Inc., Publishers
  Box 611, Jefferson, North Carolina 28640
  www.mcfarlandpub.com

For Robert, Paul, Phil, and Steve

Acknowledgments

In the course of writing any work of appreciable length, most authors have to rely on additional people who are willing to assist them, be it in the form of resource material, their personal experiences or remembrances, or simply words of encouragement and inspiration. With this in mind, recognition is due for those who contributed to my journey in making the biography of Bob Steele a story worth telling.

A chance meeting I had with Donna Halper, radio historian and associate professor of communications at Lesley University in Cambridge, Massachusetts, enabled me to learn more about the early days of the radio medium, while David Kaplan of the WTIC Alumni Association provided a vital link to Phil Steele, the third son of Bob and Shirley Steele and whose curating of the ten-volume *Bob Steele's Century* was so integral to my work. Several past members of the WTIC team who had direct contact with Bob Steele were happy to share their recollections: Joyce Mainelli was a former typist for Steele, while Sue Leroux, radio continuity writer, and Bob Scherago, engineer, provided some deep background as to the happenings in the nearest offices adjoining the studio where Steele plied his craft.

Barbara Austen and Mel E. Smith at the Connecticut State Library in Hartford directed me to material regarding the modern development of the capital city. A few blocks away, at the Hartford Public Library's Hartford History Center (HHC), much heavy lifting took place. Executive director Brenda Miller was most receptive to my project and provided crucial assistance on the bureaucratic side of their fine institution, while Jasmin E. Agosto, education and community outreach manager, and Martha-Rea Nelson, senior library assistant, were kind in handling my various research appointments. My kudos also extend to a trio of Brenda's staff who labored through the trove of Bob Steele files to find most of the images used in these pages: Elizabeth Grudzinski, HHC volunteer; Catherine Torres, the library's graphic designer; and Jennifer Sharp, HHC archivist.

This book is my third such endeavor, but as it is also my first biography,

I recognized a looming difficulty as I was contemplating how the later narrative of Bob Steele's life should be told. Helping me to conquer this instance of writer's block was Willie Steele, professor of English at Lipscomb University in Nashville, Tennessee (and, curiously enough, no relation to Bob Steele's family). Willie's reminder that "life is not even" helped me to readjust my thought process and move apace through the last chapters. Thanks also to my editor at McFarland, David Alff, for rapidly and enthusiastically embracing this book.

Among the most important primary sources that an author can gain access to are the book's subject or his/her closest associates. In my case, I found with a fair degree of expediency the three living sons of Bob and Shirley Steele: Robert H. Steele, Paul Steele, and Phil Steele. Each of these gentlemen was forthcoming in their personal stories and recollections that added much texture to the book. The Steele brothers furnished some very insightful observations that offered both corrections to the narrative as well as details that only family members would know about their father and life with the Steele family. Coming into this project as an unknown quantity to them, I valued the trust that I earned from them and sincerely hope that the finished product here has justified the faith they expressed in me as I wrote my version of their father's amazing life.

Last but certainly not least, many thanks and lots of love to my wife, Donna, who, when she tells me she's proud of my accomplishments, makes it all worthwhile.

Table of Contents

Preface

In the course of his long life, Bob Steele was a pugilist, motorcyclist, cartoonist, raconteur, wordsmith, lover of automobiles, and family man, seemingly in perpetual motion from the time he awoke until he finally retired at the end of each day. But his best known occupation was that of radio announcer on WTIC AM, a fifty thousand–watt station based in Hartford, Connecticut, whose broadcasting signal could extend south to Virginia and north to the Canadian border, with the right conditions. Born in 1911, Steele's life ran nearly the full breadth of the twentieth century and afforded him the chance to witness—and report on—most of that era's seminal events: wars, depression, assassinations, the rise of the United States to the status of a global power, the birth of the age of television, and so many more.

He was hardly alone in his role as radio announcer when one reviews a short roster of other contemporaries whose skills and deeds earned them a place in the National Radio Hall of Fame: Lowell Thomas, Edward R. Murrow, Jack Buck, and Paul Harvey to name but a few. Whereas they formed audiences on a national level or in a more parochial sense within their own localized territory, Bob Steele belonged to greater southern New England and the listenership within range of his broadcast originating in a city that was also called the "Insurance Capital of the World." The relationship he forged with those who faithfully tuned their AM radios to 1080 on the dial endured for sixty-six years, and upon his passing in 2002 at the age of ninety-one, many listeners grieved as they would upon the death of a close friend.

But what was it that endeared Bob Steele to his audience for so many decades, enabled him to capture the country's top market share for his program, and earned him the same Hall of Fame honors garnered by Thomas, Murrow, Buck, and Harvey? Steele's unbending tenor—slightly bordering on guttural—had an inflection whose purpose was to inform the listener in an unbiased way, yet immediately beneath that straight-laced vocal façade was a deft ability to charm with an unexpected pun or the dry humor that colored his programs with a lightheartedness that assured his audience that he was

1

one of them, a working stiff who rose early to be on the air at 5:30 a.m. Monday through Saturday. "He was impressed by successful people and aspired to be like them," his son Phil reflected of his father years later, and succeed he did, despite the everyman demeanor with which he comported himself.

Without actually having listened to Bob Steele, those too young to remember him may be hard-pressed to fully grasp what he meant to his audience or enjoy the timbre of the voice that held their attention and listenership for more than sixty years. He was possessed of two salient traits that are crucial to better appreciating his manner of speaking. First was Steele's personality, a soothing combination of gregariousness and jocularity spiced with more than a touch of natural avuncularity, all of which put the listener at ease. Second was the voice itself, inflected with a richness that was imbued with purpose and confidence. Thanks to modern technology, Bob lives on through a variety of selections readily accessible on the internet via YouTube, and readers are invited to take an extra step to fully inform themselves with regard to the magnificent intonations of how Bob Steele spoke.

Soon after the passing of his father, Phil painstakingly produced a ten-volume anthology that chronicled the life and career of the man who was the unshakeable voice of WTIC. *Bob Steele's Century* contains an enormous trove of information and photographs culled from the diaries, newspaper articles, and personal effects that were curated by Phil as he assembled this multi-volume compilation, an awe-inspiring feat on his part. This vast collection was ultimately donated to the Hartford History Center, located at the Hartford Public Library.

Yet, only years after Phil's publication of this compendium did I realize that no traditional biography of Bob Steele existed. So, in borrowing a challenge issued by the great historian David McCullough—that is, write the book that you would like to read—I have written such a book, namely a companion volume—in narrative form, if you will—to Phil's opus.

Enhancing my experience of exploring and writing about the life of a man who helped listeners of WTIC greet the day on countless occasions was the opportunity to add the voices of some people who knew and worked with Steele, especially Phil and his brothers, Robert H. Steele, and Paul Steele, who provided their own insights and enthusiastically supported this endeavor. Nobody knew Bob Steele better than his immediate family, and the input from the Steeles was most valuable and greatly appreciated as I strove to tell the story as accurately as possible.

The following pages are intended to bring Steele's life to the reader with the same frankness that was ingrained in his radio program, all the while avoiding any tendency towards hagiography. Bob Steele and his legend speak well enough for themselves.

1

The Birth of a Legend

Like many of you, I was born on my birthday.
—Bob Steele

America in the year 1911 bore scant resemblance to the country we know today, and the events of the day remind us that the United States was in the process of continued growth while still finding its way toward a central point on the world stage. The appalling tragedy of the Triangle Shirtwaist Company fire occurred, the United States Supreme Court ordered the dismantling of energy behemoth Standard Oil, Arizona was denied statehood courtesy of a veto by President William Howard Taft, and the Panama Canal was still three years away from opening to sea traffic. This nation's forging ahead, even in fits and starts, nonetheless served as a precursor to the power it would eventually become after surviving two world wars and a devastating depression.

At one thirty-six in the morning of July 13 of that year came the birth in Kansas City, Missouri, of Robert Jesse Steele, the latest offspring in the Scotch-Irish heritage found on both his mother's and father's sides of the family. The known ancestry dates to the late 1700s and follows the well-worn path of European immigration to North America. His paternal great-great-grandfather, John Steel, and maternal great-great-grandfather—last name Hanna, first name unknown, but both of Scotch-Irish stock—resettled in Virginia and Pennsylvania, respectively. Over the ensuing years, large families bloomed on both sides of the family tree and were typical of the age: Jesse Steel, Sr., the paternal grandfather born in 1805, was one of thirteen or fourteen offspring, while the maternal grandfather, Robert C. Hanna, born in 1840, was one of nine siblings. Hanna's own marriage to Lucinda Long would produce six boys and six girls, including Martha Susan Hanna, who was better known by her middle name.

Jesse Steel, Jr.'s marital status has been questioned—there was certainly one marriage but possibly a second—yet his union with Amy Hessler produced in 1872 one Hampton Lee Steele, who wed Susan Hanna in 1910 in

Kansas City. The addition of the last "e" to the surname Steel may be attributed to the attempt of lower classes of Scotch-Irish immigrants to gain more equal footing with "the more respectable English," and in post–Civil War America, use of the extra "e" gained wider acceptance.[1]

Robert Jesse Steele was born to Hampton and Susan in 1911, but this would be their only progeny, their marriage ending in divorce—but amicably so—on November 8, 1916. Susan was awarded custody of young Bob, and the monthly alimony payments were set at thirty dollars. It can only be speculated as to the collapse of the marriage, but as a traveling salesman for the Columbian Hog and Cattle Powder Company based in Kansas City, Hampton spent much time away from home, thus likely contributing to an estrangement between the couple.[2] After the separation, Hampton visited his son on occasion, sometimes treating him to a trip to the movies. Years later, Bob's son, Phil Steele, admitted that even Bob himself may not have been aware of the divorce's specific circumstances or otherwise internalized them. Phil believes that Bob nonetheless held a certain regard for his father, while Robert Hampton Steele, Phil's brother, concurred by observing that when Bob relocated to California in the 1930s, Hampton visited on occasion and spent time with his son. Years later, Bob would fondly recall to family members some of those meetings with his father.[3]

As a very young child, Bob and his mother spent much time with one of his father's sisters—or half-sisters—Aunt Josephine of Rich Hill, Missouri. Evidence suggests some semblance of a relationship between father and son in the form of notes that Bob wrote to his father in November 1917: "I [received] your letter … it found me well and getting along fine—Are you well?" said the primitive cursive writing, along with an update stating, "I had my teeth filled this week."[4] In a second missive Bob informed "daddy" that he had been ill with "nettle rash and ingestion [sic]" but was now feeling better. The following year, a photograph was taken showing Bob and a friend posed riding a pony at Aunt Jo's farm, with Hampton securing the small steed.

Bob Steele at the tender age of three and a half (Hartford History Center, Hartford Public Library).

And a curiosity over his given middle name also occurred. A neighborhood bully named Jesse lent a bad connotation to young Bob, and he was successful in petitioning his parents to change his middle name to Lee, thereby matching that of his father. In his adult life, Bob Steele frequently joked about his full name being "Robert L. Steele ... the 'L' is for Elmo...," but very few knew of the genesis of the alteration from Jesse to Lee.

At this time, the aura of World War I cast a pall over the nation, and in the superheated patriotic atmosphere that enveloped the United States, young Bob Steele was also exposed to the fervor of the day. He developed a deep respect for love of country while at once abhorring armed conflict, and further grew to understand and appreciate the mission of the Boy Scouts of America, whose own contemporaneous demonstrations of patriotism were consistent with those of many civic organizations. As an adult, Steele never directly mentioned to his immediate family any prior involvement with the Boy Scouts, yet he was certainly a part of the organization in his youth, and many years after such an experience he regaled audiences with tales of his deeds with the scouts. His son Phil observed years later, "It may have been from scouting that Bob learned loyalty," a trait that Steele held quite dearly for the rest of his life.[5]

Barely over six years of age, Bob began not only to demonstrate his skill at cursive handwriting but also a nascent talent for drawing, with primitive sketches indicating his potential of becoming a bona fide cartoonist. His seventh birthday was special because his present was a red and black bicycle, which unfortunately was stolen shortly thereafter. Acquiring another bike, Steele soon got a job delivering pharmaceutical prescriptions while also learning how to pedal quickly in order to safely move through "a tough neighborhood."[6] The love of drawing, writing, and cycling would be etched into his soul and serve him well in his future pursuits.

Already engaged in the typical boyhood endeavor of home delivery of newspapers, in his case the *Kansas City Journal*, Steele became an avid reader and also developed an interest in boxing, one of the premier spectator sports of the day. Enduring an appendectomy operation in 1919—in later life he referred to the procedure as an "appen/dec/tummy"—Steele demonstrated precocious ability in the classroom and completed his elementary studies in June 1923, just short of his twelfth birthday, his best grades coming in spelling, writing, "industrial work, and physical training."[7] In the meantime as an aspiring musician, he took mandolin lessons for roughly one year and followed that with a stint at the piano. But two avocations—or rather, one vice and one hobby—entered his life.

Kansas City was a sporting outpost in the Midwest, and the municipality

hosted a pair of professional baseball teams: the Blues of the American Association, and the Monarchs of the Negro National League. Home games for
both clubs meant that Muehlebach Field was in use nearly every day of the
baseball season, and it was there that the young Steele found employment as
a hot dog vendor, and he claimed to have made eighteen dollars during a
doubleheader one day by "auctioning off the steaming pups."[8] Roaming the
stands in that capacity, he also discovered that some fans were unabashed
about making various wagers among themselves on all types of action taking
place on the field. Betting ranged from whether a batter would reach base,
hit a home run, or accomplish another feat in a particular time at bat or during the course of the game. "That's where I learned about gambling—selling
hot dogs and listening to all these fans," he confessed to his radio audience
many years later. "I never realized that they gambled so much."[9] Steele took
careful note of this activity and as an adult practiced it for both profit and
loss, in some cases for extremely large sums of money.

However, another more virtuous diversion drew his attention as well,
one that presaged the career path he would follow to the pinnacle of media
fame. While working toward his elementary school certificate at Bancroft
Grammar School, Steele completed building a crystal radio set, which enabled
him to listen to various stations now beginning to spring up across the country. In the wake of advances made by Guglielmo Marconi as he pioneered
the exploration of "wireless telegraphy" in the early twentieth century, the
medium of radio broadcasting was emerging as a burgeoning industry. Steele
was a bit too young to get in on the ground floor of employment with an
existing station, but the seed had been planted in his mind about his possible
entry into the field of broadcasting.

Sequestering himself in a closet at home so he could replicate a "broad-
cast-booth effect," Steele would read magazine advertisements aloud, "imi-
tating the deep, rich voices he heard over his crystal set."[10] Over the years he
paid close attention to the fastidious manner in which several early broadcasters comported themselves on the air: Milton Cross, the future radio host
of the Metropolitan Opera; Edwin C. Hill, a popular reporter and news commentator; and Boake Carter, who narrated newsreels produced by the Hearst-
Metrotone news service. Steele was greatly affected by their demeanor and
carried this influence with him for the rest of his life.

When Steele entered high school at the age of twelve, he was also bur-
dened with a need to help support his divorced mother with whom he resided.
"He never took anything for granted," noted his oldest son, Robert Hampton
Steele, who further explained that even as a youth, Bob was the type of person
who "took responsibility at an early age."[11] Odd jobs had become a stock-in-

trade that enabled him to garner extra income to supplement the money Susan earned as a clothes presser. These small jobs drew Steele away from his high school studies to such an extent that he alternated between six months of work and a like period of time in the classroom, a schedule that prolonged his stay in high school to six years before at last achieving credit for his diploma. This travail was not lost on him: in later life, he jokingly plumped his credentials by often referring to himself as "Bob Steele, H.S.G.," the initials standing for High School Graduate, yet the truth was that he was indeed proud of this academic accomplishment.

In the summer of 1925, and in the midst of Steele's self-imposed work-study regimen, Susan acceded to his plea to swap the piano for a motorcycle. This, too, became a life-changing event, for "it was the motorcycle, not the piano, that eventually led Bob to Hartford."[12] Obtaining a used bike—whether it was a Harley-Davidson or an Indian model remains in dispute—was a pivotal point for Steele, who rode it for profit to deliver both prescriptions and telegrams. His infatuation with motorcycles, however, nearly brought tragic consequences as a result of his careless operation and driving at excessive speeds, which resulted in a dozen or more accidents that sent him to the hospital. Steele soon developed a loyalty to the Indian motorcycle, manufactured in Springfield, Massachusetts, because he supported brands that were iconic yet not necessarily widely popular.

When he was not busy with his bike, Steele filled his time by reading national publications dealing with the motorcycle trade, and when he noticed that such magazines contained no information about his racing or related dealings in his hometown, he added another entry to his growing résumé when he assumed the role of reporter for *MotorCycling*, a Chicago-based trade magazine. Further smitten when he saw his name in print, Steele realized that "he could make money with words and wit, that he could earn a living by writing and entertaining."[13] The printing of his articles, in turn, led to his creation of scrapbooks into which were pasted his many contributions to the publication, and those pages were embellished with handwritten notes and marginalia that reveal the humor and command of the English language that Steele possessed.

Barely fifteen years of age, Steele was financially compensated for his submissions to *MotorCycling*, in addition to actively competing in motorcycle hill-climbing events such as those held in Tonganoxie, Kansas, just west of Kansas City. He filed his accounts referring to himself in the third person and gained a fair degree of notoriety as "the youngest motorcycle hill climber in the United States" for 21-cubic-inch-engine racers.[14] "Krazy Kracks from K. C. by Bob Steele" was a frequent byline to his column and served as a segue of sorts to his self-given nickname of "Krazy Cracker." Cartoon artwork, again in Steele's own hand, occasionally graced those same articles.

Diversifying a bit from two-wheeled sporting as well as his secretarial duties for the Kansas City chapter of the American Motorcycle Association, Steele in 1927 added pugilism to his list of activities, supposedly in an attempt to prove his masculinity and thereby impress a young lady—two years his senior—whom he was pursuing. Boxing as a 135-pound lightweight and later as a 147-pound welterweight, he compiled a mixed record that apparently did not win him the girl's hand. He was aptly described by a local Kansas City promoter as a piece of "fighting machinery with a punch in either fist and first class boxing ability when in shape, the best welter or lightweight fighter in K.C. When out of shape, the worst."[15] Steele's experience in the ring through 1928 nevertheless fueled his desire to become an announcer and helped him several years later when he called a phantom fight as part of his radio audition for WTIC.

What draws attention to Steele is the vast amount of writing he contributed to *MotorCycling*. And not only is the volume of words impressive; so, too, is the quality of the text put to the page. Years later, his son, Robert Hampton Steele, opined that the magazine's editors may not have realized how young their intrepid Kansas City reporter was. It is often said that writers put words to paper in two ways: for the

Boxing held a special appeal for Bob Steele throughout his life (Hartford History Center, Hartford Public Library).

eye, which is to say for the benefit of a readership, but also for the voice, meaning for the benefit of a listening audience. In Bob Steele's case, the distinction between these facets is nearly seamless. Some samples here—written by a sixteen-year-old boy—demonstrate not only his writing technique, cleverly infused with wit, but for those who recall the sound of his voice over the radio, the consistency of how he would carry those words into his process of speechifying them on the air.

> In looking over the morning paper I note a little article by Herbert Corey of New York, in which he says: "I've invented a solution for the traffic problem. Chase all the cars off the streets and replace them with motorcycles." He may have been trying to be funny, but just the same he came near speaking the truth. Say, wouldn't that increase the motor-cycle business slightly? The factories wouldn't have to look for dealers any more, and the dealers could quit worrying about prospects forever. Now, who'll volunteer to chase all the autos off the streets? Step right up, men.[16]

Lamenting the demise of a local motorcycle club, Steele penned this commentary in 1928:

> Well, well, have a bit of news, thanks to the Kansas City M[otorcycle] C[lub]. The K.C.M.C. members have decided to break up the club, divide the money in the treasury among the three big shops and start an Ex-Hen[derson Motorcycle] Club, Indian [Motorcycle] Club, and Harley Club. Boys, now I ask you if that isn't real club spirit? "Divided we stand, united we fall," is the official motto of this gang, I guess. Well, whether or not it's a good idea, the majority rules, so here's to a happy funeral for the K.C.M.C. Too bad, I think.[17]

Exhibiting a maturity beyond his years and employing his artistry and writing skills to his best ability, "The Krazy Cracker" embarked on an eastern road trip in early August 1928. Chronicled in a diary replete with photographs, the journey took him from his Kansas City home to the destination of Springfield, Massachusetts, where he spent several days at the Indian Motorcycle factory. Steele's travelogue offers the reader a glimpse of his lengthy trek, which he cheekily noted would be a three-thousand-mile round-trip beginning and ending at the local Barnsdall Filling Station.

His constant companion was his trusty Indian motorcycle, but he was not bashful about introducing himself to strangers along the way. Humor leaps off some pages of the diary, including a photo of his bike parked as it straddled the Illinois-Indiana state line, and a comment about his room's dual sleeping accommodations in London, Ohio: "In order to get my dollar's worth, I slept in both beds."[18] He was fascinated by "a cañon of downtown office buildings in Indianapolis" and escaped disaster just a few miles into the Buckeye State when the motorcycle's front tire blew out "and down went Robert Steele of Kansas City, to the hard pavement of U.S. Hwy 40." Reaching

Jennerstown, Pennsylvania, he ate breakfast with a family who asked that he join them, which he did despite having already eaten his first meal of the day. "Never turned down a FREE meal in my life," he told his diary, and at Grand View Summit in the Allegheny Mountains he availed himself of "the free telescope [to look at] three states and seven counties, the states being Maryland, Delaware, and Pennsylvania, of course."

Making his way east across the Keystone State then through the capital at Harrisburg and "the chocolate town" of Hershey, he landed in Trexlertown, where he violated Prohibition by tossing back "a couple of glasses of real German beer." Crossing the Delaware River, he stopped in Paterson, New Jersey, to meet Orie Steele—no relation to Bob—who was a top-notch motorcycle hill climber. Remittance of a twenty-cent toll allowed him ferry passage to "the world's largest city, New York," where an unnamed female acquaintance provided an outsized lunch. Traveling the Boston Post Road to New Haven, Connecticut, he turned north to Hartford for the final leg of the trip and reached Springfield on August 17, nine days after departing Kansas City.

Delighting in the treatment he received at the Indian facility, Steele reveled when he "was given a factory pass, which I used when looking into the thousand wonders of the big wigwam." His enthusiasm deepened when he made friends with an Indian employee named Norman Turner, who also showed Steele some of the other sights in the greater "Springtown" area. At the conclusion of his stay on August 24, he made a less leisurely beeline back home—"I was stoppin' for nothin'," says the diary—and arrived in Kansas City at dusk on the 28th. "Home again!" he proclaimed on the top of the diary's last page, but a telling comment he scrawled in red pencil immediately below provided the continuation of the story: "Only to embark for California in 1930."

Settling in back home and continuing his "Krazy Kracks" motorcycle reportage, Steele met up briefly with his father in September, although no record exists other than a handshake photograph as to what transpired between them. Steele resumed his boxing endeavors, scoring several wins by knockout in early 1929. "Just a 1–2–3 story from start to finish[,] which is not unlike many of Bob's other fight cases," he proudly wrote of himself in the third person, his scrapbook of newspaper clippings featuring his deeds in the ring along with the marginalia of his cartoon of a boxer with gloved hands captioned, "Two fists—capable of taking care of their owner."[19] This bit of bravado punctuated what appears to be a score-settling of sorts with boxer Floyd "Red" Hall, whom Steele labeled as "cocky" because Hall apparently had tagged Steele with the pejoratively effete nickname of "Roberta." Steele's career total shows seventy bouts, eighteen fought as a professional.[20]

As if biking, journalism, and boxing failed to provide enough activity,

Steele's graduation from Kansas City's Westport High School in June 1929 thankfully provided a definitive achievement for him one month prior to his eighteenth birthday. He and his mother took the decision to open a sandwich shop that year. The R-E Sandwich Shop, at 605 East Linwood Boulevard in Kansas City, enticed customers with "man-sized sandwiches of all kinds, double-deckers, and that good coffee," all of which were served in a "12-chair sandwich emporium" financed in part by Steele's boxing winnings as well as a loan.[21] The timing of establishing this enterprise could not have been worse, however. As the Great Depression quickly commenced to cast its ugly shadow across the American landscape, few business ventures escaped the pernicious effect of a national economy now gone south. Generating adequate revenue to at least pay back the loan, mother and son closed the shop with some stains of red ink on the family ledger.

The dual tracks of Bob Steele's life, amateur boxing and motorcycling, persisted through the end of his years as a teenager. His scrapbook evinces the newspaper clippings that told of the number of bouts he fought—including many victories—together with the "Krazy Kracks" that were a mainstay of *MotorCycling*. In one instance, the two sports were conflated in the same column, wherein he reported on several "boxing exhibitions"—one featuring Bob "Knocked-out-in-the-second-round" Steele—in addition to a motorcycle endurance race.[22] As 1930 progressed, he encountered difficulty in the ring against the aptly nicknamed "Battling" Schulz, yet Steele still exuded confidence after besting "three topnotch boys" in an attempt to keep his fighting flame aglow.

Steele was nothing if not indefatigable, but the reality of his chances of advancing in the ring by defeating more skilled opponents sunk in at last, this despite a skein of ten consecutive victories heading into October 1930. Paired off against a Native American from Oklahoma named Chief Adams, Steele later recalled his fight with this foe who "had been banged around by every bum in the Midwest and couldn't bruise an over-ripe eggplant with his Sunday punch."[23] When Steele lost to Adams, the writing on the wall was clearly evident, and he left the ring, ostensibly for good. In an age when masculinity meant everything and traumatic brain injuries were an unknown entity, it is instructive that Steele counseled wisdom and quit before any physical damage could manifest itself. No longer an active boxer, he retained a fervid interest in prizefighting—as an avid spectator, ring announcer, and host at boxing-related social events—for years to come.

Bob Steele as a young man still in his teens impressed as being a product of the era. It can be easy to draw a connection between him and the Roaring Twenties: his endless ambition was emblematic of a period in American history punctuated by a spirit laden with optimism and insouciance. At the conclusion of hostilities in World War I, technological advances in communication and transportation continued to manifest themselves in the radio and automobile industries, while leisurely pursuits such as cinemas—with their talking movies—and spectator sports such as baseball—now in thrall with the current sensation in the person of Babe Ruth—conveyed a feeling that one was deriving a reward from the seeming prosperity enjoyed by so many people. Progressives scored a victory in August 1920 when women were granted the franchise upon ratification of the Nineteenth Amendment to the United States Constitution, and the only apparent blight on the good times was the earlier passage of the Volstead Act, which ushered in Prohibition.

Upon his inauguration in March 1929, President Herbert Hoover exuded the confidence that permeated nearly every corner of the country when he declared "the future is bright with hope."[24] By late 1929, at a time when Steele was hitting his stride—and his opponents squarely—in the boxing ring, the optimism fueling much of the decade came to a turbulent end at the onset of the Great Depression.

It is necessary to preface the vicissitudes of what was to follow shortly thereafter by noting that although the stock market crash of October 29 "pulled down a cloak of gloom over Wall Street," the immediate impact on the average American was slight because there were relatively few people who had investments there.[25] Indeed, conditions did deteriorate, but this was not a calamity that immediately impacted the entire nation. Bob Steele's viewpoint substantiated this status in one of his *MotorCycling* essays from late 1930:

> If you'll stand for it, I'll open this column with a word about the current "depression." Although this may have become a tiresome subject by this time, nevertheless, it is still true that people in every line of business in every section of the country are interested to know what conditions are in other sections. I found this true while on a recent trip to Milwaukee. When I told a St. Louisan I had come from Kansas City he wanted to know right away if business in Kaysee was "as bad as business in St. Louis." In Chicago I was asked if the slump had hit St. Louis as bad as it had hit Chicago. In Milwaukee they wondered if Chicago could be as bad off as Milwaukee, and so on. So I'm going to say that while Kansas City is enjoying no boom it is holding up in fine shape, everything considered. The motorcycle business in particular is hitting along at a good clip despite the season.[26]

Yet, as time elapsed in 1930, the "good clip" had also run its course in Steele's hometown. By year's end, he would join the vanguard of migrants seeking relief from the increasingly detrimental and prevalent economic woes of the Great Depression. There would be no easy escape from the hard times to come, but the stars were slowly aligning themselves to deliver Steele to the arena in which he would serve for great profit.

2

Go West, Young Man

The year 1932 will go down in history. At least I hope so. I mean, how are we going to explain the gap between 1931 and 1933 to our grandchildren if it doesn't?
—Bob Steele

As the grip of the Great Depression took increasingly firmer hold, employment opportunities dwindled and forced the migration of vast numbers of people to different parts of the country in search of employment. Bob Steele was subjected to these same economic forces, although in his case, the experience he had gained to that point in his youthful life was a bit different than that of farmers, field hands, or factory workers.

At a time when the Dust Bowl was commencing to ruin the fortunes of many Midwesterners in the early 1930s, thereby prompting their movement further west to seek a better life, Steele also sought what his eldest son later called "broader prospects." The state of California provided a lure to attract the downtrodden and the oppressed, a chance to start life anew in an ostensibly more employment-friendly climate despite instances of labor unrest that plagued farm workers in their attempts to unionize. In Steele's case, the Golden State offered a "new horizon and an exciting change of pace" that was possessed by a very active motorcycling environment that held out a greater contemporaneous hope than what he was about to leave behind in Kansas City.[1]

In December 1930, Bob Steele made his way to Southern California, and little time passed before he paid a call on the Indian motorcycle shop in Los Angeles, which became one of his haunts during his stay on the West Coast. Virtually penniless, he found employment as a messenger for the Security-First National Bank of Los Angeles, using his trusty Indian to deliver correspondence for the financial institution.

Steele's mother followed him to Los Angeles in March 1931, and Susan enjoyed the area so much that she would live there for the rest of her life.

Settling in a predominantly Mexican-American section of the city but occasionally traveling east years later to visit Bob and his own family, she had friendly neighbors, was "respected and self-sufficient" but was also supported by money that Bob sent to her.[2] In the summer of that year came another turning point that would dramatically affect her son's future. Still infected with cycling derring-do, Steele in August set a personal speed record by reaching 122.6 miles per hour on a stretch of road in Culver City, but his luck ran out shortly thereafter when he was victimized by another biking accident. His own mishap served as a precursor of sorts to the passing of Walter Pearson, another motorcyclist from Kansas City who, in early 1932, "slipped into eternity as he always wanted to go—on a two-wheeler."[3]

Undaunted by Pearson's demise, Steele soldiered on with his own participation in hill climbing events in California, and he had found employment at a Harley Davidson motorcycle shop, which may have been a jolt to his loyalty to the Indian brand but nevertheless furnished a much-needed job. Still actively racing in May—much to the chagrin of his mother—but forced temporarily to the sidelines with an injury, Steele was prevented from competing in a race in Santa Maria. When the track's public address announcer fell ill and failed to show up to discharge his duties, Steele, with alacrity, made the best of the opportunity as the substitute behind the microphone. Excelling in unexpected fashion, Steele found favor with the spectators gathered for the race, and he drew the notice of a correspondent for the trade publication *National Speedway Weekly*:

> Bob Steele on the microphone end of a Standard Oil public address system entertained the crowd with his constant prattle about the riders and what to expect next. By the time Bob had eaten a barrel of sand and countless Eskimo Pies the crowd expected most anything from him. "Happy" Weams, the Standard Oil custodian of the P.A. system, is no mean announcer himself and he interspersed Bob's wit with a little oil which sometimes was standard and sometimes quite original.[4]

This auspicious debut quickly found favor with fans, sponsors, and racing officials alike. From a small tower at Hollywood's Gilmore Stadium, Steele announced races for radio stations KHJ and KGFJ in Los Angeles, and his work drew praise from another trade magazine, *Coast Auto Racing*, which noted that "the popular announcer ... sure knows his motorcycles ... [and] consequently has firsthand information on the motors and also the riders."[5] Small-scale race events were not the only ones he handled: he was selected for the announcing duties at the Los Angeles Coliseum where the national short-track motorcycle race championships were to be staged in early July.

Notwithstanding the detour Steele's motorcycling route had taken into the realm of announcing, this did not preclude other employment to which he could apply his riding ability. Hired by Warner Bros. Studio, he and several other cyclists, including racing champions Jack Milne and Ed Kretz, performed as stuntmen. Steele himself was a double for a thirty-two-year-old Spencer Tracy in the movie *Disorderly Conduct*, a task he found rewarding—$15 per day plus $3.75 in overtime pay when filming stretched beyond 4 p.m.—but the work could be tedious due to Tracy's frequent late arrivals to the set as well as the monotony of repeated takes of the same scene. Three years later, Steele was again briefly on camera in the George Raft movie *She Couldn't Take It*.

Yet the writing and reporting chores Steele had taken on prior to his westward move hardly disappeared from his array of vocations. In June 1932 he became a staff correspondent for *Southern California Sports* and furnished accounts of various short-track motorcycle races, notably those held in Pasadena at White Sox Ball Park, a facility constructed in 1924 and used by a variety of amateur and professional baseball teams, including several Negro League clubs, but had been converted for racing purposes. Steele also began issuing a new monthly journal, *Crocker Throttle Krax*, published courtesy of the Indian Motorcycle Sales Company of Los Angeles, while at the same time working as a salesman for Al Crocker, a local bike dealer.

Steele added another option to his preferred mode of transportation in late 1932 by purchasing an Auburn convertible sedan, and in March of the following year—after sustaining an injury in a Hollywood motorcycle hill climb—he continued his budding love of the automobile. This pastime involved what would in more modern times be referred to as "flipping," a process in which Steele purchased a car in need of modest or otherwise cosmetic maintenance, performed some minor work to restore its beauty, and then quickly sold the auto at a slight profit.

Even such small financial gains in this era were crucial to economic sustainability, and Steele's ambition was manifest in this latest venture that served as an ancillary source of income. Posed astride the running board of a 1931 Auburn Brougham, he noted that he "made $ on this car," apparently after selling the vehicle for some gain.[6] Besides Auburn models, Steele also came into ownership of a Buick Roadmaster and an Austin model, among others. In later adult life this car-flipping penchant would become part of his lifestyle, occasionally putting a tremendous strain on his financial obligations but nonetheless providing one more diversion to occupy his time. Unfortunately, a far more menacing activity drew his attention and inflicted a heavier toll on his personal finances, in some instances when he could least afford it.

"I have lost all," is an ill-boding remark accompanying a mid–1933 picture of Steele taken in Los Angeles.[7] Nattily attired in a dark three-piece suit and topped with a traditional Panama hat, he seemed very much at ease in his scrapbook montage, but a diary entry he affixed to the same page tells a very different and deeply troubling story.

> Am on vacation—one week—Oct. 4 to 11 … have only gambled. At this time I have lost $350 since August 15 last and call this a major incident in my life. I have lost all I could get a hold of. Have given mother $105 in that time and have $85 coming from [former friend and motorcycle dealer Floyd] Clymer that I will give her. I am flat broke. Would have had 500 in bank by close saving by now—after having started with nothing in May 1932 with Crocker. Build up gradually, then tear down suddenly. Gambling did it. I now start anew.

Although Steele appeared to have given up boxing after the loss to Chief Adams back in Kansas City, circumstances forced his return to the ring in an effort to bolster his bleak monetary outlook. He fought at least three bouts in a heavier 175-pound weight class, winning two and losing one, but no other records are evident to indicate any participation beyond these matches. Yet as the calendar turned to 1934, an upturn in the sport of motorcycle racing ran counter to the veil of the Depression's despair. As Steele reported in May of that year,

> Twenty race tracks in the East and South plan to open within a month. Four promoters leave for Chicago where they will open one of the country's largest plants for motorcycle racing exclusively. San Diego will open sometime in May. MotoSpeedway [in Long Beach] started Tuesday night, April 24, with 7,000 people in the stands. The practice night a week previous, drew 8,000. Oakland opened April 24, and the aisles weren't big enough to hold the surplus. Earl Gilmore, the gasoline man, will open a stadium … that will seat 18,000 fans…. The National Championship motorcycle events are to be held July 1, 2 and 3, *in the Coliseum*. They will sell 60,000 seats if they sell one.[8]

In addition to his own racing exploits, Bob Steele was still in command of the trackside microphone, announcing motorcycle and midget car races and furnishing entertainment with his commentary at Gilmore Stadium in Beverly Hills. According to a note he received from the Fresno Speedway Association, Steele was offered eighteen dollars to call the action at a June 28 race. However, as if money was not enough of a bugbear for Steele, he had to pay one dollar for official American Motorcycle Association membership prior to a match race against Merrill "Andy" Anderson, plus another dollar to borrow a bike to compete in that race. Anderson worked as a starter at many of the tracks where Steele announced the races, and the competition between the two created a rivalry that bordered on feud.

Coast Auto Racing engaged Steele for a column appropriately titled "The Way It Looks From the Microphone." His tenure with the publication carried into 1935, during which time his writing, announcing, and automobile transactions went on unabated. Meanwhile, on May 2, Bob's father, Hampton Steele, passed away and was buried in Springfield, Utah. However, few details shed any appreciable light on the circumstances surrounding his death or his dealings in that state.

By 1936, "Krazy Kracks" and "Throttle Krax" were joined by "Poppings of the Day," authored by the same Bob Steele who now possessed the *nom de plume*, Professor Popper. In one of his February articles, he observed that men were not the only participants in the testosterone-fueled milieu of motorcycling. "I used to open up a column with: 'Well, boys...' or "Say, men...' or something like that. But nowadays, with so many skirts ... pardon me ... with so many girls riding motorcycles (as the pictures in The MOTORCYCLIST, Harley Enthusiast and Indian News of late will testify) I must take off my crush [*sic*] helmet and say: 'Ladies and gentlemen, how do you do?'"[9]

Prior to Steele's infatuation with motorcycles, trailblazing women had in fact accomplished some astounding feats, including a two-month cross-country journey on Indian bikes from Brooklyn to Los Angeles in 1916 by sisters Augusta and Adeline Van Buren. Descendants of the eighth president of the United States, the pair also became the first women to ascend Pikes Peak in Colorado. Perhaps as a sign that women's equality did not end with passage of the 19th amendment to the United States Constitution in 1920, women were further inspired by Dorothy "Dot" Robinson, an Australian-born cyclist who later assumed the title of "First Lady of Motorcycling" in the United States. An accomplished endurance racer even before she became a bride in 1931, Dot and her husband, Earl, embarked in 1935 on a sidecar-equipped motorcycle from Los Angeles to New York, remarkably completing the passage in just under ninety hours.[10] Although no record exists to indicate that Steele had any connection to the Robinsons' accomplishment, it is unlikely that such a feat would have escaped his notice. Thus, his acknowledgment in February 1936 of the presence of women in the world of motorcycling should come as no surprise.

Also early that year, Bob Steele had been working for the Works Progress Administration, a Depression-era initiative of the administration of President Franklin Roosevelt to put able-bodied men to work. Steele's position was that of timekeeper at a bean farm in California, a job that indicates how he made himself available for any work that he could find. He had also become friends with another motorcyclist, George Lannom, who decided to retire from active racing and segued into the role of race promoter. Now based in Newark, New Jersey, Lannom was also of the belief that the potential existed to spread the popularity of motorcycle competition events beyond the western United States, and to support this endeavor he scouted an assortment of venues as prospective race sites. He discovered one in Albany, New York, but another was located in the south end of Hartford, Connecticut, specifically Morgan G. Bulkeley Stadium.

A local jewelry merchant, Bill Savitt, and his brother Max were co-owners of the facility in Hartford, which served as home of various minor league baseball teams in the Eastern League. With a cinder track running around the bounds of the baseball diamond, the site appeared well-suited for motorcycle races, and after contracting with the Savitts to use the stadium for that purpose, Lannom quickly contacted Steele to request that he join him in Hartford. Steele's assignments would be to work as a track announcer and serve in promotional and public relations capacities. With his brief stint on the bean farm now concluded, Steele was still engaged in some radio work in Southern California, but some coaxing by Lannom in a letter of April 13, 1936, seems to have convinced Steele to join him.

With guarded optimism, Lannom spelled out some contentious issues he encountered while attempting to secure usage of a baseball park in Albany, but the impresario dangled some financial incentives in front of Steele to lure his friend east. "I had figured on letting you manage that track at say $25 per week. You would also do announcing there for an additional ten. Hartford needs an announcer and that is another ten…. If the thing goes over well in Albany you would come in for ten percent of the net profit. That doesn't sound so high but it is possible to make $2000.00 there a night if we fill the place."[11] Lannom added a caveat, noting that "there is some chance connected … *in how much money you will really make* [but] I think … that it is a very good gamble for you."[12] This became a risk that would eventually pay off for Bob Steele.

On April 28, Lannom wrote from his quarters at the Highland Court Hotel on Albany Avenue in Hartford to acknowledge Steele's acceptance. He informed Steele of the anticipated racing debut scheduled in Hartford on May 19, 1936, thereby prompting Steele to disembark in earnest from California. The Great Depression still gripped the country, and possessing but two dimes to his name, Robert Steele was delivered to Connecticut courtesy of yet another racer, Clifford Hills, who used a car rather than a motorcycle to travel east. Nine days before Lannom was to put his new charge to work in Hartford, Steele arrived in a city through which he had passed on his journey from Kansas City to Springfield back in 1928.

Now two months short of his twenty-fifth birthday, Steele was not likely to know what his length of stay in Hartford would be, nor how much of a financial benefit he would garner from Lannom's enticement. But the peripatetic, ambitious Steele was moving on to the next phase of his life, come what may, and the environs he was about to enter on the East Coast could not be any worse than the one he was leaving behind.

3

Go East, Young Man … and Meet Astrid

It must be understood by the applicant that the approval of an application does not carry with it the promise of a permanent position with this Company.
—Disclaimer on "Application for Employment at The Travelers"

In the wee hours of the cold morning of May 10, 1936, an automobile driven by Clifford "Slippery" Hills arrived in Hartford, Connecticut, stopping near Union Station. Hills's passenger stepped out of the vehicle and espied the Corning Fountain in Bushnell Park, bathed in moonlight. Bob Steele, whose pockets contained only "two thin dimes," suddenly found that he was "all by myself and I was a little bit apprehensive. I thought maybe [the fountain's decorative Indians] were gonna come after me. They had the tomahawks raised. That was the welcome I got in Hartford."[1]

Toting his "two busted-up suitcases," Steele discovered just as quickly that his twenty cents would not be able to buy him a room for the night because the tariff at the local YMCA was unaffordable at one dollar. Finding lodging in the upper reaches of the neighboring Garde Hotel, Steele finagled to delay remittance to the front desk until after he had gotten a good night's sleep, at which time George Lannom joined him and handed Steele a five-dollar bill to pay for his room and breakfast.

Such an introduction to a strange place is likely to have been a matter of routine for many who traveled during the Depression as they sought to improve their lot in life. The city of Hartford with its salient insurance industry offered a shelter of sorts against the storm of the hard economic times. "The stability of Hartford insurance companies has redounded to the benefit of their employees during nation-wide crises," opined several city historians. "The firms managed to survive the Great Depression … and two world wars

19

with a minimum of dislocation. In 1933 the impact of the bank moratorium was cushioned when the life companies became the sole source for cash payments. Most of their people were kept employed. Aetna Life, for example, laid off nobody during the Depression. Salaries were reduced only once, when the cost of living fell to such a degree that the cut was balanced by the increase in purchasing power."[2] Indeed, in 1931 Aetna had opened its massive 669-foot-long building on Farmington Avenue, bearing testimony to its confidence in its ability to carry on despite the worsening Depression.

Bob Steele came to Hartford to fulfill a very different mission unrelated to the insurance business, yet his venture with Lannom was soon to gain favorable traction. In addition to assigning Steele race announcing duties, Lannom had him put his writing talents to work by producing a series of short biographies of various motorcycle racers who were participating in the events he was staging at Hartford's Bulkeley Stadium. Informing fans with his usual entertaining flair for combining facts and wit, and doing so with the most current information available, Steele contributed to the five-cent racing magazines sold at the track, and the sketches he penned of the various race participants indicated the closeness of interaction many of them had in the world of motorcycle racing. For example, those seeing races at Bulkeley Stadium were apprised that Stanley Lipsky's "return match with Joe Sypek, who defeated him two weeks ago, should provide lots of action tonight," while Gordon Schautz "is with us tonight and is bound to be a star whether he wins all his races or loses them all."[3]

As was also a common practice in this age, major league baseball teams played exhibition games against local squads. Hartford jeweler Bill Savitt, who along with his brother Max owned Bulkeley Stadium, sponsored his own ball club, the Savitt Gems. In late July 1936 as the St. Louis Cardinals traveled from Boston to Brooklyn, they stopped in Hartford for an afternoon contest against the Gems, and Savitt used the occasion to present watches to several members of the famed "Gashouse Gang," Frank Frisch, Dizzy Dean, and Leo Durocher, who had cut his professional teeth as a member of the Hartford Senators in 1925. Dean was also an aspiring announcer and went to the press box to call a few innings' worth of action, but "[h]e talked so fast and so much that Bob Steele[,] regular announcer[,] could not get a word in edgewise."[4]

The 1936 motorcycle racing schedule in Hartford began to wind down as Labor Day approached, but Steele had already been hopeful of seeking a more permanent position to ply his trade. In early July, the studio manager of radio station WDRC informed him that a local advertiser was initiating a program to review news of the week and was interested in having Steele serve as the announcer. His audition did not find favor, however, and as the summer ebbed, it appeared that Steele's prospects of remaining in Hartford were on the wane. As the month of September drew to a close, he was about to leave for the West Coast in an effort to pick up where he had left off prior to his departure from Southern California just a few a months earlier.

Seeking to stave off boredom on the afternoon of September 30 as he waited in downtown Hartford for his ride, possibly from Hills, Steele learned from the box-office attendant at the old Princess Theater on State Street that the next showing of a mystery film in progress would not start for another twenty-five minutes. He followed the attendant's advice and elected not to enter immediately and catch the end of the movie, which would have spoiled the surprise ending of the film. With a little more time to kill, however, Steele wandered across the lawn of the Old State House and impulsively entered the Central Row building that comprised part of the Travelers Insurance Company's campus.

Asking to be taken to the studio of radio station WTIC—whose call letters were taken from the company name—on the sixth floor of the adjoining Grove Street building, Steele upon arrival met with the station's chief announcer, Fred Wade. With nothing to lose except for the few minutes to spare before the movie's next screening, Steele inquired as to any job openings, and Wade replied, "We just auditioned about thirteen guys an hour ago. We'll give you a shot if you want to go in."[5] Go in, indeed, he did, setting in rapid motion events that put him on the air the very next day.

A decade beyond the turn of the twentieth century, the industry of the radio broadcast business barely had a pulse. Although Guglielmo Marconi initiated wireless telegraphy in 1901, this method of information conveyance was employed "almost exclusively for ship-to-ship and ship-to-shore communication, ending the perilous isolation of large vessels at sea."[6] The most dramatic moment in the nascent stage of such usage occurred in April 1912 when the ocean liner *Titanic* became imperiled in the North Atlantic Ocean. A young New York City–based radio operator working for Marconi at the time, David Sarnoff, was actively involved with radio transmissions related to rescue operations, and just three years later at the age of twenty-four, Sarnoff implored an executive with Marconi's company to consider using the new medium as a means to transmit music into private homes for entertainment purposes. "I have in mind a plan of development which would make radio a 'household utility' in the same sense as the piano or phonograph," Sarnoff envisioned. "The idea is to bring music into the home by wireless."[7]

In reality, years would pass before Sarnoff's theory took form and rooted itself in American households for the benefit of the average person. When

General Electric aligned with the Radio Corporation of America in 1919, Sarnoff had maneuvered into a position of power at RCA, this coming at a time when the growing mass production of affordable radio sets for the home combined with the increasing number of broadcasting stations that continued to sprout up across the country. This symbiosis had by the early 1920s served to make interest in radio more than the passing fad it was perceived to be.

As Sarnoff forged ahead with his plans and began to turn RCA into a communications titan based just beyond the border of southwestern Connecticut, outlets in the Nutmeg State commenced their own gradual entry into the world of broadcasting.[8] The first station on air is acknowledged to be WCJ, a subsidiary of the A. C. Gilbert toy company, well known for the production of the Erector Set and, in the late 1930s, American Flyer toy trains. WCJ endured a rocky fourteen-month existence and went off the air by December 1922. In the meantime, another station, WQB in Hartford, started to broadcast without officially obtaining a license from the Interstate Commerce Commission, there being no Federal Communication Commission until 1934.

In May 1922, WDAK in Hartford went on the air as an adjunct of the *Hartford Courant*, the capital city's morning newspaper. However, the generation of revenue via commercial advertising was not allowed during the early years of broadcasting; therefore, many stations were challenged to pay their expenses unless they were connected with a large business entity that was able to absorb such overhead. Some outlets cleverly traded for music records or equipment by mentioning on the air that those goods were furnished by a particular local merchant. In the case of KDKA in Pittsburgh, announcers would intone that their broadcasts sounded better on a receiver made by Westinghouse, that entity, of course, being the parent company of the station.

But in many instances "community goodwill" was the only net gain for the station rather than necessary income. After generating a loyal listening audience, WDAK nonetheless became a financial burden to the *Courant*, and in the summer of 1924 it fell by the wayside and ceased operations. Other small stations in the area soldiered on, yet there was no single broadcaster that was on the air in a high-powered capacity. That situation changed in early February 1925 when the Travelers Insurance Company launched WTIC, which grew into a fifty thousand–watt powerhouse four years later.

Along with other technologies such as automobile transportation and electricity making their way into the modern world of the twentieth century, wireless communication was finding an increasing presence in industrialized society. Radio technology was part of this phenomenon, and a new station in Hartford came to life at 7:45 p.m. on February 10, 1925. Employing the power of a 500-watt Western Electric transmitter and a pair of 150-foot towers mounted atop the Grove Street building of the Travelers Insurance Company, WTIC commenced its programming with inaugural remarks by company vice-president Walter Cowles.

Speaking on behalf of the company, Cowles told his listeners, "This service has been installed purely and simply as a new means of publicity. It is a method by which we are able to come into close personal relationship with the public.... The hope and constant aim of this station will be to earn the goodwill, friendship and confidence of those who hear us."[9] The station's maiden voyage featured musical selections by male and female singers as well as piano accompaniment, and the evening's program lasted less than three hours.

Pre-recorded music at this time was of such inferior quality that it was more practical to broadcast live performances, and WTIC hired a variety of musicians to furnish various entertainments, including vocal and piano recitals, dance bands, and concerts by the Travelers Symphonic Ensemble, a group formed in 1926. By 1929, the station had installed on Talcott Mountain a fifty thousand–watt transmitter purchased from the Radio Corporation of America, thus establishing the high-powered mechanism to extend its signal up to hundreds of miles under certain atmospheric conditions.[10]

Administratively, this year was notable for WTIC's hiring of two key personnel: Paul Morency as the station's first president, and Leonard Patricelli, a scriptwriter who later became program manager and held several executive positions when television programming entered WTIC's endeavors. It was Morency who in the short life of the station "was acutely aware that WTIC had already developed its own personality [and] had become more than just a publicity vehicle for Travelers."[11] This level of perspicacity worked symbiotically when Bob Steele came aboard, although it would take time for their relationship to flourish.

By the autumn of 1931, WTIC had added self-produced dramas to its programming in an effort to compete with other popular radio shows of the era, such as *The Lone Ranger*. Three years later, the duties for a "carefully scripted" morning program called *The Musical Clock* were assumed by Ben Hawthorne, who became the first radio personality to ad lib parts of his show rather than rely solely on formulated material.[12]

Although news, weather, and sports were standard features that found space on the air waves, such information was sourced from the two local newspapers, the *Hartford Courant* and the *Hartford Times*. Not until the catastrophic flood of March 1936, which crested at a record thirty-seven and one-half feet in Hartford and inflicted $35 million in property damage, did WTIC begin to devise a methodology for "accurate, responsible and community-oriented reporting" when "WTIC became the focal point for disaster information [because it was] the only station able to remain in constant operation."[13]

When Bob Steele arrived in Hartford barely two months after the deluge—and with but twenty cents to his name—he was thinking only of his business dealings with George Lannom and the short motorcycle racing season in the next few months, with little consideration for what may lie beyond.

Although the order of events is lost to time, what did occur when Bob Steele stopped by the studios of WTIC that fateful afternoon was his completion of a two-page application for employment at "The Travelers" as well as his audition. On the application he informed his prospective employer of his parents' ethnicity as well as his status as a single man—who had graduated from high school—who was now boarding with a Mr. Morehouse at 12 Marshall Street in Hartford. Of current job relevance, he listed George Lannom as his most recent employer, his duties being an "announcer and publicity writer" whose reason for leaving this most recent position was because "business season [was] over."[14] Nowhere on the form do the words "motorcycle" or "motorcycling" appear, yet their markings were in abundant evidence: Lannom was the racing promoter; the "business season" was the just-concluded racing schedule; Steele's second most recent employment was with motorcycle dealer Al Crocker, whose business closed and prompted Steele to come east; besides listing Bill Savitt as a personal reference, two of the other three names given for such

Bob Steele shortly after beginning his tenure at WTIC in 1936 (Hartford History Center, Hartford Public Library).

purpose—Fred Marsh and Floyd Clymer—were racers; and the final entry for additional information shows Atlantic Boulevard Speedway in Los Angeles as a previous employer.

Also conspicuous by its absence was any space on the application for the prospective employee to indicate exactly what position he (or she) was applying for, although the form did reference clerical jobs and secretarial functions. For the information that Steele provided, he answered in the negative, as would be expected, with regard to any tasks related to typing, stenography, and operation of a typewriter, Dictaphones, or Ediphones.

For the all-important audition, Steele read some typical news items and introduced several pieces of classical music to demonstrate to his prospective employer "if I knew anything about composers like Bach, Beethoven, and all those fellows." Years later in a startling admission, he confessed, "I'd never heard of them, but they gave me the sheet and I read them just the way they looked. I didn't know how to pronounce them [because] I had never gone to college."[15] Although Steele's verbalizing of those composers may have come out as "Batch" and "Beet-hoven," the station's boss, Paul Morency, told him that if he could drop his Midwestern "Missoura" accent—in which "hog" sounded like "hawg" rather than a preferred Eastern "hahg"—Steele would be given a six-month trial "reading station breaks and commercials."[16] A deal was then struck for employment at a weekly salary of $35 with a probationary period of one month—as shown in the employer notes section of the job application—rather than the supposed six months.

In the event, a new era in radio broadcasting opened just one day after Bob Steele walked into the offices of WTIC on a lark. He had already signed off from his motorcycle announcing chores in Hartford both at the microphone and in the last edition of the racing program, but he anticipated his return to the track in 1937. "Good bye, folks," Steele wrote, "I hope to be bothering you again next year when George Lannom resumes his most spectacular, most sensational and most run-for-the-money thrill show here at Bulkeley Stadium."[17]

Many years later, Steele reflected on the momentous afternoon that changed his life forever. "I went in and just asked, 'Do you need any announcers here?' This was in 1936. You couldn't buy a job in those days," he recalled, obviously alluding to the prevailing economic throes.[18] Thus, with no guarantee of employment upon his intended return to California, he was content to take a sure thing in Hartford even temporarily rather than leave it to chance back on the West Coast, where another possible stint working on a farm—or any other menial job—held little appeal for him. And few people would have suspected that the motorcycle racing world's loss of one of its premier announcers would turn out to be a windfall for the most powerful radio broadcast facility in southern New England.

The new world—specifically the state of Connecticut—into which Bob Steele was stepping had a landscape of divided politics, a manufacturing industry that was in a state of uncertainty, and shifts in demographics among its population. A respite from the upheaval of the Depression was slow to make itself evident in southern New England.

At the State Capitol, Democrats held a slight edge over Republicans in the Senate, 17–15, who were joined by three Socialists; the House was decidedly Republican, 180–85, with two Socialists; and New Haven's Wilbur L. Cross, another Democrat, occupied the governor's office. With deterioration in Connecticut's production of hardware, machinery, and firearms evident from the economic realities of the 1920s—increasing labor and transportation costs were to blame—the state's manufacturing climate was further wracked by the Depression. Governor Cross, fearful that assistance from federal government programs might lead to loss of his control over the state's affairs, resisted consigning the state to aid from Franklin Roosevelt's New Deal efforts until 1936, when the General Assembly at last succumbed to implementation of "modest public works programs" lest the state lose Social Security benefits coming from Washington.[19]

Connecticut was fortunate in one important aspect: various new commercial enterprises were formed and began to fill the need for production of automobile parts, equipment related to generation of electrical power, and, most notably, aircraft engines from Frederic Rentschler's Pratt & Whitney Aircraft Company. Skilled manufacturing labor, in some cases left behind by businesses that had moved from the state, was in ready supply, thus easing the burden among these industries to find able workers, and previously vacated factories found new life.

Ethnic characteristics continued to evolve as well. An influx of immigrants from Poland and other eastern European countries settled in central Connecticut and took up trades to the advantage of hardware, machine, and metal parts producers, as well as Colt Firearms and the Underwood Typewriter Company.

Residents of greater Hartford had access to a pair of major newspapers, the *Courant*, published continuously since 1764, and the *Times*, an afternoon paper founded in 1817. Voice communication via telephone continued to expand by the 1930s, at which time the Southern New England Telephone Company counted tens of thousands of subscribers, and although the New Haven Railroad continued its passenger and freight service as the region's major rail provider, it was laden with debt and soon to declare for reorganization before the end of the decade.

This review of the climate of greater central Connecticut is useful to understanding Bob Steele's milieu as he cast his lot with WTIC and began rooting himself here rather than return to California. Various press and media outlets, including the trade publication *Billboard*, heralded his new appointment to fill the position once held by announcer Graham Gladwyn, yet Steele's career turn did not dim his motorcycling reportage, as he continued to file columns for *Motorcyclist*.[20] By 1937 he was immersed in radio work, served as master of ceremonies at civic events, and was lined up to again handle his plum assignment of motorcycle races in Hartford and Albany.

In the spring of that year, Steele was to become preoccupied by an interest that had nothing to do with motorsports or announcing. Meeting a female passenger on a Travelers elevator one day as he ascended to the radio studio on the sixth floor, he soon after inquired of the cab's operator who the young lady was who happened to be heading to her job on the eleventh floor. Steele's attention was seemingly transfixed, and his quest for a date with her quickly ensued.

When Oscar Hanson and his future wife, Esther, emigrated from Sweden near the turn of the twentieth century, they had traveled on the same ocean

In his earliest days at WTIC, Bob Steele is shown with some of his contemporaries. From left: Bunny Mullens, Bob Steele, George Bowe, Phil Becker, Fred Wade, and Ben Hawthorne (Hartford History Center, Hartford Public Library).

liner yet never became acquainted until after their arrival in America. He became a successful stonemason whose forte was the building of chimneys, and upon their marriage, the Hansons began their family that would eventually include five daughters, the youngest of whom was Astrid Shirley. Her first name meaning "star" in Swedish—and correctly pronounced *AHS-trid*, not *ASS-trid*—Astrid was born in Hartford on February 5, 1915, yet she was reticent when it came to discussing her Scandinavian ethnicity in her formative youthful years.[21] While her parents were bilingual, Astrid and her sisters wanted to be considered truly American and did little to learn their parents' native tongue, although with a family of her own years later, she was renowned for making sumptuous Swedish pancakes.

An aspiring pianist as a young girl, Astrid attended Hall High School in West Hartford but finished her studies at a local business school. After a stint at Aetna Insurance Company, which she terminated because of "advances from her boss," Astrid was hired by The Travelers Insurance Company to work as a secretary.[22] And so it was on the telling day when she was riding an elevator to reach the floor of her office that she unwittingly became the interest of a another passenger. Smitten by her good looks, Bob Steele inquired of the elevator operator who the young lady was. Astrid was unaware that she had captured the attention of a budding radio star, and a note from Steele asking her for a date was soon in her hands. He was excited for the opportunity to trade on his celebrity as an announcer and used this to his advantage by letting her know of his vocation. When she accepted his offer, a bit of legerdemain was also at work thanks to a fancy automobile parked near The Travelers' premises.

> We had an engineer by the name of Al Jackson [who] had a 1930 Cadillac touring car … with the tonneau windshield in the back, a classic thing. It was a terrific piece of machinery. He parked it outside the station on Grove Street. Everybody who walked past used to admire it. [Astrid] thought I owned the car. She thought I was the guy. So she wrote me a little note saying okay [to a date]. When I called for her, I was on foot. I didn't have a car. I didn't even have a bike.[23]

Regardless of the means by which the suitor reached his lady, there is absolutely no doubt that Bob Steele had found the woman with whom he was prepared to spend the rest of his life. While his profusion of writing about motorcycling continued along with this radio announcing, Steele also produced a seemingly endless stream of correspondence—much of it on stationery featuring the letterhead of "The Travelers Broadcasting Service Corporation"—addressed to Astrid, the new, unqualified love of his life.

All these missives, at times hopelessly cloying yet undoubtedly sincere, demonstrate without question Steele's avid pursuit, much of this effort punctuated with his trademark humor as well as a trove of comic drawings, all executed in his own hand. Determined to win her heart, he sent letters to Astrid in the late summer and early autumn of 1937 that were replete with wit, and the envelopes that delivered these messages were embellished with his whimsical artistry.

In late August, which appears to be the early stage of this budding romance, there is a hint of her reluctance to return Steele's written correspondence. On the 30th of that month, he was at Yankee Stadium for the controversial Joe Louis—Tommy Farr boxing match, in which Louis was declared the winner after fifteen rounds but was unimpressive in his performance. Writing to Astrid the next day, Steele created a cartoon of the bout featuring an announcer telling his NBC radio audience, "This is Bob Steele at the ringside folx, and th' most important thing I can think of right now is that Astrid didn't keep her promise and write me from New York…," and he closed with a plaintive postscript: "Maybe you could STILL write that letter…. HUHHHHH?"[24] In mid–September while in the Albany area, he sent her a telegram expressing his regret—CANT SEE YOU THURSDAY NIGHT—while nonetheless conveying his devotion—BUT AM THINKING OF YOU EVERY OTHER SECOND FURTHERMORE I LOVE YOU.[25]

One month later as the barrage of charm continued, Steele penned a note at "nine-thutty o'clock Wednesday morn" in which he twice told her "Honey—I love you" and signed off—as if there could be any doubt—"Oh, yes—and I do mean YOU. All the love & kisses you'll ever be able to use, XXXXX from your Bob."[26] Although no clear date of a marriage proposal is in evidence, it likely occurred at this time. A photograph of the loving couple simply labeled "Fall '37 engaged" indicates a future wedding, and Astrid had to have asked him one final question known only to both of them. His answer—unadorned with any cartoons, completely serious in tone save for the self-given title of "General Mangler, WTIC," and using his formal signature of Robert L. Steele—read,

> Dearest Girl:
> I do. Definitely.[27]

Their engagement did little to curb Steele's enthusiasm for his bride-to-be. More letters posted with ten-cent special delivery stamps followed, as did at least one telegram: HEY HEY HAD TO STAY I SAY LOTS OF LOVE ANYWAY WHAT DO YOU SAY: ROBERT L.[28] Clearly evident—and remaining remarkably consistent in the ensuing decades—was Steele's unwavering love for this woman, whose name would transition from "Astrid" to her middle name "Shirley" and, years later, to "Mama." About the time that their engagement took shape, "Brother Bob" became a member of Lafayette Lodge Number 100 of the fraternal order of Freemasons, thereby attaining the first of the degrees which he carried proudly for the rest of his life.

The marriage of Bob and Astrid occurred in early 1938, albeit under circumstances that were a bit chronologically vague. Many years later, their son Phil wrote, "The story in the Steele family was that Mom and Dad were engaged in the fall of 1937 but eloped to get married in Baltimore on January 7, 1938. The part about being engaged and eloping was true enough, but the marriage certificate clearly shows that the nuptials took place not in January but in March. No doubt the birth of their first son, on November 3, 1938, was the reason for celebrating their anniversary in January."[29] Indeed, Baltimore's Court of Common Pleas has the record of the event of March 24, 1938, in which one Robert L. Steele and one Astrid S. Hansom [sic] "were by me [C. Carroll Bailey, minister of the Gospel] united in Marriage."[30] Soon thereafter the couple settled into an apartment on Ashley Street, near Sigourney Square Park in Hartford.

Life as a newlywed did little to divert Steele's attention from the vocational and avocational pursuits that had long held his interest. Holding forth with his announcing chores, including work with WTIC's renowned Playhouse troupe, he continued to write his "Professor Popper" articles for motorcycle-related publications. Steele was on the front lines as a reporter covering the aftermath of the devastating Great New England Hurricane, a Category 5 storm that swept the Northeast on September 21 and resulted in

The loving couple, Bob and Astrid (soon to be better known as Shirley) Steele (Hartford History Center, Hartford Public Library).

the deaths of nearly 700 people. In late October he was among the noted media members and athletes who spoke at a "Sports Review" held at the Connecticut State Prison Auditorium in Wethersfield, and just days later the additional duties of fatherhood entered his life upon the birth of Robert Hampton Steele in early November.

As the calendar turned to 1939, Bob Steele grew comfortable with paternal tasks. In the spring of that year, he was posed on a stationary motorcycle while cradling his son in his lap, the baby's forehead adorned with a pair of racing goggles. A photograph of the occasion was printed in *The Motorcyclist*, and Steele jokingly remarked that "Bob H." was reading the magazine and absorbing all manner of the sport. Steele further penned an essay from his wife's perspective—under the alias of "Mrs. Prof. Popper"—to inform readers of what life was like in their home, which now was occupied by "a loving police dog" in addition to an infant.[31]

Steele was trying to maintain control over his career path but nonetheless kept in the back of his mind a possible reunion with his mother, who still lived in Southern California. In private notes Steele scratched to himself, he confessed that he was "writing to KFI—KHJ and KNX Los Angeles—trying to get announcing jobs there," and he was cognizant of the newest medium about to gain entry in American markets: "Television experimented with."[32]

Nineteen thirty-nine would mark the end of an era of tentative global peace, a wary tranquility that was shattered on September 1 when Nazi Germany's invasion of Poland plunged the world into warfare that exacted a toll soon to reach unfathomable proportions. But in the Steele household, the vivacity of new family life was only beginning.

4

The Sportsman Goes
on *The Morning Watch*

*Yelling "Hot Dogs" possibly gave him the strong and clear voice
he has, which is excellent for sports broadcasts.*
—WTIC promotional biography
of Bob Steele, circa 1939

*Good morning! How many of you folks are getting up this
morning? MOST of you, I hope.*
—Bob Steele's comment to open
his inaugural morning show

Bob Steele's familiarity with major sports had been in his veins long
before his arrival in Hartford, so it was perhaps natural for him to suggest to
his employer that WTIC create a new sports program that would cater to
fans of every stripe. Learning the final results of sporting events could easily
be the highlight of any aficionado's day, yet the timeliness of the delivery of
those results often meant waiting for desired information to be made available
in the next edition of a newspaper.

However, anxious fans could be better placated if results were relayed
to radio stations and put on the air in a more punctual fashion compared to
the involved process necessitated by the print media. "We didn't have a sports
program back in 1938," Steele recalled years later, "and yet there were baseball
games every day, all day games. People at six o'clock in the evening would
tune in their radios to get the scores. We didn't cover them and being a fifty
thousand–watt station, I thought that we should have a sports show. Our
news at the time came from Boston; we lacked our own local stuff. So I cooked
up the idea of doing a sports show and took it to my boss."[1]

Steele won support for a new program, and he was tabbed to be the
show's announcer. Slated to begin Monday through Saturday at 6:15 p.m.—
a half-hour later on Sundays—and run for fifteen minutes, *Strictly Sports*

became a forerunner in sports programming. Formally commencing in 1939 and introduced in an era when the preponderance of baseball games were still played in the afternoon, "[t]he show quickly became Bob's ticket to broadcasting popularity," wrote Bob's son Phil many years later, alluding to the more timely broadcast of scores and other news from various sporting venues compared to the inherent tardiness of the printing of newspapers.[2]

Continuing to announce vaudeville-style shows sponsored by a social organization known as The Travelers Club—comprised of Travelers employees—Steele gained further publicity for his work as noted in trade publications such as *Radio Daily*, which in April 1940 ran a full-page advertisement for WTIC with the primary purpose of informing its readers of his outstanding credentials. "A sportswriter for 14 years and now one of the most popular radio broadcasters in Southern New England, he knows his stuff and how to put it over," crowed the ad, which also reminded radio industry clients that with fifty thousand watts of power, WTIC was "[a] 'must' for a big job in the big Southern New England market."[3]

Steele's career focus remained in the realm of sports, not least of which was his coverage of a July boxing match in Hartford between Carl Dell and black fighter Ernest Robinson. The outcome of the fight was controversial because of the close final decision in Robinson's favor. Having acquired a dubious reputation for his poor track record in predicting the winners of various sporting events, Steele "throughout the fight had been arguing with the sports writers at ringside" that Robinson would emerge victorious.[4] To the consternation of many, Robinson indeed was declared the winner, thus prompting a show of respect from *Hartford Times* sports editor A. B. McGinley, who wrote that the "[r]eal importance of [referee Louis] Kaplan's decision was the fact of it establishing Bob Steele, WTIC sports commentator, as a boxing authority."[5] Steele would soon meet legendary fighter Jack Dempsey and strike up an enduring friendship with the "Manassa Mauler."

Yet mixed in with his sporting duties was a foray into scripting his own version of the children's classic "The Ugly Duckling," replete with cues for sound effects and musical passages.

About this time, another child entered Bob and Shirley's life, when son Paul Alan was born on October 3, 1940, and "The 4 Steeles" soon became the featured motorcycle riders drawn by the family patriarch as part of a whimsical Christmas message sent to family and friends.[6]

But as war in Europe continued, the United States government was taking steps to be prepared in case of the nation's entry into the conflict. Less than four weeks after Shirley delivered their second son, officials of the Selective Service conducted a draft lottery in Washington, D.C., and from a fishbowl containing about nine thousand capsules, Steele's number of 3298 was eventually drawn, though he would not be called to the colors. And with the general election of 1940 just days away, Steele "stood within arms [sic] length" of Franklin Roosevelt when the presidential incumbent made a campaign stop in Hartford.[7]

At a time when FDR was partway through his second term as president, he founded the March of Dimes organization to raise funds that would be directed toward research to fight polio, an infantile paralytic disease with which he was afflicted as an adult. WTIC general manager Paul Morency partnered with the *Hartford Courant* to devise a clever way to raise donations of ten cents, in the form of dimes, as an easy way for the average person to help the cause. Events were staged in which contributors—individuals as well as groups such as youth scouting organizations and civic clubs—placed dimes side by side along a mile-long ribbon to fulfill the mission of completing a "Mile o' Dimes."[8] Bob Steele was an event announcer on such occasions held in Hartford, and some famous personalities were persuaded to lend their names to the cause and draw even more people to add to the coffers. Steele interviewed George Raft when the actor came to Hartford in late January 1941, and the total collected for this event alone exceeded sixteen thousand dollars. Over the station's fifteen years of participation, it was one of Steele's favorite charitable ventures, earning national acclaim and ultimately raising over $1.1 million.[9]

The addition of Paul Steele to the family meant that it was time for a bigger home, and in mid–June they relocated to a modest home on Buckland Road in neighboring Wethersfield. One of the oldest towns in Connecticut, Wethersfield would be called home by Bob and Shirley for the rest of their lives. In their new homestead, the Steele sons continued to grow quickly under their parents' love and care, but Bob kept up his hectic pace by attending midget auto races, speaking at testimonial dinners in the greater Hartford area as well as programs at the Wethersfield prison, and adding to his dubious reputation as the predictor of winners in various sporting events.[10] After successfully forecasting that the Brooklyn Dodgers "would blitz to top honors in the National League," he failed in a subsequent prediction when the "Beloved Bums" fell to the New York Yankees in the World Series.[11]

Beginning in the summer of 1939 and running through the fateful year of 1941, Steele included small entries in his scrapbook to denote the milestones that were related to the commencement and continuation of World War II. "Germany declares war on Russia!" he exclaimed on June 22, noting Hitler's attack on its former ally in Operation Barbarossa, and the gravity of the times struck the American home front when the United States was set upon by the

Empire of Japan. "[Eight] days ago Japanese attacked Pearl Harbor. So now U.S.A. is at war with Japan, Germany and Italy (The "Axis"). We're preparing for the worst in [Hartford]. Getting air raid precautions lined up. No planes yet but two scares last week. Thought enemy planes were on the way—but not. San Francisco, however, was visited by enemy reconnaissance fliers," he wrote in a scrapbook. Trying to salvage a small ray of optimism by way of pleasant weather, he concluded ominously, "Nice day today. But War! Too bad—war."[12]

The weight of current events in the country cannot be understated, and the importance of WTIC as a media outlet, as demonstrated during the 1936 flood, meant that the station was also subjected to necessarily protective measures. "The station was kept under guard, and the usual flow of visitors was severely restricted. These security precautions seem a little quaint [in modern times], but they were in keeping with a local and national concern over security. WTIC was, after all, a vital link in the communications network."[13] General manager Paul Morency allowed the governor of Connecticut, Raymond Baldwin, unfettered access to the station for any official purposes he deemed necessary in the public interest.

Steele's time on the air was reduced to three days per week, and a corresponding cut in pay resulted. Yet the pace of his schedule seemed not to suffer in the least because of his ongoing involvement with boxing. In late January 1942 he paired with announcer Keyes Perrin to broadcast a fight in Hartford between Willie Pep and Abie Kaufman from the Governor's Foot Guard Hall. An advertisement in the *Hartford Courant* put potential listeners on notice that they would need a new frequency modulation radio set to hear the action on station W53H. Operating on 45.3 megahertz, WTIC's affiliate was in the vanguard of the latest in broadcasting technology, but "radio's latest miracle," as the ad stated, was accessible only with FM sets.[14]

W53H, which would change its call letters to WTIC FM in November 1943, recorded bouts in Hartford with Steele at the microphone for the purposes of late-night replays on WTIC AM "for the benefit of war workers and less important stay-ups."[15] Fights in Providence and at New York's old Madison Square Garden found Steele among those in attendance—only as a fan rather than an announcer—but another cause occupied his time when he served as master of ceremonies at a war bond drive at the Hartford Auditorium. Another such duty took him to the grounds of the Old State House, just across Central Row from The Travelers main office, where he announced a boxing exhibition headlined by Willie Pep that was staged with the intent of helping a two-week effort to raise $1.5 million through the sale of war bonds and stamps, "enough to buy six four-motored bombers."[16]

His voice now infused with more than a tinge of celebrity, Steele received a "request" from station GM Morency—but actually came from the federal government's Office of Coordination of Information—to record a two-minute segment of local sports news "done in a light manner for a short wave broadcast to Connecticut troops stationed in various parts of the world." Wishing to ensure the quality of the content, Morency added, "I suggest that you come in and talk it over before you write it up."[17] Some passages from one of those recordings that passed muster, and now found in the Library of Congress, contains the following:

> Howdy men, this is Bob Steele, speaking to you from WTIC in Hartford, getting all set for about two minutes of *Strictly Sports* for you Connecticut boys. Tuesday, September 22 [1942] was a big night for Willie Pep, Hartford's undefeated featherweight. Willie beat one of the toughest boys in the business, Vince Dell'Orto, before a crowd of sixty five hundred at Bulkeley Stadium.... Paul Revere, who used to bring me the late baseball scores on his trusty plater [a low-grade racehorse], Porter's Hat, has joined the Civilian Pilot Training Corps, U.S. Army Enlisted Reserve. Speaking of baseball scores and baseball, Hartford finished seventh in the Eastern League, Springfield eighth.... Ted Williams, the kid himself, leader of both leagues in batting, home runs, and runs batted in, is coming to Hartford September 28 to play center field for the Savitt Gems in a game with a Connecticut semi-pro team to be named. The Red Sox slugger was a little backward about coming at first. Bill Savitt offered him five hundred dollars to appear, but Ted declined. Next day, Savitt offered him $750 but got no answer to his wire. Well, Bill told me about it. I suggested offering Williams a thousand dollar war bond, same outlay to Bill, $750, but who could refuse a thousand dollar bond? Bill wired the offer; Williams wired acceptance within one hour. Till next time, this is Bob Steele in Hartford, saying "So long, men."[18]

On the heels of his twenty-fourth birthday, Williams did travel to Hartford and was accorded a grand reception, which included a luncheon at the Empire Restaurant hosted by Savitt, a brief tour of the city, and a visit to the Wethersfield State Prison, where he posed for a contrived mug shot as prisoner #3600. Williams was interviewed by Steele before the game, and soon thereafter the Boston star went on active military duty.

The war continued to influence the radio station's programming, and the United States Coast Guard Academy, located in southeastern Connecticut, hosted a Saturday morning program, *The United States Coast Guard on Parade*, from the gymnasium on its campus. Prior to the Japanese attack on Pearl Harbor, WTIC enforced a strict policy of impartial reporting of the news and world events, and announcers were threatened with dismissal should they violate this mandate. After America's entry into combat, however, the station threw its weight fully behind the quest for victory, which in 1943 spawned a brief audio clip that remains in use to this day.

On July 4 of that year, WTIC debuted a new tone that was played to indicate the exact time at the top of each hour. British prime minister Winston Churchill was famous for his "V for Victory" hand signal, and the "V" was further co-opted by the United States armed forces for the usage in a correspondence system known as Victory Mail. V-mail, as it came to be labeled, was employed to save shipping space by reducing the size of traditional letters sent overseas, and the Morse code for the letter V was *dot dot dot dash*, which, in turn, could be musically interpreted as the four opening notes of Beethoven's Fifth Symphony. When programmed electronically, these notes became WTIC's signature time-check tone, and was a standard that Bob Steele faithfully followed to remind his audience *precisely* of the beginning of a new hour. For other time checks, which he also signaled precisely on the minute, he used a Deagan chime that he struck "with the care and precision of a musician."[19]

One year following Pearl Harbor, Steele made a note of his night out with Shirley, on which the couple enjoyed a movie and a nice dinner—prime rib for her, flounder, "which tastes like cardboard soaked in milk" for him—but he pointed out the real privations that the war was visiting on the American home front: "Meat scarce. To be rationed soon. Coffee, sugar, gasoline rationed already. I get 3 gal[lons] a week. May as well sell car. Can't drive it anywhere."[20]

Despite the limitations, Steele found himself in constant demand for appearances beyond his radio job. Speaking engagements and serving as master of ceremonies at events hosted by public and private groups kept Steele virtually in perpetual motion. Wartime exigencies being what they were, he encouraged people to support blood drives, believing that "it was the plain duty of every red-blooded man and woman to donate a pint of his or her blood" as part of the on-going war effort.[21] Steele's friend Bill Savitt, recuperating from a broken foot in early 1943, joined him for a blood drive intended to accommodate first-time donors. Before leaving the blood drive site, each of the seventy-one participants received a card on which to record their donations, which stated, "This certificate signifies that its possessor has rendered a patriotic service by giving his or her own blood for the treatment of the seriously injured."[22] Steele was later awarded a certificate of appreciation by the American Red Cross for his assistance in the campaign. In fact, his devotion to support blood drives through radio advertisements "was ongoing … a regular item on his show right up until his retirement," and he was very proud to use the airwaves for such purposes.[23]

A well-known, landmark department store in Hartford, whose origin dated to 1847, was G. Fox, located on Main Street directly across from Christ

Church Cathedral at the upper edge of downtown. The owners of the spacious, multi-level store were the proud sponsors of WTIC's *Morning Watch* radio program, which until the beginning of World War II had been hosted by Ben Hawthorne. Catching the patriotic fervor of the day to do his part in the conflict, Hawthorne in 1942 chose enlistment in the army, and his broadcasting duties were taken over temporarily by his wife, Travilla. At a time when jobs in many fields previously filled by men were now open due to their conscription or enlistment in the armed forces, women stepped in to alleviate the labor shortages that existed in farming, manufacturing, and other war-related industries, thereby giving rise to "Rosie the Riveter" as the iconic female worker.

The departure of Ben Hawthorne presented an opportunity for his spouse, but by early 1943 change was in the air. Already popular in his own right, Bob Steele auditioned to take Travilla's place upon her departure, and he successfully won the chance to become the new host of the popular show. Steele was well-credentialed and needed little introduction to listeners, and he simply carried into the *Morning Watch* the same type of material from which he had been drawing for years.

Reading from scripts that he personally wrote and typed, he introduced himself to listeners at seven o'clock on the morning of March 11, 1943, employing his trademark humor and style.

> This is Boob.... BOB Steele, friends, taking over for Travilla Hawthorne, and inviting you to have BREAKFAST with me. I just sent Brother Kingsley down for an egg sandwich, three large coffees and two small waitresses to take out. Now we have a perfectly faskinating [*sic*] selection of transcribed and recorded music this morning. We have all kinds of recorded music. Fast, slow, slower, too slow, sweet, bitter, curdled, classic, semi-classic, semi-conscious, UN-conscious, popular and unpopular, and ... well, ALL kinds, as I said.[24]

He then advised the audience that the upcoming tune would be Glenn Miller's "Juke Box Saturday Night," and at the song's conclusion, Steele resumed his schtick. Years later, his son Phil observed, "Bob developed the knack of being able to deliver a script he'd written for *The Morning Watch* while sounding like he was ad-libbing."[25] This preparation became his standard procedure, but there were times when the pages of the script combined with lots of other material—the text of advertisements, correspondence from listeners, and information gleaned from teletypes at the station—to make for an overwhelming sheaf of papers. A seeming disaster struck one day when the breeze from an open window scattered his material, and with no time to rearrange and recover his place, Steele was forced to improvise on the spot.

This untimely accident provided Steele with a valuable lesson: it proved that he did not have to rely on a script and thus enabled him to move confidently forward—slowly but surely—without one. Considering the fact that his "written voice"—as he very ably demonstrated through his many essays and commentaries for *Motorcyclist* magazine and other publications—was so well aligned with his "speaking voice"—as shown in his days as a race announcer and later his appearances as a master of ceremonies and featured guest at other engagements—it should come as no surprise that he could transition from one to the other so smoothly to the benefit of a readership or a listening audience. Steele's consistency in his train of thought, which is to say his ability to quickly evaluate any given situation and explore the opportunity to present a pun or joke, conflated with the acute sensibilities and timing of a stand-up comic to fuel the wit that endeared him to so many.

As prominent as this trait was, the many scripts Steele did use are wonderfully laced with a trademark charm and humor that are further embellished by the phonetics he inserted to remind himself of how passages were to be presented to listeners. The following segment is an example of how he told an early *Morning Watch* audience of the difficulties of being precise with articulation, and exacting though he tried to be, his script contains a minor misinterpretation and misspelling of the last name of the popular music conductor Andre Kostelanetz.

> This pronunciation business is a pretty good sized headache for a poor old radio announcer ... he can't say anything right, no matter how he sez it. If I said Kosta Lahn YETS ... I'd get four hundred letters wanting to know why I didn't throw away my silk hat and eyebrow arching outfit. I think a hundred people say Kostalanetz, where only I would say it the way this letter suggests.... For Ypres [the city in Belgium], I couldn't say Wipers. It has to be Eepr ... yet I wouldn't say Paree.... I would say Paris. And we radio announcers have to sort of "try ON" a word and see how it fits.[26]

Elaborating on this point the following year, Steele penned a column describing the plight of radio announcers who were bound to mispronounce a word or proper name despite their best efforts to avoid doing so. Writing in the *Hartford Times*, he stated his case, not to evoke sympathy but rather to prove the difficulty of trying to be an on-air perfectionist, which he always strove to be. Coming at a time of global conflict when news reports were replete with the names of foreign cities and countries as well as the people associated with those places, Steele pointed out how achieving any level of uniformity of pronunciation—to say nothing of being correct—even within one particular language could be daunting.

The column also evinced the pride he had in his level of self-inculcation and his diligence in his attempts to be as precise as humanly possible. "Not being a professor, or even a college man, I suppose I have no right to bat out an article on the pronunciation of proper names. However, I can claim to be a radio announcer who has been educated the hard way these past eight years at WTIC."[27] After listing several tongue-twisters—Przemysl (Poland), Pszczyna (Polish Silesia), Llwchwr (Wales), and Soerabaja (Java)—and providing the proper phonetic pronunciation, he ended by offering readers simple advice as to how to follow in his footsteps to enlighten themselves in the same manner he did: "You'll find 'em in Webster's New International [Dictionary], unabridged, if you're the curious type."[28]

Steele's work schedule remained busy enough: in addition to *Morning Watch*, he continued to serve as a regular announcer and was still hosting *Strictly Sports* in the early evening. The thirty-two-year-old Steele, whose draft classification was III-B (or 3-B) meant that he was "deferred both by reason of dependency and occupation essential to the war effort," privately noted the hardships of the ongoing world war and the prospects that lay ahead as Allied forces in North Africa fought against Germany's Erwin Rommel, "the Desert Fox" of the Axis mechanized army.[29]

"All meat rationed," he wrote, but his family was fortunate to have two young boys who added to the ration points the Steeles could accumulate and redeem for food, even though sons Robert and Paul, both under the age of five, were far from able to consume as much as an adult. Observing the travails of the daily war news, Steele commented, "British + U.S. running Nazi's Rommel and Van Arnim out of Africa. Getting set for invasion of continent and Germany. Will be bloody. Long war ahead—seems to me."[30]

On Memorial Day 1943, before Steele commenced his program with his traditional tune, "A Hunt in the Black Forest" composed in 1894 by American bandmaster George Voelker, he somberly reminded listeners of the significance of the day, by which time approximately 100,000 American servicemen had perished. "Good morning, everyone … this is Bob Steele … welcoming you to the G. Fox *Morning Watch*. No foolishness this morning … this is a day for remembering our valiant men who have gone down fighting—fighting for the right to live and work and worship as we please … men of the USA who have died in the service of our country."[31]

Another staple made its way into Steele's lineup in the early days of *Morning Watch*. Perhaps cognizant of having left home himself without an important item that he intended to take, he occasionally reminded his listeners to remember those articles before heading off to work or running errands. Colloquializing his script, Steele would intone, "Gotcha Lunch? Spoon? ID? Badge? Wallet? Change? Don't get onna bus [with a] $10 bill. Glasses? That letter you wrote last nite? G. Fox Charge Plate? Book yez gonna return to the library yestdy?" There was also an appropriate addendum for members of the recently formed Women's Army Corps who served at the airport in nearby Windsor Locks during World War II: "You WACs at Bradley Field—don't forget your Base Pass. That reminder is a special request from some soldier gals at Bradley."[32]

Reminders also went out to listeners who were reluctant to participate in blood drives—"I think 999 out of a thousand of you would [donate blood to save a dying soldier] yet not more than one in TEN is contributing at the blood center here in Hartford"—nor was he bashful about encouraging the purchase of war bonds, signing off one of his shows by importuning, "'Til [tomorrow], it's Good-by[e] … spelled B-U-Y … WAR BONDS FOR VIC-TORY."[33] Yet Steele found humor in minor annoyances, as when he vowed to invent a new type of chewing gum that would bounce back and adhere to persons who thoughtlessly discarded it on the sidewalk.

In July of 1943, Bob and Shirley embarked on a trip to Texas for the marriage of her sister, after which Shirley remained in the Lone Star State while he returned to Connecticut. Steele kept Shirley regularly informed of events back on the home front by sending typed letters to her at the Hotel Stephen F. Austin. He had taken their sons to the circus despite the sweltering conditions, but he happily observed that the boys enjoyed the show. It was also at this time that Steele penned an article for the August edition of *Esquire*, detailing the life of a twenty-one-year-old boxer christened Guglielmo Papaleo.

Born in Middletown, Connecticut, Papaleo later changed his name to Willie Pep, and fighting as a lightweight he rose to the top of his weight classification. This local-boy-made-good found favor with Steele, who had never lost interest in prizefighting, and Steele furnished a profile of the boxer who now called Hartford his home. With glowing admiration, Steele noted Pep's accomplishment: "Sixty-two successive professional victories Willie scored in a row, eight of them after he was champion. It is the most amazing winning streak in the annals of boxing."[34]

The essay brought Steele a bit of additional renown—as well as a $125 payment from the magazine—in the form of a full-size billboard, which was his endorsement of the Villanova Restaurant, an eatery just up the street from WTIC's studios. "Bob Steele says in Esquire magazine…. Famous for its Italian cuisine," gushed the outsized advertisement, and he indeed had firsthand experience with the eatery's veal scallopini that was "cooked to a King's taste."[35]

For all the prodigious amounts of writing that he did for his radio programs and various publications, Steele continued to find the time to leave many private notes and personal thoughts in diaries and scrapbooks. As the

Allies fought valiantly in both the Pacific and European theaters of the war, the need for servicemen grew without remittance, and the expansion of conscription drew Steele's notice. "War going okay for us just now," he wrote. "Fathers are going to be drafted starting October 1 unless they're in essential industry. At least that's what Washington says now."[36] Still insulated from the service because of his 3-B classification, he nonetheless kept a wary eye on his possible call to the military. And his attention to happenings in the Steele household was ever present, from leisure time spent with his family, the tedium of cleaning the garage or cutting the lawn, and the ingesting of vitamin pills, which he termed a recent "fad" that helped to re-invigorate him through his busy days.[37]

Steele's ardor for his job, his home life, and the manifold of extracurricular activities in which he engaged had by the end of 1943 begun to exact a medical toll. An examination and X-ray of Steele led a physician to conclude that he was affected by duodenitis, the condition likely brought about because "[t]his man being a radio announcer probably has considerable nervous stress and this may be the explanation of the functional disturbance in the small bowel."[38]

A popular segment of Bob Steele's personal appearances was his presentation of "The Lion and Albert," a poem written by the Scottish scriptwriter and poet Marriot Edgar.[39] Written by Edgar and performed famously by English actor Stanley Holloway, the piece was recorded by Holloway sometime after 1930. Steele was so taken by the story—a Mr. and Mrs. Ramsbottom took their young son Albert to a zoo in Blackpool, where, after teasing a caged lion, the boy was eaten by the beast—that he delighted in reciting it on the air, complete with Cockney accent, and he carried a small copy of the tale to speaking engagements in case there was a demand for a performance by an interested audience. "The Lion and Albert" thus became ensconced in Steele's vast repertoire.

Though he was not a certified professional accountant, Steele maintained diligent watch over his personal finances, as evidenced by the many entries in the various diaries he kept over the years. For example, on January 31, 1944, he performed a brief skit that he wrote himself for which he was paid a ten dollar appearance fee, and the following day he was to collect fifteen dollars for being the master of ceremonies at an Army Services Show sponsored by G. Fox. He also tried to navigate his radio listeners through some of the more intricate portions of the Internal Revenue Service's tax code and paperwork: "If you paid in September and December as well, you'll get credit for it when you enter it on line 21b or on Form 1040–13b or c on Form 1040A…. Just don't let Form 1125 CONFUSE you…."[40]

The self-deprecating side of Bob Steele never left him in spite of the celebrity status he was constantly accreting. Always quick to display this humorous trait, a glowing mini-biography published in the March 12, 1944, edition of *The Hartford Courant Magazine* concluded with a quote that proved how well-grounded he was in the realization that fame could be fleeting for anyone, himself included: "Nothing recedes like success!"[41] But the article was compelling because it revealed a trade secret or two about the man listeners had come to love.

> On the air he talks at a rate of 150 words a minute, and in the course of his day's work he pours into the microphone an average of ten thousand words, a good many of which he pronounces correctly…. His special programs permit much ad-libbing, and when a crisis develops, which happens occasionally with even the best of announcers, he peeks into his little black book, pulls out some intriguing combination of letters like "garrandis," "ribbaforsen," or "snarmenhampers" and trusts to luck that his listeners will forget what he forgot what he was talking about…. And he always has on the tip of his tongue, or makes up, some cheerful filler-in. He fairly dotes on the one to the effect that "many a true word has been spoken through false teeth."[42]

The growing popularity Steele enjoyed at the time nevertheless led one of his sons to speculate many years later that his father may have been casting about for an unspecified change in employment. Citing various documents found among his father's scrapbooks of the mid–1940s, including scripts infused with one-liners, short jokes, and the like, Phil Steele opined, "They look more like a radio network audition than material aimed at getting after-dinner speaking engagements. But he was grateful for his job. His roots now included a family and home. If he was actively pursuing another job, he never told anyone about it."[43] Indeed, the fertile mind of Bob Steele, firm in its grasp of humor and puns for any occasion, could easily have put him on a path to join the likes of other popular entertainers of the era—George Burns, Milton Berle, and Bob Hope come to mind—had he so chosen.

A brief article in the April 27, 1944, issue of *The Sporting News*, nicknamed "the Bible of Baseball" for its extensive coverage of the national pastime, informed readers of Steele's interview with Army Air Forces Captain Walt Stewart, who had recently flown bombing missions over central and eastern Europe. In his conversation with Steele, Stewart confirmed that servicemen overseas were thrilled that baseball continued to be played in spite of the acute shortage of major-league-quality players. Lost to time is the fact that in the late summer of 1918, there was no clear end to the First World War in sight, and with many ballplayers having been drafted, baseball curtailed its season and braced for the possible cancellation of the 1919 season due to lack of able talent.

When the United States entered World War II, baseball commissioner Kenesaw Mountain Landis asked President Franklin Roosevelt directly "whether professional baseball should continue to operate."[44] The timing of the commissioner's query was crucial given that by mid–January 1942 baseball teams were soon to embark on their annual spring training endeavors. FDR's prompt reply, which became known as the "Green Light Letter," stated that in his personal opinion the game of baseball should proceed in order to furnish "a chance for recreation and for [people to take] their minds off their work."[45] This blessing by the president allowed baseball to move forward during all of World War II even though the quality of players was noticeably lacking. When Steele asked Stewart if servicemen were "really glad that baseball is rolling again," the captain answered unequivocally, "Why, Bob, when those fellas over there get the news that Brooklyn beat the Phillies, 8 to 2, like you just reported, they'll go through the roof.... They want baseball. If they ever discontinue it, I'll betcha half those guys wouldn't even want to come home."[46]

The preservation of the game in time of war also meant that *Strictly Sports* would proceed unimpeded. Had no games been played at either the major-league or minor-league levels, there would have been no sports news on the baseball front, and the lack of such information almost certainly would have resulted in a reduction or suspension of the program's schedule until a resumption of play at the conclusion of hostilities. Thankfully, the major leagues carried on their business—as did prizefighting, much to Steele's delight—and the American League champions of 1944 helped Steele salvage his reputation as a poor prognosticator of pennant winners. Picking the often hapless St. Louis Browns in recent years to capture the AL crown, Steele finally won out with his persistent choice of this perennially woebegone team.

The summer of 1944 was significant in world events: Allied forces liberated the city of Rome, and their launching of D-Day on the beaches of Normandy, in which Steele's brother-in-law Herb Swanson participated, was a hard-fought success. Locally the city of Hartford witnessed the tragedy of the Ringling Brothers and Barnum & Bailey circus fire in which 167 people died, with over seven hundred suffering various injuries. The season was noteworthy in a positive sense for the Steele family when Shirley delivered a third son, Philip Lee Steele, on August 22 at Hartford Hospital. And as the autumnal equinox approached, the three-time father struck upon an idea that served as a cornerstone of his legacy. "Suggest word-a-day usually mispronounced" was a simple message scrawled in one of his scrapbooks, and Steele's ability to influence his faithful audience and instill in listeners a new level of learning was at his disposal thanks to the fifty thousand–watt power of WTIC. In years to follow, his "Word for the Day" segment, like his humor, became a staple of his morning program.

And that humor found yet another public outlet when Steele wrote a series of weekly "columns" using the alias of Judge Underdunk Fnoost. These articles, really a compilation of one-liners and short jokes, were actually advertisements for his friend Bill Savitt, the mention of whose jewelry business was always cleverly embedded in each piece.

Steele's position as a boxing broadcaster came to the fore in the aftermath of a controversial bout in Hartford on the evening of November 15. Willie Pep, the favorite son of local fans, was ultimately victorious over Charles "Cabey" Lewis, but the fight was marred by a false claim made by Lewis's manager, Tommy Dio, that the bell ending the fourth round had rung prematurely, just at the moment Pep was struggling to regain his feet after being knocked down by his opponent. At the referee's count of six, the bell chimed to end the round, saving Pep from possibly being counted out, but Dio, who was not at the fight but was thought to be in New York at the time, nevertheless spread the word that the bell sounded at two minutes rather than the regulation three. With Pep saved by the bell, he forged ahead and bested Lewis, but the imbroglio drew quick notice due to Dio's allegation.

All boxing officials associated with the event, with the exception of Dio, were vindicated when WTIC's recording of the fight, with Bob Steele handling the broadcast, was played back and conclusively proved that the bell ending the fourth round did indeed ring at the three-minute mark. In the end, Dio was assessed a fifty-dollar fine by the Connecticut Boxing Commission for making the false accusation, but there was a surreal, concluding anecdote to the affair. Shortly after the tempest subsided, Steele wanted to show beyond all doubt that round four was of official length, so he announced that the recording would be aired on *Strictly Sports*. "Get out your watches, men," he bellowed. "Time the round! Perceive how science never lies!" and with that, the recording was played—only to have the replay short-circuited when an ill-timed power outage struck the station at the two-minute mark! Scrambling to save face when the power was restored ten minutes later, "Steele's anguished voice returned ... beseeching his [audience] to understand that the power had failed and assuring them that the demonstration would go on again the following Tuesday."[47] The next replay, unhindered by technical difficulties, put the matter to rest, and the episode garnered Steele much acclaim not only in the United States media, including *Newsweek* and broadcasting trade publications, but in the Canadian press.

When Allied forces successfully moved off the beaches of Normandy and continued east in their drive toward the heart of Nazi Germany, the outlook for an end to the war in Europe seemed justified. But when Hitler's troops unexpectedly arose as 1944 drew to a close, Steele noted on Christmas day, "War news not as good as has been. Two weeks now Germans have been counterattacking in Belgium + Luxembourg, driving Yanks back."[48] Such an observation was consistent with Steele's unflagging hope for peace.

The year 1944 had been a good one for Steele in many respects, and his naming by the *New York Enquirer* as one of the country's top boxing announcers further burnished his glowing credentials. Public service work in support of the war effort remained on his task list, as he solicited donations of harmonicas and phonograph records to be dispensed to soldiers for their entertainment pleasure, and he continued to lend his name in support of Red Cross blood drives.

Adopting a clever tag line—"This is your good friend and mine, Bob Steele"—he never slowed down in his career while at once tending to the needs of his expanding family. During a break in his duties at WTIC, he found the time to post a brief note to his wife, Shirley, as the spring of 1945 loomed. "I love you. Guess who!" he wrote, signing off with the classic cartoon face he was so accustomed to drawing.[49]

This circa 1940 cartoon, drawn by Bob Steele, combines his love of family with his love of motorcycles (Hartford History Center, Hartford Public Library).

The voice of Bob Steele was helping WTIC to grow into one of the top radio markets in the country, which, given the location of Hartford in the Northeast, was a heady accomplishment when one considers the competition of other major outlets in Boston, New York, and Philadelphia. Fortified by "your good friend," Steele's employer was poised to sink its roots ever deeper into the soil of a medium soon to enter a postwar era that would also give rise to a new form of competition: television.

5

"I'm a big slob
from Missouri too ...
just like them"

He's big time.
—Lou Black's praise for Bob Steele,
New Haven Register, June 1945

By early 1945 the résumé of Bob Steele had acquired a fair amount of heft, and material that was created for WTIC's promotional purposes comprised two typed pages written in the trademark casual and fluid prose that, not surprisingly, impressed as a Steele-esque script that could be read on the air. At the top of the first page, the salient trait of "color" was credited as putting him in the same league as other charismatic sports personalities of the era such as Leo Durocher, Dizzy Dean, and Jack Dempsey.

Listed was a host of areas of specialty (boxing, racing, baseball) and roles that Steele had filled over the years (writer, cartoonist, gagster, speaker, announcer, sportscaster), and his glowing credentials were burnished with notes specific to his recent work in the field of boxing, not least of which was the resolution of the Willie Pep—Cabey Lewis controversy. "Call it a flair if you will ... call it a personality factor. Call it the result of 'knowing his stuff.' It all adds up to 'Color.' Color is equally valuable in selling sports or merchandise. Bob Steele can do both!"[1]

The demand for Steele's time continued to grow, whether it be for commercial advertising purposes at the radio station or personal appearances away from the studio. His popularity remained on the upswing, and his voice both on-air and in various columns and articles that he authored for publication remained remarkably consistent. When director Albert Lewin's motion picture adaptation of Oscar Wilde's *The Picture of Dorian Gray* was released in March 1945, Steele even briefly became a movie critic—of sorts—following a screening of the film at Avery Memorial Hall for the benefit of the local press. "[T]he most compelling thing I ever saw—as gripping as my landlord standing in the door on the second of the month," he joked, adding, "Seriously: it's absorbing, engrossing, brilliant." These comments, in turn, were re-worded into "Exceptionally absorbing! Gripping! Brilliantly different!" and appeared in a *Hartford Times* advertisement for the film.[2]

Although Steele never served in the armed forces, his scrapbook notes indicate a deep respect for those in the military. The surrender of Nazi Germany in May 1945 ending World War II in Europe meant that troops in the various branches of the service would begin returning to the States, and shortly after V-E Day Steele joined two other sports figures on a visit to a station hospital set up at Bradley Field to accommodate wounded veterans making their way home. The goodwill visit by Steele, professional golfer Bud Geoghegan, and *Courant* sports editor Bill Lee delighted all present, and when Steele served as "quiz master" in asking soldiers a range of trivia questions, he was astounded at the knowledge they displayed.[3]

Not only had Steele been accorded special access to the facility: he also proudly noted that when the first groups of bombers of the Army Air Forces arrived, he "interviewed crews when they first set foot on U.S. soil."[4] Steele lent his voice as WTIC joined other Hartford stations to solicit donations of old radios that would be repaired and given to military hospitals in neighboring states. In July he also was aboard a military plane that participated in a simulated airborne attack staged at Brainard Airport near the Connecticut River in the south end of Hartford. Because the conflict in the Pacific was far from over—there was no public knowledge of the development of the atomic bomb that would soon be used against Japan—the demonstration was part of another war bond drive that ultimately raised in excess of $1 million, and Steele reported on "the reactions of the men as they hit the 'drop zone' where they were to parachute to the ground."[5]

When the bomb was indeed dropped over Hiroshima and Nagasaki weeks later to force Japan's capitulation, the news spread quickly via teletype. The printed output was very much worth saving in Steele's view, and it found a place among his mementoes. While the formal surrender was yet to occur, the bulletin stated that "[t]he Japanese government are [*sic*] ready to accept the terms of the Potsdam Conference…," to which Steele added his own marginalia: "This is it! The real beginning of the end."[6] World War II in the Pacific theater concluded with the formal signing of surrender documents in September 1945.

In late November, the *Bridgeport Herald* printed a story that told of a battle shaping up between the Hartford radio stations. The article provided

a compelling footnote to Ben Hawthorne's prior departure for military service, which created the morning show vacancy subsequently filled by Bob
Steele. Recall that Hawthorne's wife, Travilla, initially took Ben's place, but
the *Herald* spoke a bald truth by pointing out that her stint on the air "left
something to be desired when she tried to match the sparkling performance
of her husband."[7] With Ben having fulfilled his obligation to the armed forces,
he was primed to return to his chosen field of work in the Hartford market,
but Steele was firmly entrenched in Hawthorne's old spot, so the two other
stations in the city, WTHT and WDRC, sought past WTIC personnel to compete with the capital's fifty thousand–watt outlet.

Despite Hawthorne finding a new home at WTHT, where he revived his
once-popular *Breakfast with Ben* program, and WDRC taking on former
WTIC announcer Roy Hansen—both were slotted head-to-head with Steele's
Morning Watch—there really was no contest. Steele noted that a Hooper poll
in early March 1946 indicated that for 7–8 a.m. programming, at least thirteen
radios were tuned to WTIC, only four for WTHT, two for WDRC, and one
for WHTD.[8] Although the survey may have suffered from the small sampling
size, it nonetheless seemed to indicate that Steele's show was by far the preferred choice of listeners.

Steele's mother, visiting the family in Connecticut over Christmas for
an extended stay, returned to Los Angeles courtesy of Greyhound Bus Lines,
and shortly thereafter he noted that with war now a thing of the past, the
economic recovery of the country was far from brisk. "Strikes rage in nation,"
Steele commented, "steel strike just settled but plenty of peace yet to be made
in industry." This situation was especially acute for a man infatuated with
automobiles: "No cars being made yet. Don't know when we'll get a new
buggy. Been without one 2½ years."[9] But just one month after registering this
mild complaint in his scrapbook, he took delivery of a new Ford from Gengras
Motors.

The spring of 1946 provided the chance for Steele to again act as prognosticator for the coming baseball season, and he struck gold by choosing
the Boston Red Sox to win the American League pennant and the St. Louis
Cardinals to take the National League crown, which both teams accomplished
the following autumn. Of greater import and more notoriety were a trio of
WTIC programs—including Steele's *Morning Watch*—that garnered honors
from *Billboard*, a broadcasting trade magazine. WTIC was the nation's only
station to have three shows so recognized, but not every member of the audience was enamored with his material.

Steele's fan mail included at least one missive in which "a 'slowly going
mad' Hartfordite" singled out his penchant for whistling during his show.

Although Bob Steele hit it lucky picking the 1946 baseball pennant winners, most of his predictions failed to come true because he often picked the underdog. This Christmas collage is also representative of Steele's outstanding cartooning ability (Hartford History Center, Hartford Public Library).

"Why can't you ack [sic] like normal people? Why don't you stop whistling? I must give you credit for playing some decent music, BUT WHY SPOIL IT WITH YOUR STUPID ASSININE [sic] WHISTLIN'? WHY??? I'm disgusted and from now on will do my own whistling in the morning."[10] Rather than take offense at the listener's rant, Steele used such otherwise unflattering correspondence by turning it into more self-deprecating fodder for the many events at which he was a guest speaker.

As if to assume the role of a bookkeeper with his sleeves rolled up and a visor over his brow, Bob Steele noted that even though World War II was a thing of the past, the lingering policy of government-regulated cost control still impacted what people paid when shopping for groceries. Several months prior to the entry of the United States into the war, the federal Office of Price Administration had been established by executive order for the purposes of harnessing inflation lest it have an overall deleterious effect on the economy. The OPA was also responsible for the rationing of a variety of food items including meats and sugar, gasoline, coffee, tires, as well as other major consumer products. When OPA constraints were removed in early July 1946, Steele recorded that the price of butter jumped over 50 percent (eighty-one cents a pound to $1.25) while the cost of ground beef more than doubled (forty-three cents a pound to ninety cents). Such huge increases led OPA to reinstate its controls by the end of that month in order to provide a degree of stability to the economy.

Fully aware of what was taking place in the world, Steele also privately observed at the time that there was "trouble in Palestine—King David Hotel bombed recently—Jews protesting fact that only a small number can get into foreign countries from Palestine [sic]."[11] While he left the reporting of these events to WTIC's news staff, Steele was on the local beat to inform listeners about fire prevention, conducting on-site interviews with public works employees and Hartford fire officials. His typical schedule had him on *Morning Watch* Monday through Saturday from 7 to 8 a.m., followed by announcing tasks that lasted until 1:15 p.m. (except on Saturdays), and *Strictly Sports* aired in the early evenings of Tuesday, Thursday, and Saturday from six fifteen to six twenty-five.[12]

In the postwar era, the mode of air transportation was slowly gaining currency in the public realm, but the frightful prospect of a disaster dissuaded more than a few potential passengers. "Air crashes numerous past 3 or 4 weeks," Steele told his diary. "People won't fly. Ride pogo stix if have to," he commented, and further cited the deaths of Prince Gustaf Adolf of Sweden and twenty others in a crash in Copenhagen, along with a later remark about fifty-two people who perished when a plane went down in Utah.[13] However, by early 1948, Steele found himself on company business traveling to Miami to broadcast a fight between Willie Pep and Humberto Sierra of Cuba. Aboard an Eastern Airlines "New-Type Constellation" for his round trip originating at Newark Airport, Steele's mind was diverted from the possibility of the plane going down, at least on the return flight. He breakfasted on "grapefruit, melba toast, sweet roll, butter, [and] coffee" and enjoyed the company of former boxing champion Jack Dempsey, who had officiated the bout in which Pep knocked out Sierra in the tenth round.[14]

This most recent Pep fight drew Steele into the national spotlight even though the bout was poorly attended—held at the Orange Bowl, the fight drew fewer than eight thousand fans as rainy weather took its toll at the box office—and the fight promoters suffered a loss of over forty thousand dollars. Steele was on hand to broadcast the fight back to WTIC in Hartford, but one of the event's handlers offered the opportunity to give him wider exposure. "How about you broadcasting on a [Mutual Broadcasting System] hookup? Would your company object? This might be the big break you've been looking for," read the tempting note from one of Steele's friends.[15] Indeed, Steele enthused upon his return home, "Broadcast received very favorable comments from everyone. Must have had terrific audience. On air 42 minutes before fite [sic] started—kept it rolling and got the plaudits."[16]

In the spring of 1948, Steele finally conceded that something had to give in the lengthy list of personal chores to which he was committed. "Stalling Around ... with Steele" made its final appearance in *Motorcyclist*, and he later confided to his scrapbook that "some readers didn't like [the column]—not enough stuff about motorcycles. Jokes too deep!"[17] By that summer, he found reason to slacken a bit: his mother came in from California for a month-long visit, and he had been named the top disk jockey in Connecticut by *Radio Best*, a media trade publication.

Steele's son Phil endured a minor medical calamity, having swallowed a dime but then passing it three days later. The situation was not lost on his father, who cheerily and frugally observed that the coin was "blackened but still worth 10¢!"[18] But a far greater concern arose when it was noticed that Phil's left foot was not growing properly, leading doctors to believe that he was suffering the effects of Kohler's disease, whereby the navicular bone in the foot collapses due to a lack of blood in the bone tissue. The youngster's foot was placed in a cast for four months in hope of a cure, and when doctors suggested treatment at the Newington Home for Crippled Children, Bob and Shirley blanched at the thought and sought a different opinion.[19] Another specialist, a Dr. Jones who disagreed with the original finding, recommended removal of the cast, and Phil, no longer encumbered by the implement, sprang to life and demonstrated his mobility by shinnying up a street pole near the Steele home.[20]

The financial condition of the Steele household was in great shape, in large part because WTIC was happy to reward their top man for the job he was doing and would have been foolish to do otherwise. Competing stations in the greater Hartford area also sought his services, but Steele was content taking a smaller salary from his current employer. "Was offered 5 year contract @ 17 thous[and per] year by Dr. Ben Sachner of WBIS Bristol or 15 per and 5% of sta. [ownership]," he noted a bit cryptically in early 1949.[21]

Coming at a time when the median annual wage in the United States was just under three thousand dollars, Steele—who was driving a new 1949 Cadillac—was living quite comfortably and earning enough to support his family and lifestyle, although the offer from WBIS appeared to be extremely generous. After discussing the matter with his boss, Paul Morency, Steele turned down the proposal and was satisfied to remain in the employ of WTIC, a clear manifestation of the loyalty he felt he owed to the enterprise that had benefited him so much and given him the opportunity to enjoy the additional income that resulted from his on-air exposure.

G. Fox had long underwritten *Morning Watch*, but even though they cut back their sponsorship to thirty minutes beginning in 1950, this adjustment had no impact on Steele's schedule as he was to remain on air for his normal full hour. Meanwhile, Shirley and Phil departed for a New Year's vacation in Florida, and in her own correspondence back home, she exhibited a bit of the Steele traits emblematic of her husband.

Traveling by rail, she was logging expenditures—forty-five cents or more for a series of luggage fees, fifty cents for pillows on the train—complaining about the "greedy red caps" who charged full price for Phil's meals even though he was only a child, and telling about a restive night en route to Fort Lauderdale. She explained that she "just couldn't [sleep] as I was helping the engineer keep the train on the track. Remote control[,] of course...."[22] The missives she sent home—portions of which Bob used on his program—indicate that she loved her husband as much as he loved her. During Shirley's absence, he was called away on business, serving as a broadcaster for the Willie Pep—Charlie Riley championship fight that took place in St. Louis on January 16.

In a pre-bout visit to the studios of radio station KSD, owned by the *St. Louis Post–Dispatch* newspaper, Steele attracted a crowd among the personnel there, and when he commandeered a typewriter in one of the offices, he banged out a letter to Shirley with his usual flair. "I guess they figure I'm just a hick from [Connecticut]," he told her, but since he suspected that the locals may not have been aware of his own roots, he also confided, "They don't know that I'M A BIG SLOB FROM MISSOURI TOO ... JUST LIKE THEM..."[23]

A possible strike of communications workers nearly ruined plans for the fight's broadcast, but when a delay in the job action was brokered, Steele went on the air unimpeded to call Pep's fifth-round knockout. Accompanied by Bill Lee and A. B. McGinley from the Hartford newspapers, Steele enjoyed their company on the round-trip rail excursion. He complained mildly to Shirley that he was not paid for the work he did covering the fight in St. Louis, but he noted that WTIC did compensate him for the three *Morning Watch* programs and two sports shows that he missed while he was out of town.

While Shirley was soon to end her hiatus in Florida, her son Robert took after his father by penning her a clandestine note to provide a status of affairs back at home in Wethersfield. The boy had been ill and "felt bad" because he was unable to go on a hike and "use some of my Boy Scout things that I got for Christmas," but he delighted in the souvenirs that his father had brought home from St. Louis.[24] All parties were looking forward to Shirley and Phil's return to Connecticut, a reunion which, of course, would alleviate the head of the household—and especially Grandma Hanson—from all the recent familial chores.

In the spring of 1950, Steele joined three other disk jockeys from across the United States in an appearance on *The Sammy Kaye Show* to relate some of their personal experiences to the bandleader who was now hosting a new television program that debuted in June. About the time the Steele family was to journey to Casco Bay, Maine, for vacation, hostilities erupted in Korea between the north and south, and he lamented to his diary two weeks into the conflict that the situation was looking bleak. He later grew concerned over "talk of using 'a' bomb" in the hopes of bringing a quick end to the fighting through the use of an atomic weapon. "Peace is an elusive thing," he wrote philosophically, and in a rare reference to religion, he concluded, "But war is human nature it seems. There will always be wars—until the very end, says the Bible."[25]

Steele was buoyed, however, by the anticipation of another addition to the clan: Shirley was again pregnant. And the Steeles also enjoyed local weekend trips to Cornfield Point in Old Saybrook, where Shirley's sister Florence kept a summer cottage just west of the mouth of the Connecticut River on Long Island Sound. Steele's popularity and the attendant compensation it brought him afforded the luxury of purchasing fine automobiles and time away from the studio to enjoy the state's shoreline. The earnings also paid for the $1,380 remodeling of the family home in Wethersfield, which relative to the time was a significant outlay of money.

In the early morning of December 9, Steven Michael Steele was born at Hartford Hospital, and despite the fact that this was Bob and Shirley's fourth child—all boys—the new mother wrote to her sister informing her that "Bob was like a man without a head all day[,] he was so dazed and happy."[26] When Steele announced the new arrival on his show a few hours after the birth, it prompted a flood of well-wishes from listeners who sent over four hundred cards and letters within a matter of days.

By the beginning of 1951, Steele evinced the pacifism that he favored in world affairs. The Korean War was in its seventh month, and he confided to his diary that there was a rumor that armed forces of the United States and the United Nations might initiate a complete withdrawal. "We lose face," he noted, alluding to the fact that such a pullout would be embarrassing to America's struggle against communism, but of greater importance to him would be the "sav[ing] a lot of GI's from LOSING FACES."[27] These observations were strictly private because although he kept track of "national and international politics [he] never commented on them on the air."[28] On April 11, his neutrality was tested when he took to the streets to get opinions on the biggest news item that day: "MacArthur fired by Truman!" he wrote in large letters in his diary.

The dismissal of General Douglas MacArthur by President Harry Truman was extremely controversial because many Americans recalled the popular warrior's famous declaration, "I shall return," stated upon his forced departure from Corregidor and the Philippines in 1942—and his subsequent victory in the Pacific theater that made him a military icon. As hostilities in Korea continued into early 1951, Truman thought that he might be able to broker a peaceful settlement with China, which had been North Korea's biggest ally. But MacArthur was persistent in his desire to carry on the fighting, thus undercutting Truman, who dismissed the general and, in turn, was reviled—especially by Republicans—for removing a venerated military leader.

Truman's handling of the affair won few supporters among the MacArthur crowd, but neither did the commander-in-chief endear himself to another branch of the nation's military when he previously sent a letter to a congressman in which he called the Marine Corps "the Navy's police force" that was enabled by "a propaganda machine comparable to Stalin's."[29] The remark drew outrage from the Marines, at least one of whom saw fit to reconfigure the lyrics to "The Marine Corps Hymn" in order to deride Truman for his mean-spirited comment, and the revised words to the song eventually became material for Bob Steele, who later employed them "for historical and patriotic, rather than political, value."[30] Among the verses recited were these:

From the halls of Montezuma
To the shores of Tripoli,
We'll police old Harry's navy
As long as they're at sea.
First to fight the Army's battles
And to win Korea fights
And still our good friend Harry
Tries to louse up all our rights.

Later that spring, Steele was tapped by WTIC to travel to the Indianapolis Speedway to report on the time trials for the 1951 Indianapolis 500, and in late June he served as the host of a tribute in Hartford paid to Connie Mack, the longtime owner and recently retired manager of the Philadelphia Athletics. The event contained not a little historical foreshadowing: Mack spent seven decades in baseball, which was only a few years longer than Bob Steele would devote to working for WTIC. There soon followed in Steele's diary an entry in large writing that played to a time-honored cliché in commemoration of his birthday: "40 Today! LIFE BEGINS!"[31]

Life for Bob Steele obviously began much sooner than age forty, and in a commercial sense he continued to curry favor with advertisers. His *Strictly Sports* program was sponsored by Camel cigarettes and the United Aircraft Corporation, the latter enterprise eventually transforming into United Technologies Corporation. But Steele also drew the notice of *Broadcasting* magazine's feature article on Hartford National Bank and Trust and the positive results the bank experienced thanks to its sponsorship of Steele's morning show. The publication informed readers, "Live commercials were carefully planned by the bank, the [advertising] agency ... and the station [WTIC].... He was given full latitude to put the announcements into his own words with occasional historical and humorous references to the bank."[32]

Ostrom Enders, president of the financial institution, proudly wrote to Steele and commended him on the "wonderful job which you have done for the bank. Somehow you manage to make the endless talk about a relatively dry subject interesting...."[33] Hartford National came to know what Camel and United Aircraft—along with other Steele sponsors such as the Mennen Company, Sterling Salt, Manhattan Soap, and Lehigh Coal—already knew: Bob Steele had a likeable voice that inspired trust, and his appeal further bolstered the confidence of advertisers who wisely chose to cast their lot with him.

Already well documented in these pages is the indefatigable spirit of Bob Steele, a man who seemingly never took a break from his career, family chores and duties—which he tended to with alacrity—and the extracurricular activities that rounded out his life. As if all this were not enough, however, in the spring of 1952 he became involved in yet another venture: a car wash business.

Operated by his friend Jack Moore, the Quick Auto Laundry was a partnership in which Steele invested, and his diary entries reveal a great deal of angst that accompanied the launching of this enterprise. Moore oversaw the construction of the facility at 155 Airport Road in the south end of Hartford, and he would handle its day-to-day operations once completed. But a series of delays and problems hampered efforts to open the new business, not least of which were some legal issues that stalled the laying out of the plot of land on which the building would be constructed. Once this had finally been accomplished on May 24, Steele informed his boss at WTIC, Paul Morency, about his entering into the deal with Moore. Morency sanctioned the arrangement with one caveat: "Don't publicize it."[34]

Concrete footings were poured in early June at the Moore-Steele Auto Laundry, but Steele fretted three months later that it may take another six weeks for all the work to be done. "Jack raising hell because Auto Laundry so slow being finished. It's really an ordeal for Jack. He's there all the time. Painters, plumbers, carpenters fail to show up," Steele confided to his diary, and the site was struck by disaster when a "BOILER blew up today—about 10:30 a.m. and if door hadn't been open in boiler room Jack and a young labour[er] would have been hurt or killed. Tremendous blast. Neither was even scratched. Close!"[35]

As the calendar turned to November, Steele noted, "Money is running short. Gotta get rolling," and after all the turmoil subsided and the contractors at last completed their tasks, the Auto Laundry opened following a ribbon-cutting ceremony attended by Hartford mayor Joseph Cronin on November 6.[36] Steele, ever vigilant of the bottom line, was discouraged by problems with the conveyor system as well as other glitches that limited the number of cars processed that day to 248, and he would be frustrated further when bad weather discouraged customers from patronizing the business. But as the weeks and months progressed—and as additional snafus were addressed— the volume of traffic at the state-of-the-art facility continued to rise, peaking at about one thousand cars in one day in early 1954.

Potential entrepreneurs took notice of the success enjoyed by what Steele himself nicknamed "Quick": "Everybody wants to get into the act—[phone] calls every day. How to get into [the] business? Where [to] get machinery? How much? Etc."[37] A little over two years after he became involved in establishing the car wash, Steele received a proposal to sell most of his share in the business to Jack Moore—while retaining a 10-percent interest—but another deal was consummated on June 11, 1954, whereby he sold all of his stock to his partner.

When Steele was initiating the venture with Moore, he also observed that the new medium of television was strongly rumored to begin broadcasting from Connecticut's capital. "No channel assigned to any station, though," and he expressed a reluctance to embrace the latest technology: "Everybody talks about it but me."[38] Indeed, Steele's blasé reaction reflected the attitude taken by the management of WTIC.

As a growing number of radio stations in major cities added television broadcasting to their offerings, "the impact was tremendous. Some of the really popular radio programs—the daytime soaps, for example—disappeared almost overnight."[39] And as a growing number of modern appliances made their way into more American homes, the transition from listening to the radio to watching television was underway.

However, as the alumni association of Bob Steele's employer observed, "WTIC had always been responsive to change. There was, naturally, a concern for programming that sold. Using instinct, knowledge of market and ratings, management made adjustments in the station's programming to fit the changing tastes of the public. WTIC had always maintained continuity ... but was not allowed to become stagnant. Quality local programming filled the void left by network radio's retreat."[40] That quality programming was fronted by Bob Steele himself, and it would later prove compelling that one of WTIC's shows, *Mind Your Manners*, which aired from 1947 to 1954 and focused on a younger audience, was hosted by a thirty-year-old continuity writer named Allen Ludden, who would later move on to emcee the popular, long-running television game show *Password*.

A national figure already etched in the public's mind was Arthur Godfrey, the popular radio host who gradually segued to television in the late 1940s. In mid–September 1952, Steele privately indicated that a "Mr. Chapman," who was a board member of the Columbia Broadcasting System, was interested in reaching out to him to possibly "get me on at CBS as a Godfrey assistant, understudy, successor, or what have you." But Steele also was leery of such an offer, opining, "Sounds like HOKUM to me."[41]

Yet, an avocation that would not entice Steele away from the studio was active participation in softball, which he did once in a *Hartford Courant— Hartford Times* benefit game held between radio announcers and members of the city newspapers. Not only was the radio crew trounced 20–9 in the contest at Bulkeley Stadium despite a 3-for-4 performance at the plate by

Steele, but he loudly complained of the resultant and immediate pain in muscles he had not exercised in quite some time: "IT IS 4 a.m.—I'M UP! MUSCLES in legs and left arm so sore I'm going off my rocker. To bed at 8 p.m. after scalding bath."[42] At least the take for the game was a success—$700 was raised to support children's activities at Camp Courant and the Times Farm.

The year 1952 faded into 1953, but the calendar change was not kind to Bob Steele, who was hospitalized in late December for surgery on hemorrhoids, and then three weeks later he broke his left hand. Nonetheless, he was not out of action for very long, and soon after resumed his work at WTIC as well as his personal appearances at various social and civic functions. Resumed, that is, until he was felled by a back sprain in the second half of May, and as if to prove the point that misery loves company, his oldest son broke a leg and ankle playing baseball. Steele's diary entry for this mishap borrowed from the former great pitcher Dizzy Dean: "Robert ... playing [second base] was taking throw from outfield as Ed Greene <u>slud</u> into him."[43]

One year after the Quick Auto Laundry began operation, it remained the only such facility in Hartford, and there followed the opening of another modern structure that was emblematic of the flourishing love affair that post–World War II America had with the automobile. "Opened up G. Fox's new parking garage," Steele told his diary on November 5, 1953, and in an age when grand, city-based department stores remained crucial to the vibrancy of urban business districts, it was a wise move on the part of G. Fox's management to offer parking to cater to those customers relying more heavily on their personal cars.[44]

And by further extension of increasing auto traffic, a pernicious problem also began to foment not just in Hartford but across the country. Steele and his family reluctantly went to a family gathering on the Connecticut shore, wavering not because of the company but they "[h]esitated to go because of SMOG. Atmospheric conditions of past 3 or 4 days have kept smoke from disappearing—hence fog and smoke pall has hung over area. Many wrecks—esp[ecially] on parkways where long chains of cars (50 in one case) banged into each other."[45]

In early 1954 as The Travelers was vying for a television license for Channel 3 with a local enterprise known as Hartford Telecasting Company, Inc., Bob Steele became an unwitting subject of legal testimony over the Federal Communications Commission's definition of what constituted a live broadcast, as opposed to one that was recorded. Steele obviously used recorded music several times during his shows, but the FCC's mandate required that "live" programs employ recorded music "only for themes, background, musical bridges, and so forth."[46] Although the competing interests of WTIC and

Hartford Telecasting actually related to the ability of either enterprise to properly finance adequate programming for the proposed television station, it
was interesting to see that the format of Bob Steele's show—with him clearly
serving as a live radio host—had been brought into the court proceedings.
The process of WTIC acquiring Channel 3 would extend through the remain-
der of the year.

Regardless of the FCC's interpretation of "live," Steele in mid–April had
fifteen minutes added to his show and was now on the air Monday through
Saturday from 6:45 a.m. through 7:30 a.m. for *The Bob Steele Show*, which
then immediately segued into *Morning Watch* and ran until 8 a.m. His *Strictly
Sports* also aired those same days for ten minutes beginning at 6:15 p.m., and
the salary for all these efforts amounted to about $6,200 per year, excluding,
of course, fees he picked up from scores of speaking engagements.[47]

Steele took a break during the early summer to travel with sons Robert
and Paul on a western motor trip to Los Angeles to visit his mother. Giving
the slightly underage youngster some practice behind the wheel of a new
Oldsmobile 98 convertible, Steele bragged in his diary that "Robt drove 1500
mi[les] in desert!," although the son explained years later that his father would
give driving lessons to all the Steele boys in their turn.[48] Once in Southern
California, their sightseeing led them to lunch at the home of Hollywood
star Virginia Mayo and her husband, the actor Michael O'Shea, who was a
native of Hartford. The actress further noted the terrible sunburn that young
Robert received due to traveling with the Olds' top down in the stifling Southwestern heat. Steele faithfully sent postcards and letters back home to Shirley
and their other sons in addition to placing long-distance calls on at least
eight occasions to keep tabs on the home front.

Keeping an active eye on the boxing scene also earned Steele a chance
to voice his opinion in a new sporting publication. He, along with several
promoters and politicians, offered views on the state of boxing in answer to
a question posed by *Sports Illustrated* columnist Jimmy Jemail: What can be
done to clean up boxing? Steele replied that "a national czar," whose position
would be commensurate with that of the baseball commissioner, would help
to remove some of the recent unsavory characteristics that were infecting
boxing. Not least of this tawdriness was the second-round knockout of Willie
Pep in a February 1954 fight in which it was later claimed that the Hartford
ring hero had taken a dive in order to receive an underhanded payout of sixteen thousand dollars.[49]

At the close of 1954, a logistical change at WTIC did not find favor
among certain staff members. "Announcers grousing about new set-up in
Studio F—Near the 'Brass,'" he penned in his diary, and he observed that the

engineers' former duty to maintain the logs of program information was now the responsibility of the announcers themselves.[50] Such a formalization of paperwork protocol, however, may have been initiated by the FCC and thus out of the control of station management, yet the level of comfort now reduced by closer physical proximity to those in charge of WTIC's operations presented some unwelcome apprehension.

This particular year also marked the establishment of an enduring, landmark service. The Travelers Insurance Company, in conjunction with WTIC, founded The Travelers Weather Service under the leadership of former MIT professor Dr. Thomas F. Malone in an effort to "provide its listeners with more meaningful and understandable weather forecasts ... and help residents better prepare for the unpredictable Connecticut Valley weather."[51] Among the key information passed on to WTIC's audience were features that described the significance of barometric readings and sun spot activity, an explanation of the jet stream, and other valuable aspects of meteorology.

The timing of the Weather Service's creation could not have been more propitious given that in the very next year, southern New England was ravaged by two hurricanes, Connie and Diane, the latter being the far more devastating storm. Weather advisories and public service broadcasting became WTIC's stock-in-trade to assist the vast population affected by the event that wrought $600 million in damage to the area.

Bob Steele remained the most visible luminary—perhaps the busiest ever—at WTIC, yet other personnel such as Floyd Richards and Ross Miller were also instrumental to the station's ongoing efforts and resultant success. All the while, the management was in a protracted struggle to add television to its media lineup, a situation that took its toll on Paul Morency, the WTIC mogul who was removed from the office by wheelchair at the end of October, apparently suffering from the stress associated with trying to acquire the rights to Channel 3.

In the early 1950s, television was a distant runner-up to the more deeply entrenched medium of radio, which had no fewer than sixty-five licensed stations all over the United States broadcasting at fifty-thousand watts—six alone in Chicago and five in New York—with many more operating at lesser power, many of them affiliated with the Columbia Broadcasting System, the National Broadcasting Company, the American Broadcasting Company, and the Mutual Broadcasting System.[52] It is also important to note that millions of newspapers across the nation continued to be printed each day, many areas serviced with morning and evening editions that provided information on all manner of news, advertising, and entertainment features.

While newsprint had a longer history and commercial radio was only in its fourth decade, the tide was slowly shifting toward television, and WTIC was determined to participate in the latest broadcast technology. This radio outlet's brightest star would soon play a role in that endeavor as it sought a better footing in the competition for its share of a new audience.

6

Moving into the Age
of Modernization

I'd like to forget TV and just keep rolling with good old, comfortable, sane radio.
—Bob Steele, diary entry of September 13, 1957

The decade of the 1950s tells a story of the American dream coming to fruition for many in the country's middle class. With the privations of the Great Depression and World War II now in the past, the United States had much to look forward to, not least of which was the growth in economic power that fueled the formation and rise of a consumer culture. Prosperity in the postwar era, according to the historian James T. Patterson, "broadened gradually in the late 1940s, accelerated in the 1950s, and soared to unimaginable heights in the 1960s."[1]

Hartford, Connecticut, was not isolated from the forces influencing the middle decade to which Patterson refers, although manufacturing industries in the greater Northeast were beginning a slow migration to more southern and western parts of the country. However, a saying of the day—"What's good for General Motors is good for America"—conveyed the ambience of the era in which it seemed that so much was going right for so many people.

Adding its own contribution to the blooming growth in America was the purchase of household appliances now on offer. As the construction of new homes—notably in Levitt Town–style developments—created new residences, those same homes were increasingly filled with the accouterments of the modern American household: vacuum cleaners, washing machines, and, catering to the latest in media technology, television sets. Entrepreneurs such as Eugene Ferkauf saw the future developing before their eyes and formed retail outlets to ensure that the demand for all manner of home goods would be met, thus his launching of the discount store chain E. J. Korvettes, where consumers flocked to buy not only hair dryers and toasters but large appliances as well. This was the milieu of the mid–1950s, a time when The Travelers Insurance Company ultimately succeeded in its acquisition of the rights to Channel 3 and also when Bob Steele commemorated his twentieth anniversary of service to WTIC.

Shortly before the oldest Steele son was packed off to Amherst College in the autumn of 1956, The Travelers finally succeeded in securing the rights to Channel 3 on July 25. Despite the bureaucratic victory, the insurance company was nonetheless precluded by the Federal Communications Commission from beginning construction on its television broadcast facility until late February of the following year. But Paul Morency, WTIC's president, noted, "Within five months … our downtown TV studios were built, our transmitter and studio equipment installed and tower erected, ready for wiring. Despite uncontrollable delays, including a new FCC ruling prohibiting the use of a temporary antenna tower with which we had planned to begin operations, we have kept the pledge we made back in September 1947 to 'proceed to construct a station with the greatest possible speed' after we received the go-ahead signal."[2]

A trade publication indicated that once WTIC-TV became operational, the programming schedule of "the new independent station … [would rely] heavily on features plus news, sports and weather to attract viewers," and those features were to include syndicated shows as well as packages from Movietime U.S.A., United Artists Award, Screen Gems' Hollywood Premiere Parade, and others.[3] Enabling the broadcast of all these programs was the new state-of-the-art studio furnished with "[a] wide variety of lighting and floor equipment, mechanical devices for providing scenic effects, draping for background purposes, an excellent art department, and the necessary tools to build sets and props [to] make the station a 'producer's dream.'"[4]

All of this hardware was set up on the sixth floor of the Travelers' Grove Street and Central Row buildings, which were adjoining edifices that comprised part of the company's downtown Hartford campus. Nearly twenty-thousand square feet of space was apportioned for media operations, with twenty rooms and offices dedicated to television, twelve more reserved for radio, and another seventeen spaces used for both radio and TV purposes. Walter Johnson, WTIC's general manager, was concerned that the construction of a new adjacent building on Main Street—also to be part of the Travelers' property and connected to the Grove Street building—might cause "some construction noise [to leak] into microphones on a few occasions," but in the end, the logistics worked out well as the station carried on with its broadcasts.[5]

Radio station WTIC began regular coverage of the Boston Red Sox on April 20, 1957, a tradition that has lasted well into the twenty-first century, yet its new television partner carried the Cleveland Browns as its pro football attraction. But the foray into television broadcasting was an entirely different venture, and it was one that caused no small amount of angst for Bob Steele. An early evening in mid–September found Steele returning home following a third day of dress rehearsals for the new version of his *Strictly Sports* program, the televised edition called *Close-Up on Sports*. He told his diary,

> TV is new to me—and hard. Geo[rge] Ehrlich is helping me prepare the [program] but isn't a real big help. Seems to be nice guy [however]. After I do radio sports (10 min[utes] at 6:15) I have to do a TV rehearsal for 10 min[utes] at 6:30—then the show— 30 min[utes] of talking—all under pressure—and it's wicked. Right now as I look toward opening night Sept 23—I feel I'll never make it.... I wouldn't even predict that I'll go thru opening night.[6]

In a newspaper preview celebrating the launch of WTIC-TV—which, not surprisingly, featured a full-page opening photograph of Steele seated at the studio desk—Steele tried to put a humorous spin on the landmark event by informing readers, "We're going to bend every effort to present the best and

Judging by the look on Bob Steele's face, he was never comfortable in front of a television camera (Hartford History Center, Hartford Public Library).

most comprehensive TV sports show that can be packed into ten minutes.... When those cameras and all that other expensive equipment pick up my likeness on the magic lantern, something may well explode. We can only put our trust in a good make-up man and hope for the best."[7]

The stark reality of live television laid bare everything before the viewing audience, and there were few means to prevent or recover from miscues that might happen on air, such as the studio crew's failure to display the proper photographs that correlated to the story being read at the moment. "There was too much that could go wrong," noted Steele's son Phil years later, "and as a perfectionist, Bob could be quick to anger over such mistakes."[8] When this snafu occurred during one program, "Bob was so upset that the minute the show was over he let out his displeasure by punching a fist through the studio wall."[9] A few years later as black-and-white television began to be supplanted by color broadcasting, Steele had a rude introduction to the latest version of this technology when he interviewed New York Yankee manager Johnny Keane at a sports banquet. Steele was not aware that his conversation would be filmed in color, carping afterward to his diary that when he dressed the morning of the event, he clad himself in a "black and white striped shirt, black tie, shoes and sox and gray suit! The truth!"[10]

On WTIC television's opening night, there were a multitude of issues, and Steele was quick to vent to former WTIC radio host Ed Begley, who served as the master of ceremonies for the occasion. "[Steele's] colleagues were not always comfortable with the exacting way Bob strove to meet standards for himself and his profession," observed Phil Steele, and not all of the inaugural broadcast issues were under the control of those personnel who were on the air; in some cases the transmitting signal was so strong that it caused reception problems in some areas.[11] Despite the assortment of troubles, upper management of WTIC nonetheless expressed its appreciation for the effort put forth by Bob Steele. "[Y]our presence on the program helped create a warm friendly feeling, a most difficult ingredient to inject into any program, be it radio or television. You made a lot of friends for both yourself and the station on that Opening Night...," read a personal memo to Steele.[12]

Steele likely appreciated such attention, but with his duties on radio as well as the demands on his time for speaking appearances continuing to cut into his days, he found television to be among his least favorite obligations. As television sunk its roots ever deeper into the cultural milieu of the United States, the country's landscape was being subjected to a transmogrification that plunged the nation into an age of modernity. The state of Connecticut was not immune to the forces of economic development that were girded by

an ideology upholding a doctrine that newer was better, and the city of Hartford also was swept along with this tide of progress.

Many books and studies have detailed the scale and scope of a multitude
of construction projects across America throughout the 1900s. The physical
and radical transformation in the decades following World War II spoke
directly to the industrial might unleashed in the United States during the
conflict, and creation of new housing, highways, and commercial buildings
impacted the lives of tens of millions of people. The most widely known—
or demonized, depending on one's point of view—person who led the charge
into rapid urban growth was Robert Moses, the autocrat who shaped and
reshaped the metropolitan New York City region throughout the middle of
the twentieth century. But just as greater Manhattan was a constant work-
in-progress for Moses, the late 1950s were fertile ground for the planning
and creation of other enduring landmarks: the interstate highway system,
Dodger Stadium on the fringe of downtown Los Angeles, and the iconic,
scalloped skyscrapers of Chicago's Marina Towers to name but a very few.

In Connecticut, there were a number of projects underway, and although
some of them were less ambitious in scope than something Moses may have
engaged in, they nonetheless indicated that the Constitution State was hardly
being left behind in the forward march of progress. TURNPIKE LARGEST
PROJECT EVER UNDERTAKEN BY STATE, blared a headline that spanned an
entire page of the October 23, 1957, *New Haven Evening Register*, and the
accompanying article presented readers with an astonishing array of facts
and details related to the 129-mile stretch of highway from Greenwich to
Killingly, most of those miles being incorporated into the new federal highway
system as Interstate 95. An important adjunct to I-95, Interstate 91 would
also be constructed, running north-south between New Haven and the Massachusetts state line. But in the process, I-91 would inflict damage to the economy of the businesses on the Berlin Turnpike, an existing state highway
running parallel to the new roadway and from which traffic and shoppers
would be diverted.

Two years later that same newspaper provided a status of the various
development projects around the state, trumpeting the plans for New Haven
as the "most ambitious." Indeed, the Oak Street section of the Elm City by
late 1959 was purged of a "42 acre site considered Connecticut's worst slum"
and had been made over into a complex featuring "the City's largest office
building, a multi-colored modern apartment building, [and] a streamlined
business and shopping center."[13] Most major municipalities, including Bridgeport, Waterbury, Stamford, Bristol, New London, and New Britain, joined in

the rush to upgrade because "[l]ike a woman with her face lifted, a redeveloped city gets a new lease on life, redevelopment advocates say."[14] Hardly left behind, the state capital found itself in the thick of the action as well.

Proposals for urban renewal in Hartford were directed at the eastern side of the downtown area, and those targeting this part of the city had several good reasons bolstering their argument. What was known as the original Front Street district had consisted of several blocks of structures dating to the 1800s that had been populated by evolving ethnicities. Historian Peter C. Baldwin wrote that "shiftless and unkempt housing" put a blight on the East Side, the tenements of which contributed to a "slum [that] bordered so closely on downtown office buildings and department stores that the middle class could see the squalor."[15]

The misery already impacting the East Side was compounded by the floods of the 1930s and persistent neglect by landlords insensitive to the needs of their tenants. As Irish, German, Scandinavian, Russian, Polish, Jewish, and Italian immigrants passed through Front Street over a number of decades, the neighborhood acquired a smarmy reputation for social restiveness, and "[t]he atmosphere reflected not simply the different cultures of the immigrants, but especially the fact that the East Side served as Hartford's skid row and red-light district."[16] No better remedy to eradicate the problem could be found than subjecting the area to a modernization that would displace the ill-fortuned residents, raze the blighted buildings, and create a new, clean, urban space catering to commercial enterprises.

An attempt to soften the blow inflicted on the displaced tenants came by way of a proposed plaza and "roof garden" that would conceal the parking garages built underneath the pedestrian concourses and provide a manufactured green space connecting a series of new commercial buildings. "Civic leaders wanted to redevelop a run-down ethnic neighborhood … known as Front Street. The plaza was the answer," said one landscape architect, explaining that "The Travelers Insurance [Companies] led the charge, envisioning a public space that would be occupied and enjoyed not only by the building inhabitants, but also *all Hartford residents*."[17] Little charity underpinned the true motive for this urban improvement: "One of the [architectural] designers recalls a Travelers executive saying he believed the plaza would ensure the long-term value of the company's downtown property."[18]

Thus, the decade of the 1960s dawned with plans being rendered to transform what some critics referred to as a slum on Hartford's East Side into a fine example of the benefits to be gained through the initiative of urban renewal. Ground was broken for what was named Constitution Plaza, a project that cost $42 million and was eventually completed in 1964. In the decades since it debuted, Constitution Plaza has been alternately lauded and berated: praised for the improvement it brought to an admittedly ramshackle district yet condemned for the impersonal evisceration of a minority population whose ethnic diversity and antiquity are what twenty-first century romantics find crucial to the preservation of cultural characteristics.

In the first years of Constitution Plaza's existence, the beneficial value of the project was neatly summarized by *Look* magazine, which enumerated several assets that gave the place an air of synergy. When financial problems set in during the early stages of development, The Travelers intervened with a heavy infusion of cash, and "Phoenix Mutual Life Insurance Company reversed its decision to move away from Hartford and projected its new, ship-shaped building as an extension of the plaza. Constitution Plaza proved to be just the vote of confidence in the city that was needed."[19] The publication also cited a host of other worthy projects: the expansion of the nearby G. Fox department store, the construction of new headquarters of the Hartford National Bank and Trust Company one block to the west on Main Street, a Travelers computer center and graduate school for Rensselaer Polytechnic Institute minutes away to the north, and, two blocks to the south, a new wing at the Wadsworth Athenaeum.

By the mid–1960s, the example set in Hartford encouraged at least one other municipality to explore a similar initiative, when an official from Pontiac, Michigan, visited Constitution Plaza to see firsthand the transformation of the downtown area. Mayor Les Hudson was trying to stem the flow of his city's businesses to suburban areas, an unfortunate migration that was bringing desolation to a previously thriving commercial district.

Not mentioned in the *Look* article but nevertheless a key component in the site plan for Constitution Plaza was a new venue for the studios of both the radio and television operations of WTIC. Moving to Broadcast House on September 3, 1961, where bright, contemporary facilities awaited the staff, crew, and management, WTIC opened a new chapter in its storied history. Yet Bob Steele and his comrades did business there for barely thirteen years before WTIC—now divested of the television side of its enterprise—relocated to another new edifice emblematic of the strength and power of the capital city, the Gold Building.

Life in the Steele family carried on with its expected ups and downs, and in early 1958 the paterfamilias observed that he "[m]ay be doing too much work."[20] Bob Steele's diary indicated that a house call by his personal physician produced no conclusive causes for the stomach woes he was suffering, but through it all there was no easing of his on-air duties. Steele's radio morning show ran Monday through Saturday from six forty-five to nine fifteen, and his evenings on those same days were taken up with evening sports reporting on radio from six fifteen to six twenty-five and then in the television studio from six forty-five to six fifty-five. All the while, his sons were growing up before his eyes: Robert was in his second year at Amherst, Paul contemplated enrollment at Hobart College or Bates College—another Small Ivy school in Maine which won out as his choice—Phil was soon to move up to Wethersfield High School, and Steve was about to finish second grade at Charles Wright School. And the boys' mother, the love of Steele's life, "is fine and still a beautiful girl."[21]

Even though his own job was secure, Steele was troubled by a downturn in the U.S. economy and the rise in unemployment. What some labeled the Eisenhower Recession was of brief duration, and although conditions improved by May, the shockwaves it generated caused no small amount of worry. As the economy slowly recovered, Steele and son Phil embarked on a summer road trip to California to visit Steele's mother and his old friend George Lannom. Destinations enjoyed during the three-week journey included the Grand Canyon, Disneyland, and even a stop at Abraham Lincoln's home in Springfield, Illinois. The trip to see Susan was poignant in its timing as it would be the final time that she would see her only child.

In Steele's diary entry for November 16, 1958, he wrote, "[W]TIC-TV Ch[annel] 3 has CBS-TV for [the] first time," a landmark event that removed the television station from its status as an independent outlet and affiliated it with the Columbia Broadcast System, an association which endures to this day even though WTIC-TV became WFSB in the early 1970s.[22] He further recorded the occasion of a family dinner—sans the oldest sons, who were in college—at the Simsbury House restaurant, but of far greater importance was the lengthy paean he wrote to memorialize his mother. It can only be left to speculation as to why a man so fastidious with the maintenance of a diary would have delayed the mention of the passing of someone who was so dear to him. But on the one-month anniversary of his mother's death, Bob Steele took the time to fill nearly two pages of his diary with some of the most heartfelt words he had ever set to paper.

After cheerfully commenting that the owner of the Simsbury House had invited the Steeles to be his guests for Thanksgiving dinner, Steele poured his heart out because his mother was not able to join the traditional feast.

Wish my Mom could be with us. She passed on Oct. 16, 1958, at Los Angeles—cancer. I flew out and was with her 2 days—or 3—before her death. Left Oct. 15 at 9 p.m. not knowing how long she might linger. Aunt Mayme [was] with her. Death came a few hours after I left. I lost the most wonderful mother who ever lived and I'm ashamed that I didn't insist that she live with us in her last years. But she liked California. Phil and I went out in July and took her (and Phil!) to Disneyland, a night drive to Beverly Hills, Hollywood, the hills above Hollywood, the Brown Derby for dinner (on Wilshire)—a wonderful dinner and a fond memory. Then the 3 of us drove east in the Rambler Ambassador [auto dealer Harvey] Lipman gave me for the trip, and enjoyed it—the best of the desert, the noise and activity of Las Vegas, the beauty of Utah and Colorado—and left Mom with Aunt Mayme in Topeka. I'm glad we were with Mom—and she with us—another month or two would have been too late. She felt fine on the trip but cancer was beginning to take her, though she didn't suspect. Or, so she told me. She was the kind, though, who might have known and wouldn't say. Every day I realize more and more—it becomes clear to me—that she was a most remarkable person with a tremendous strength of character—that I could never begin to match. Mom, I love you more each minute—but now it's too late—too late. Why must that be the old, old, story?

God Rest You and Bless You, Mom.[23]

Susan Steele, aged seventy-nine years, took with her more than the fond memory of her son's most recent trip to see her. The sense of pride knowing the heights of fame he had achieved at WTIC was far removed from what she may have envisioned for his future when they lived together in Kansas City years earlier, especially as the Great Depression began to cast its shadow across the nation.

To atone for that time regretfully lost, Bob Steele read on air a few weeks after his mother's passing a poem, "Why Do We Wait?," intended to be at once cathartic for himself as well as friendly advice for his listeners. Although anonymously written to address a masculine subject, the message contained therein was unmistakable.

Why do we wait 'til a person's gone
Before we tell him of his worth?
Why do we wait, why not tell him now
He's the finest man on earth?
Why do we wait 'til a person's gone
To send him flowers galore,
When a single rose would have meant so much
If we'd take it to his door?
Why do we wait 'til he cannot hear
The good things we might say
Why put it off, why not tell him now
And share his joy today?
Of course, we're busy—that's our excuse
—But why, oh why do we wait
To tell a person our love for him
Until it becomes too late?[24]

By the spring of 1959, the Steeles were ensconced in their new residence, less than one mile from their previous house. Even though the family's ranks had been thinned a bit with sons Robert and Paul away at college and Phil nearly ready to depart for that same purpose, they moved into a new four-bedroom home at 384 Wolcott Hill Road that also featured an attached two-car garage. An English major with a minor in Russian, Robert would soon graduate from Amherst and then spend six weeks traveling to Russia as part of an exchange program in mid–1960 prior to his entering Columbia University's Russian Institute. The excursion of the eldest Steele son came at a time when the premier of the Soviet Union, Nikita Khrushchev, was engaging in an instance of Cold War saber-rattling. Bob Steele noted in his diary that "Khrushchev has just told U.S. not to lay a hand on Cuba or Russian rockets could reach USA. Doesn't sound good."[25] Thus, by well over two years Steele observed a presaging of what would develop into the Cuban Missile Crisis of October 1962.

Garnering the honor of Connecticut's "sportscaster of the year" for the second straight year was one of Steele's highlights in 1961, but his silver-anniversary year at WTIC was also complicated by a springtime surgical procedure and subsequent ten-day hospitalization.[26] The wedding of eldest son Robert to the former Elizabeth Ann "Betsy" Truex occurred in early August— and was followed in April 1962 by the arrival of the first Steele grandchild, Kristen—while Paul, entering his senior year at Bates, became engaged to a junior classmate, Carol Long of Auburndale, Massachusetts. Paul, finding employment as an English teacher at the high school in Plainville, Connecticut, and Carol became husband and wife in June of 1963.

A significant transition occurred on September 23, 1961, when WTIC vacated its Grove Street venue within The Travelers campus and moved to Broadcast House at 3 Constitution Plaza, yet the relocation of the studios rated little with Steele. Among his trove of mementoes was a printed program devoted to the opening ceremony held two months later, with some of the contents highlighting the station's on-air personalities, but Steele included no marginalia or other commentary offering his opinion on the brand-new, $3-million facility. However, another article in a Steele scrapbook read that the dedication of the new building "was carried out in good taste with the governor and mayor present, stars from the opera, a fine orchestra, solo harpist, some comedy relief by Bob Steele, the early morning favorite, and well-tailored speeches by J. Doyle DeWitt, Travelers president and Paul Morency, president of the Travelers Broadcasting Service."[27]

In the event, this was the dawning of a new age for WTIC, whose fifty thousand–watt signal remained a beacon of the radio airwaves in New England that proudly carried its affiliation with NBC, and whose connection with CBS anchored the station just as firmly on the television side of the business.

Mysteriously, Bob Steele's thoughts on the aforementioned Cuban Missile Crisis of October 1962—one of the most frightful episodes in U.S. (or world) history—went unrecorded. However, decades later, his eldest son Robert provided a recollection of the excruciating anxiety of that trying time. Still associated with Columbia's Russian Institute in the autumn of that year, Robert understood better than most the machinations of the crisis: he had agreed to join the CIA as a foreign affairs officer, and in his work as a research assistant at the Ivy League school, his advisor was Zbigniew Brzezinski, who later served as national security advisor in the administration of President Jimmy Carter. Commuting by train from Byram, Connecticut, where he and Betsy resided, Robert found himself in a room at Columbia's library in the early evening of October 22, where he and about forty students watched President John F. Kennedy's address in which JFK informed the nation about the Soviet Union's placement of nuclear missiles in Cuba.

Kennedy announced a blockade of the island nation, and Robert recalled the "extremely somber mood" of his small viewing audience. At the conclusion of the speech, Robert called home in Wethersfield, where he spoke with his father. Bob expressed his support for the stand that JFK was taking against the Russians, which was the possibility of a full, retaliatory response should any missiles in Cuba be launched against the United States or its allies. Father and son were in agreement that "this was what the President had to do" to discourage any further belligerent action on the part of Khrushchev.[28]

Bob Steele was most concerned that his son and his young family, living in the section of Greenwich, Connecticut, closest to Manhattan, would surely fall prey to an attack on New York City, a site assuredly selected as a target of Soviet missiles. Bob tried to persuade Robert and Betsy to move back to Wethersfield to be out of harm's way, if there could be any chance of being somewhat safe given the circumstances of the threat.[29] However, the crisis was diplomatically defused about one week later, and life eventually returned to normal, but it remains the most harrowing moment of the Cold War era.

At the beginning of 1963, Steele's show was expanded from 6:45 a.m. to 10 a.m., yet the rewards for his hard work and his continuing renown in the field of sports brought him more awards, including honors as Connecticut's best sportscaster for the fourth straight year. He was feted in May at the Hotel Statler Hilton for the twenty-six years he had been on the air with WTIC, and the guest list for the occasion included luminaries from the print and broadcast media, the sports world, and, not surprisingly, politics: Red Smith of the *New York Herald Tribune*; Arthur McGinley of the *Hartford Times*; Charlie Blossfield, past owner of the Hartford Chiefs, a minor-league affiliate of the Boston Braves; Sol Taishoff, the publisher of *Broadcasting* magazine;

Robert Lee, head of the Federal Communications Commission; Steele's boss, Paul Morency; Connecticut governor John Dempsey; and Steele's longtime friends, jeweler Bill Savitt and George Lannom, the motorcycle racing promoter who brought Steele to the Insurance Capital where his broadcasting legacy soon commenced.

Supplementing the notable attendees was a galaxy of baseball stars who telegrammed their regrets of not being able to participate: former Red Sox Ted Williams and Johnny Pesky, Yankee manager Ralph Houk, New York Mets skipper Casey Stengel, and a contingent of Milwaukee Braves including Warren Spahn and future Major League Baseball commissioner Bud Selig, who at the time was a major Braves shareholder. Missives from Boston Celtic legend Bob Cousy, Connecticut U.S. senator Thomas Dodd, and another old cycling friend, Floyd Clymer—whose typed, three-page tribute was a short biography of Steele's early life—added to the accolades. The five hundred guests in attendance included Shirley Steele and the couple's sons, and as might be expected of an honoree whose charitable work was as famous as his broadcasting career, McGinley reported that "at Bob's direction any surplus from the dinner receipts would go to the Shriners' Hospital for Crippled Children and the Newington Home."[30]

Just as the passing of Bob Steele's mother prompted him to record his most somber reflections, so too did the tragedy of November 22, 1963, move him to register his observations and personal thoughts upon one of the watershed moments in American history. An extensive passage in his scrapbook provides a coherent timeline consistent with the manner in which memories are forged when people first learn of a significant event. That Steele was an accomplished diarist—and in this particular instance, even logging the time at which he wrote the entry—enabled him to leave a detailed and compelling account of that afternoon as he lived it.[31]

> 11–22–63 Written at 5:20 p.m. Friday
>
> President Kennedy was assassinated today at Dallas, Texas. He was shot in the head by a sniper's bullet during a parade. He was riding in a Lincoln convertible with his wife, [Jacqueline,] Governor [John] Connally of Texas and his wife.

After describing some aspects of the initial erroneous reports emanating from Dallas, such as the killing of a Secret Service agent, Steele placed the tragedy in the context of his own experience.

> I first heard the news in a restaurant in Hartford where I had just had lunch. A man ran into the restaurant, shouting "They just shot Kennedy—the President!" The restaurant radio was turned on and everyone listened quietly as the announcer reported that it was not known how serious the wounded men were. A man I shall never again have any respect for said, "Good! I hope the S.O.B. dies!" I couldn't believe he had said it.

Others looked at him in disbelief.... About half an hour later I drove into Pierce Buick to have my new car serviced at the 1,000 mile inspection point and found everyone talking about the shooting and expressing shock in subdued tones. Everything seemed to have slowed down.... Herb Woerz, manager of the company, came out of his office, walked straight to me and said excitedly but gravely, "He just died. The President is dead." I found myself starting to cry several times, as I drove home and kept thinking only of the shooting.... Lyndon Johnson was sworn in as President aboard the presidential plane by a woman judge, who administered the oath, the reports say, in tears.... I've been watching TV for an hour and CBS has announced cancellation of all commercials and all entertainment programs until after the funeral. My sports shows on radio and TV have been cancelled for tonite, so I'm home at this hour—now 6 p.m.... This has been a historic and tragic day.

The lucidity of Steele's narrative belies a stream of consciousness that might otherwise be tinged with exaggeration, hyperbole, or other flaws. He undoubtedly maintained accuracy by committing his thoughts to paper shortly after arriving home that afternoon; his record is at once bold and sincere, and it mirrors the reaction of millions of Americans to that sad event in Dallas.

Although Bob Steele quite likely never made this observation, he may well have regretted not being around when the automobile was first invented. As we have seen, the unflagging passion he exhibited throughout his life for cars and motorcycles was manifest at an early age, and it would have been only fitting had he been given the opportunity to partake in operating the very first powered vehicles. Nevertheless, as the years rolled on and Steele enjoyed his unending purchases of new cars, he put those vehicles to their intended usage. "Bob never lost his love of the open road," his son Phil observed. "His favorite vacation was just to drive somewhere."[32]

Such was the case in the summer of 1964, when he, Shirley, and son Steve embarked on another western excursion that ultimately delivered them to the Pacific Coast. The trio took in the majestic sights of the Grand Canyon, spent time with some of Bob's old motorcycling coterie in Los Angeles, and visited San Francisco as well as Joshua Tree in the Golden State. Bob acted as tour guide on a swing through his native Kansas City, where Steve posed for a snapshot in front of his father's old elementary school.

The motor trip was not the only pleasurable aspect of the summer. Upon Steele's return to work in early August, he learned that he had merited a pay increase at the same time his schedule was reduced because he would no longer have to do his Saturday evening sports program. "After Sat[urday] a.m. show I'm off till Mon[day]. Feels good," he noted with relief.[33] Barely one month after this adjustment, Steele served as an honorary foreman when he helped to direct the placement of the first beam of structural ironwork used in the construction of the new Hartford National Bank building at the corner of Main and Pearl Streets, the first of the contemporary behemoths that would slowly but surely redefine the city's skyline.

As the season shifted from summer to autumn, it turned out that Steele was not completely separated from weekend sports after all. He was assigned to the role of "insurance quizmaster [for] a series of 60-second commercials, broadcast over Channel 3 during NFL games."[34] The purpose of the advertisements was to educate—through a series of questions and answers—the viewing audience of the virtues of the insurance industry and "why the Insurance Companies of Connecticut are so good for the *people* of Connecticut."[35] A promotional publication for the ad campaign was further infused with a swipe at the American Football League, which at the time was only in its fifth year of play and trying to make firmer inroads against its better established rival. "This fall the best football in the world will be seen on Connecticut's Channel 3—through its exclusive coverage of the country's best professional games, played by the teams of the National Football League."[36]

A busy first half of 1965 found the Bob-Shirley-Steve triumvirate again on the road, first to Daytona, Florida, immediately after the running of the annual Daytona 500 auto race, and then to the New York World's Fair. The sadness of the passing of Shirley's grandfather, Oscar Hanson, in mid–May was countered by the arrival of the second grandchild for Bob and Shirley when their daughter-in-law Betsy gave birth to another girl. Steve's parents later took him on a weekend visit to Philadelphia in the fall. As autumn evolved into the typical winter that brought inclement weather to New England, Steele divested himself of the chore of reading the no-school announcements because it interrupted the flow of his personal program narrative, this duty now delegated to his booth announcer.

Bob and Shirley saw their third son, Phil, complete his undergraduate studies at Amherst, where he earned cum laude laurels, yet the eldest Steele continued to insist that the only higher education he had was a result of his enrollment in the "College of Hard Knocks." One of the vicissitudes of that "school" came in the early summer of 1966 when his physician made a house call to the Steele residence. The head of the household complained of chest pains but later sloughed it off as mere "muscular soreness."[37] Shortly after this medical scare, Steele celebrated his fifty-fifth birthday with a home-cooked family repast, and on October 1 he marked the occasion of his thirtieth anniversary with WTIC. This in itself was a milestone, yet no one knew—certainly not Steele himself—that he was not even halfway through his eventual tenure at the station.

Steele displayed a consistent anti-war stance throughout his life—"He was no hawk," according to his son Robert—and trepidation about conflict among nations, as opposed to battles in the boxing ring, was never far below the surface of his persona.[38] In the mid–1960s, troubles in Communist China and Southeast Asia worried him, as he told his diary, "They're talking Peace— very slight chance it will come. I pray it will."[39] The deep respect he held for the American armed forces was evident as the nation descended into the deepening quagmire of Vietnam. "U.S. resumed bombing of No. Viet Nam today. Too bad—that war," he recorded in his diary in early 1966, yet at a local social affair he was proud to engage Staff Sergeant Barry Sadler, a Green Beret medic who achieved fame as the singer who recorded "The Ballad of the Green Berets," a song that was the country's top hit single for five weeks.[40] Sadler and Steele shared a common childhood link, both experiencing the divorce of their parents when they were young children.

The end of 1966 signaled what Steele's son Phil labeled the end of an era, when Bob Steele was accorded the title of chief announcer for WTIC, a post that had previously been held by only three other individuals since the station's operations began in the mid–1920s. Through the mechanism of a promotion, Steele was relieved of his evening sportscasting duties on television and given supervisory responsibilities over all sixteen announcers on WTIC AM, FM, and Channel 3.

This change in Steele's job status meant that he was able to distance himself from George Ehrlich, WTIC's television sports announcer with whom Steele did not see eye to eye, but it also was framed in a way that, according to Phil, "would not appear to be a demotion." As Steele's son explained the reality of the circumstances, "Bob's morning program was WTIC's bread and butter, and it no longer made sense to have him burning the candle at both ends. And Bob thought he was getting too old, too bald, and too fat for TV and had never been as comfortable on TV as on radio.... At age fifty-six, Bob welcomed the relief from the grueling schedule of working mornings, afternoons, and evenings."[41]

This may have been the end of an era, but considering Steele's tepid embrace of television since its debut at WTIC, his exit from the TV side of the business could only be seen as a move that could add years to his life.

With benefit of historical hindsight, we see that 1967 would prove to be a transitional year in United States history. As the counterculture movement attracted more young people into its fold, the historian William Manchester observed, "The great year of the hippy may be said to have begun on Easter Sunday, March 26, 1967, when ten thousand boys and girls assembled in New

York Central Park's Sheep Meadow to honor love."[42] The "boys and girls" referred to by Manchester were in reality young adults ranging in age from their late teens to their twenties, and indeed, such gatherings bore testimony to an ostensible innocence cloaking the American landscape. However, the year's ensuing "Summer of Love" played out against a backdrop of increasing racial strife that erupted in several major cities, especially Detroit and Newark, and current events foretold of more ominous clouds billowing over the nation's deepening involvement in the Vietnam War.

The conflict was the subject of a program aired by CBS that spring, but when WTIC's management previewed the film and deemed its content to be an inaccurate representation of the conditions in Saigon, Channel 3 was not among the outlets to broadcast the eponymous documentary. In the opinion of the station's program committee, *Saigon* presented "a totally distorted viewpoint as to the position of Americans in Vietnam," and therefore chose to run two episodes of Danny Thomas's popular situation comedy *Make Room for Daddy* on the evening of March 14.[43] Scores of angry viewers flooded WTIC's telephone switchboard to rail against the blackout, and these callers were joined by about a dozen protesters who assembled at the station's Broadcast House, bearing placards reading "Give Us the Right to Know," "A Free Press Equals a Free Society," and perhaps the most clever, which used Channel 3's call letters as an acronym for its message, "WTIC: Where Truth Is Censored."[44]

Subsequent letters to the editor of Hartford's newspapers reflect the increasing division of opinion in the United States over the prosecution of the war. Those favoring the American effort—and who would likely have had little issue with the cancellation of the airing of *Saigon*—believed the program to be nothing more than "propaganda making our troops look like sadists," and accused peace activists of "never howl[ing] when the Viet Cong murder entire families of innocent non-combatants but yell bloody murder when an American bomb falls amongst North Vietnamese civilians being used as camouflage to hide an anti-aircraft missile site in Hanoi."[45] Countering the hawkish view were opinions expressed by citizens who sought to expose the harsh realities of events in Vietnam and who "[did] not need an all-knowing 'big brother' to decide for us where the truth lies."[46]

Steele observed that the "public is 'down' on WTIC-TV for suppressing a documentary on Saigon recently.... Quite a furor," yet in an aside he penned in his diary, he privately commented, "Editorials in both papers. (Mostly, I think, by people who like to see their words—not necessarily their actual thoughts—and names in print.)"[47] In spite of the sanguine outlook presented by the American military brass, who at the time continued to see a fabled light at the end of the tunnel with regard to the supposed progress being made in the fight against the Viet Cong and North Vietnamese Army, Steele dourly commented, "The Viet Nam War drones on—200 U.S. killed every week now—it's grim. Peace is mentioned but that's all. Looks bad."[48] The Six-Day War in the Middle East between Israel and its neighboring countries provoked further anguish over a "tough situation," but Steele stated the obvious regarding the outcome: "Israel big winner—also triumph for [United Nations]."[49]

Late summer in the Steele household brought another hospitalization, but this time the patient was Shirley, who endured a difficult bout with colitis for most of August. Already possessed of a slim build, she recovered but lost thirteen pounds in the process, and moving forward she had to be very conscious of her diet. Just weeks later, Steele's air time was extended by forty-five minutes, the opening of his show now moved up from 6:45 a.m. to 6:00. To commemorate the tenth anniversary of Channel 3's debut, Broadcast House was opened to the public for tours, which, according to Steele, drew thousands of curiosity seekers who took advantage of the opportunity to see the point from which WTIC's broadcasts emanated. And although his beloved Chicago White Sox failed down the stretch of that year's amazing American League pennant race, he and Shirley experienced the thrill of the final World Series game at Boston's Fenway Park—yet Steele admitted that "Mama and I snuck out [at the] end of the 8th [to] beat the crowd"—where the St. Louis Cardinals were victorious against the overachieving hometown Red Sox.[50]

Youngest son Steve was away at school in Pennsylvania, although he frequently flew home on weekends. For all intents and purposes, Bob and Shirley were empty-nesters who, like all Americans, were swept along in the wave of turmoil that turned 1968 into one of the most disturbing years in American history. The end of March marked the denouement of President Lyndon Johnson's administration when he announced that he would not seek a second term—in his own right—and Steele noted that the United States and North Vietnam might be heading to the negotiating table to discuss a settlement to the conflict. But on the heels of this glimmer of hope, America was rocked by the assassination of the most prominent leader of the civil rights movement.

On the evening of April 4, the Steeles were dining with good friends, Bill Savitt and Jack Smith and their spouses, when they learned that Dr. Martin Luther King, Jr., had been killed in Memphis, Tennessee. "This will precipitate riots and unrest all over the country," Steele wrote that evening, and his observation came true, as he noted the next day, "Race trouble in many cities—some in Hartford—damage in north end—even in downtown Hartford. NINE arrests made."[51] Disturbances in Hartford paled in comparison to those in other major cities, but the gravity of the tragedy was not lost on local leaders: John Dempsey, the governor of Connecticut, declared the day of King's funeral to be a state holiday observed in conjunction with the national day of mourning sanctioned by President Johnson.

In the wake of the shooting, Steele wrote to son Steve, "The country is certainly having its problems," but he also hoped to buoy the youngster's spirits—and likely his own—with the enticement of an invitation to take in a light-heavyweight boxing match in New York between Bob Foster and Dick Tiger. But those problems persisted when Robert Kennedy was shot at the conclusion of the California Democratic primary in Los Angeles in early June—"Sen. Kennedy lingers between life + death," Steele told his diary, and Kennedy succumbed to his wounds two days later.[52] As if the pair of assassinations were not bad enough, the city of Chicago erupted in rioting during the Democratic National Convention in August.

The subsequent presidential election afforded Steele the opportunity to remark about the outcome, although like many of his prognostications about various sporting events, his commentary about the United States Constitution's Twelfth Amendment did not come true. "It's official—[Richard] Nixon elected—[Hubert Humphrey] concedes at noon. Humphrey's popular vote slightly bigger than Nixon's—but Nixon got 287 electoral votes (270 needed [to win]). *I look for abandonment of the electoral college system.* They've talked about it for years—but now will do something, I think."[53]

In the Steele household, there were doses of welcome news, all related to life changes that signaled prosperity and traditional expansion of family. Robert, the senior of the sons, and Betsy added Jeffrey Robert Steele to their fold in September while Paul and Phil entered the world of high academia, the former moving on from Plainville High School to Potomac State College in Keyser, West Virginia, while the latter accepted a position at Washington & Jefferson College south of Pittsburgh. Paul, in turn, soon moved to Concord, Massachusetts, to begin a lengthy tenure teaching English at Lexington High School beginning in 1969. Paul's wife, Carol, gave birth to Mark Conrad Steele, born in December 1968.

As the decade of the sixties drew to a close, Bob Steele commented about a new phenomenon that was plaguing a narrow segment of the travel industry. "Air liners being 'hi-jacked' to Cuba—the big craze now. Two or three a week!" he noted, this coming decades before the federal Transportation Security Administration was even dreamed of.[54] In May 1969, Steele was at ringside to call the action of the fight between defending light-heavyweight champion Bob Foster and Bob Kendall in West Springfield, Massachusetts, and although

the telecast was not shown in the greater Hartford area, the broadcast on
ABC Television went nationwide and garnered Steele kudos from many
friends around the country who viewed the event. At about this time, his
oldest son, Robert, was making his first inroads into the political arena by
seeking the Republican nomination for Connecticut's Second Congressional
District in the 1970 midterm election, an effort in which he was successful.

The spectacular achievement of the *Apollo 11* mission that landed the
first men on the moon in July 1969 was matched—figuratively speaking—
barely three months later when the formerly hapless New York Mets stunned
the baseball world by upsetting the powerful Baltimore Orioles in the World
Series. "I pickt Balt! Natch?" moaned Steele, again alluding to his continuing
inability to forecast a winner, but at least he and friend Bill Savitt had a good
view of the historic fifth and final game from their mezzanine box seats
behind third base at Shea Stadium.[55] Rounding out the year was a family dinner of ham on Christmas Eve—since Steele was due in the studio for his show
the next morning—and he enlisted son Paul to assist with cleaning up in the
kitchen.

The transition from the 1960s into the 1970s provided little relief in Bob
Steele's routine or in the heights of popularity he had achieved and maintained
in southern New England's radio market. Steele certainly had hit his stride with
the locals, but he also captured increasing attention on the national level.

7

"I'm thankful for everything I have in this world"

His show has had a waiting list of advertisers.
—*Billboard Magazine*, January 1970

Mr. Robert Steele is the greatest thing ever to have come out of Kansas City.
—Arthur B. McGinley, May 1970

The shifting of the calendar to a new decade did little to slow down Bob Steele's juggernaut of popularity. One of the biggest media trade publications declared in its January 1970 edition that the pantheon of top-flight morning radio hosts was not limited only to large-market personalities such as John Gambling, Jr., of station WOR in New York, Bob Van Camp of Atlanta's WSB, and WJR's J. P. McCarthy in Detroit. Also capturing and maintaining their adult audiences with a pleasant blend of talk and music was Steele, a small-market host but one who for years provided WTIC with a powerful drawing card.

Billboard magazine informed its readers that although Van Camp drew between 35 and 60 percent of Arbitron ratings in his market's audience, Steele was attracting 57 percent in WTIC's broadcast area because he "keys his show on humor and he plays the music he likes, ranging from rinky-tink [*sic*] piano to fairly hip, but adult-aimed, records."[1]

Hartford Times sports editor emeritus Arthur McGinley, writing a tribute for yet another Steele testimonial banquet, reinforced the acclaim showered on the Connecticut Boxing Guild's Man of the Year: "Countless citizens along the New England countryside insist upon having for breakfast each new day orange juice, cereal, eggs, toast—and Bob Steele."[2] More than belonging to Hartford alone, Steele had grown into a regional institution, and as one trade publication, billing him as "the hottest radio property north of New York," observed, "A Connecticut media specialist describes Steele's year-in-year-out rating as 'monstrous for radio. Around a 6 or 7. The kind of rating TV personalities pull. He owns that market!'"[3]

The institution Steele had created for himself was not beyond reproach, however, as he learned in the late spring of 1970. The earliest stage of what

Even in his older age, Steele's love of boxing remained a constant in his life. Here he is mugging with promoter Manny Leibert and ring opponent Chico Vehar to promote the 1972 Connecticut Boxing Guild dinner (Hartford History Center, Hartford Public Library).

became known as the Women's Liberation Movement was hitting its stride and serving to fuel the burgeoning effort to formulate an Equal Rights Amendment to the United States Constitution. Women across the country grew increasingly vocal in their demands for equal pay, improved working conditions, and property rights—among other things—that were commensurate with their male counterparts, this particular issue remaining in the public domain even to this day.

During his program of June 1, Steele mentioned to his listeners that a female athlete had occasioned to win at least two thousand dollars in an event. He further commented, "That's a lot of money for a woman" and then "went on to enumerate the many silly things she would have spent it on: shoes, clothes, pocket books, etc."[4] Made with tongue in cheek, the remark was indicative of a type of humor that relied on "a kind of lighthearted battle of the sexes" that was part of the act of George Burns and Gracie Allen, or the characters on the television series *The Honeymooners*.[5] Feeling offended rather than amused, one woman in the audience from Hartford took extreme exception to Steele's observation and lashed out in a letter to him:

> Did it occur to you that she might possibly use it to care for an aged parent, or to put a younger member of the family through school? She might invest it so that she would have something to fall back on in her old age and not be a burden on society. Who knows, she might even spend it to take care of a lazy, good-for-nothing man who spends his money on booze, the ponies and other useful and admirable things. I wish you and other people who address the public would get over your patronizing way of speaking about women.

The writer closed by indicating that she "[did] not belong to any Women's Liberation Movement and probably never will. But I do think that the odds of this [woman athlete] or any other would use her money at least as usefully as the average male are at least fifty-fifty."[6]

In the twenty-first century, provocative radio hosts would not only call out such a listener on the air but no doubt add further insults in order to heighten the inflammatory rhetoric. Steele, however, pleaded his case on a program days later that he commented only in jest and noted the intelligent manner in which his critic expressed herself. First tweaking his challenger a bit—"This woman, I'm sure, is more interested in making me feel uncomfortable than in furthering JUSTICE and fairness for womankind"—he went on to compliment her.

> She has the expertise[,] the gift of language to roast me to a turn. She certainly writes well.... A woman this sharp would KNOW I was JOSHING when I said "first prize of 2000—that's a lot of money—for a woman." To say a thing like that and mean it—I'd have to be a real dunderhead.

Steele then defused the controversy by imploring the distaff members of his audience to be discerning when listening to his attempts to be humorous: "Let's call off the duel—I apologize to Rosy—and I ask the rest of you girls to be sensible—and I know you will be."[7] In his opinion, it was better to atone for a misstep—even one that was perceived to be—than to risk damaging his hard-earned and long-held reputation.

During a later show in which he implored motor vehicle operators to use their directional signals, he called out women specifically to do so "well before the turn," but then—having learned a lesson the hard way—immediately qualified his remark with a playful twist. "Every time I talk about women drivers, sort of downgrade them, I get a letter, from a woman, someone who's running the head of a woman's lib group or something, you know, and they really lambaste me. But girls, it's only a joke. I don't believe in downgrading the ladies.... I think the women get the best of it—it seems to me. For instance, diamonds are a girl's best friend, right? Man's best friend is a dog."[8]

The summer of 1970 furnished a significant moment to the Steele family when son Robert captured the Republican nomination as the candidate for the seat of Connecticut's Second Congressional district. He had been chosen in a special election to fill a vacancy occasioned by the death of William St. Onge in May and then won a full term in November. While Bob—Robert's father—was happy "to put in a good word for his boy who was unable to attend" a rally at Lake Compounce in Bristol, he never indulged in promoting his son's political aspirations on the air.[9]

During Robert's Congressional campaigns, and also a later run for governor of Connecticut, listeners of Bob Steele's show would never realize that his son was seeking the office because he never mentioned it on his show: "[H]is father can't campaign for or mention his son Bob Steele ... because he IS the well-known Bob Steele and does not take sides in politics."[10] Of course, because Steele was notorious for his incorrect predictions on many sporting events, it was perhaps wise that he kept his thoughts to himself rather than share them with his radio audience.

Not lost on him, however, was the work that his eldest son was already doing on behalf of one of the most important industries in Connecticut, the Electric Boat division of General Dynamics Corporation, based in Groton and builder of submarines for the United States Navy. Steele noted in his diary that Robert was "elated over [government] contract for 7 nuclear subs to Electric Boat. He 'worked like a tiger' on it."[11]

Robert also received publicity for his work to combat the importation of illegal drugs to the United States from Turkey and Asia as well as exposing the nefarious dealings of Major General Ngo Dzu of the South Vietnamese

Army, who was fingered as a kingpin in the trafficking of heroin on American military bases. He was honored by the United States Jaycees as one of the nation's ten outstanding young men of 1971, and Steele was among six members of the House and Senate recognized by President Richard Nixon for their leadership in passing a three-year, $1 billion drug abuse prevention and rehabilitation bill—the direct result of a report the young congressman had co-authored.

After several decades of handling fame with a relatively even temperament, Bob Steele at last had to make a concession to keep admirers at bay. Phil Steele indicated that his father "responded faithfully to his mail but phone calls were another matter," and in mid–March 1971, "he finally resorted to an unlisted number" at the Steele residence in Wethersfield.[12] While the content of those calls can only be left to speculation, perhaps there may have been a complaint or two regarding the choices of music on some of WTIC's programs. A gathering of select members at the station, including Steele, discussed the need for "more 'contemporary' music on [the] morning show, especially 7 to 8 [a.m.] (biggest listening audience)."[13] Such action may have been in response to Steele's occasional singing of his favorite tune, Ray Noble's 1934 jazz standard "The Very Thought of You." Times were changing as were tastes, and management did not want to lose the younger listeners of Steele's program because of what it believed to be a catering to outdated musical selections.

Yet more Steeles entered the family fold with the birth of a daughter, Vanessa Shirley, to Paul and Carol in September 1970 as well as two sons, Dana to Phil and Cheryl on November 24, 1970, and Bradley Hampton Steele to Robert and Betsy on July 9, 1971. But the autumn of that year brought a significant honor to Connecticut courtesy of the World Series victory of the Pittsburgh Pirates over the daunting Baltimore Orioles. Pitcher Steve Blass, a native of Canaan, won two games in the Fall Classic, the second of which earned the Pirates their victory in the deciding seventh game. Bob Steele interviewed Blass's mother by telephone and was on hand to chat with the Series hero in person when his hometown celebrated "Steve Blass Day" on October 22.

In 1972, the state of Connecticut inaugurated a lottery program as a means to increase its revenue, and the first drawing was held at Bushnell Memorial Hall. The February 24 event was hosted by Governor Thomas Meskill, and Bob Steele served as the master of ceremonies. Weekly drawings were conducted in the lottery's early stages, and the state's Gaming Commission secretary, Joseph Burns, felt that the payment of Steele's $300 appearance fee was reasonable in order to secure a local celebrity to help promote the

"Money Tree" program. Steele had been earning such fees for many years; in fact, he charged them as a way to discourage organizations, with the exception of charitable causes, from asking him to appear at various events, but sponsors were only too happy to pay up. But when the revelation of the commission's remittance came to light, there was a stern backlash in the state press.

Rather than criticism being directed at Steele, many newspaper editorials decried the state's decision to spend $8,100 for the twenty-seven dates for which he was to be engaged. The *Meriden Record* told its readers, "Under the circumstances, one can't blame Steele for taking the job. But one can blame the Commission for the extravagance," while the *Hartford Times* opined, "The fact that the M. C. in question is a widely known and liked radio personality, Bob Steele, is beside the point. The readiness of the commission to spend $8,100 a year for his services at half this year's drawings deserves another look."[14] Trying to distance himself from the fray, Steele said of the commission, "They came to me," indicating that the job of emcee was one he had not sought.[15]

With his personal integrity at stake, he followed a directive from WTIC president Leonard Patricelli and relinquished the position, and although Steele understood the need to stanch the bad publicity, he privately mused, "[B]ut what did I do? Rob somebody?"[16] The tempest was quelled when the executive director of the lottery assumed the duties of drawing the numbers, but another spat erupted soon after when the *Hartford Courant* increased the cost of its daily newspaper to fifteen cents. The price hike occasioned Steele to remark on his April 3 program, "[Hartford] has 3 income groups— low, middle, and those who buy the morning paper.... The *Courant* is up to 15¢ this morning—but I don't see that the news is any better," and his jab, as playful as he may have meant it to be, drew a quick rebuke from station management.[17]

On the heels of Lee Trevino winning the Greater Hartford Open held at the Wethersfield Country Club—Steele picked black golfer Charlie Sifford to win, but as usual his prediction was wrong—the world was stunned by the attack at the Summer Olympic Games in Munich, where a group of Black September terrorists kidnapped eleven Israeli athletes, coaches, and other officials. A failed attempt to rescue them led to a battle between captors and police that resulted in the deaths of the Israeli contingent as well as all but three of the terrorists. "Last night all hell broke loose at Munich airfield," Steele somberly noted in his diary. "Terrible day at Munich."[18]

The general election that November saw Steele's eldest son prevail by a wide margin over his Democratic challenger who had been endorsed by the *New York Times*. "[T]he largest 2nd District plurality in history of Connecticut politics! 67,000 [votes]!" Steele proudly exclaimed in his scrapbook when Robert the incumbent swept into Congress for his second term.[19]

Bob Steele was often prone to use all capital letters in his written notes as a means to denote something worthy of being emphasized, or what with today's word processing applications can easily be italicized. But on January 22, 1973, he penned an entry in his diary that indicated a sea change that was in store for the Hartford media—indeed, the entire Connecticut market— and the opening word signaled the gravity of the situation.

> BOMBSHELL of news explodes at Broadcast House. Before 150 employees at 2:30 p.m., [President Leonard] Patricelli announced that WTIC is about to be sold to The Washington Post, owner of stations in Miami, Jacksonville + Washington, Newsweek Magazine, and other companies. Roger Wilkens, chairman of the Travelers, said it may be a year or a year and a half before the deal is consummated and there is a chance it may not go through at all, since it must be approved by the [Federal Communications Commission] and that is not automatic. WTIC Radio would not be included but would be sold to some other buyer. Price: 40 million for both stations—Radio + TV.[20]

The volatility of media enterprises became more evident as ways by which people received news and entertainment programming changed. By the 1960s, the general public enjoyed greater availability of low-cost, portable radios as well as expanded national evening news shows on TV which, in turn, allowed easier and more timely access to the day's news, thereby reducing the demand for newspapers, especially those editions published in the afternoon.

By the mid–1960s, the reality of declining readership may have been most obvious in the nation's largest city, as reported by its flagship newspaper. "In 1900 the reading public in New York had a choice of 15 daily newspapers of general circulation," the *New York Times* told its readers in May 1966, adding, "The list has now dropped to four."[21] As an adjunct to the changing realm of the print industry, broadcasting was undergoing its own transformation.

"The late 60s and early 70s were times of transition at WTIC," related a commemorative publication released by the station. "The most difficult period came in the early 70s. The Travelers decided to get out of the broadcast business. The reasons were complex. The sale of the WTIC broadcast properties came as a shock to long-term staff members." However, in an attempt to have the radio part of the business remain under the control of someone with Connecticut ties, "Mr. Patricelli made every effort to keep WTIC AM and WTIC FM as locally owned operations."[22]

However, the purported reasons for the sale may not have been that complex at all. The insurance company no longer needed to rely on ownership of a radio station—and subsequently a television station—to retain its public image as it believed it had a few decades earlier. And almost certainly the expenses of maintaining a media business had become a burden The Travelers no longer wanted and thus felt that sound economic sense dictated its divestiture. As WTIC had outlived its space on the campus of The Travelers and was forced to move to Constitution Plaza, so too had WTIC outlived its usefulness to its parent company.

Ownership of the television station was transferred to the *Washington Post*'s consortium Post-Newsweek, which came under the corporate umbrella of Graham Media Group, and the $35 million deal was capped with a change in Channel 3's call letters to WFSB to commemorate Frederick S. Beebe, the president of the now-separated TV entity. In realizing its goal of local control for the radio operation, WTIC succeeded in consummating a deal with real estate developer David Chase, who "had grown up listening to WTIC and recognized its importance to the Southern New England community."[23]

Both AM and FM operations would be brought into a newly formed business, The Ten Eighty Corporation, and not only did Chase furnish financial backing to pave the way for continuity of the freshly minted enterprise but the radio stations would be housed in brand new studios located in a building under construction on Main Street just a block away from Broadcast House. Officially named One Financial Plaza but better known by its color-related nickname, Chase's "Gold Building," retains its eponymous and reflective glow on the Hartford skyline, and commencing on September 3, 1974, it served as WTIC's home through the early years of the twenty-first century.

The new radio corporation sought to maximize the benefits that Steele's program had for its sponsors, as well as to break a logjam of advertisers waiting to be associated with his show. Twenty hours of daily broadcast time Monday through Saturday were not hosted by Steele, but Lou Palmer's *Afternoon Edition*, which found favor with its own audience, was partnered with Steele's program in order to allow advertisers a chance to rotate sponsorship in morning and afternoon time slots. The theory was to have more advertisers swapping in and out than to have others hoping to gain air time on Steele's show be shut completely out of the process. A flyer from WTIC contained information explaining the scheme referred to as "Maximum Traffic Plan" and a table of time slot options that "enables advertisers to take advantage of listeners going to and from work, as well as reaching housewives at home. An advertiser will reach a much broader audience and still achieve broadcast continuity."[24]

The Steeles were saddened by the loss of a dear family member when Shirley's mother passed away in late March 1973 after a lengthy illness. Bob's spirits were buoyed a few months later, however, when he was honored by the University of Hartford with the presentation of a Doctor in Humane Letters and, to his consternation, an award as the Man of the Year presented by the University Club of Hartford. "Looking at other [past] recipients I still don't know why me!" he mused upon discovering that he was in the company of recent honorees including Igor Sikorsky (of aviation fame) and Connecticut governors John Dempsey, Raymond Baldwin, and Thomas Meskill.[25]

Although the country was only in its earliest stages of putting the Vietnam War behind it due to the withdrawal of American troops, controversy swirled around statements by Jane Fonda, who was denounced by Congressman Steele for labeling prisoners of war "liars and fakes," and the realm of domestic politics was becoming increasingly steeped in the Watergate affair, as the divulging of details into what happened and who was responsible for it unraveled. "Pres[ident] Nixon said he'd have to assume responsibility," Bob Steele noted in his diary, and weeks later in mid–May he complained, "Watergate! Watergate! That's all you see and hear. Questioning of principals is on TV about 7 hours daily."[26] Come the fall, he was randomly questioned in an ABC News man-on-the-street interview about the scandal, at which time he revealed that, in his opinion, Nixon had not been treated fairly by the media and was otherwise innocent until proven guilty of the allegations surrounding the imbroglio.

Neither was the country's unsettled political climate the only cause for alarm among the citizenry. When the Yom Kippur War erupted in October, the Organization of Arab Petroleum Exporting Countries—what later came to be called OPEC—declared an embargo aimed at countries that supported Israel in that conflict. As the demand for oil grew in the United States through the middle decades of the twentieth century, the importation of crude rose to satisfy the need to refine it for fuel used in motor vehicles and—with less demand for domestic coal to provide residential heat—home heating oil. With winter approaching, the Arab oil embargo could not have been more ill-timed.

The major disruption in the supply of oil reaching the U.S. caused a rapid escalation of prices for gasoline and heating fuel as well as shortages of both commodities. In his role as a congressman, Steele's son Robert personally pleaded the region's case with President Nixon, who was increasingly besieged by Watergate, to get Washington to focus attention on—and relief for—New England as the days of autumn waned. Steele told the president that New Englanders were incensed by the indifference to the problem shown by John Love, the director of the Office of Energy Policy.

Whether by accident or design—and to the "complete surprise" of the congressman—Love resigned three days later, having been replaced by a new "energy czar," Bill Simon, who delivered the action that was needed to divert millions of barrels of residual oil from the South to New England. But as the political wheels were slowly turning, back home Bob Steele recognized the worsening peril for the nation, not just in terms of high fuel prices, writing in early December:

> National speed limit now 55 [mph]—Connecticut's: 50! Truckers don't like it—threatening strikes. Dow Jones closes at 788! Confidence in the nation seems to be at a new low. People are suspicious of the [Nixon] administration and fearful of the coming winter with heating oil and gas scarce. Unemployment is growing—auto sales sharply down—oil-dependent industry closing or slowing.[27]

The pinch for consumers, including Steele, was palpable:

> Hard to get gasoline. One has to hunt for a station that's open—then wait in line for 10 minutes to ½ hour. Some stations open for 2 hours, then close, then open again later.... Today's prices: regular 49.9 cents [per gallon], premium 54.9. Some stations serve gas by appointment only. Display their phone number + suggest you call![28]

After all the work that Congressman Steele had done in nearly four years in Washington, he announced his candidacy for governor of Connecticut in early April 1974, and after winning the Republican primary in late July, he moved on to face the Democratic challenger, Ella Grasso. The GOP candidate's father remarked little about the resignation of President Nixon two weeks later, but he was an enthusiastic supporter of his son along the Connecticut campaign trail—yet never on his radio show.

The November mid-term election was marked by the tangible fallout resulting from Nixon's inglorious departure from office, although not exactly in Bob Steele's hyperbolic terms. While it was true that Democrats won in a national landslide and his son lost his gubernatorial bid by 200,000 votes, Ella Grasso was not "*one of millions* of Demo[crat]s swept in all over [the] USA," even if the sting of Republican losses across the country may have felt that way to some.[29]

Robert's bid for Connecticut's highest office may likely have been more successful had his father used the power of his voice on WTIC to encourage voters to choose his son, but Steele's conscience and integrity guided him in 1974 as they did during the two previous congressional elections. Personal appearances on the stump were one thing—and Bob was not bashful about participating in those—but the only support for his son over the airwaves came via paid advertisements. The *Bristol Press* commended the radio host's comportment:

> More neutral observers, such as we sometimes claim to be, were interested in the question of how Bob Steele, the veteran radio personality, would resolve the problem pre-

sented to him by the candidacy of his son. So far as we listened to his daily program, there was never any mention, by the father, of the son's candidacy. There were, on the program, political commercials for Steele and for Grasso, but we did not hear the elder Steele give the slightest hint that he knew there was a campaign going on.[30]

Two footnotes in the election's aftermath are worthy of comment. Retiring from the political arena, Robert became the president of Norwich Savings Society in January 1975 and enjoyed a very successful career in finance. And to celebrate the fiftieth anniversary of WTIC, a gala was held at the Hartford Sheraton in February 1975 that was attended by over five hundred guests and dignitaries. Given the honor of cutting a cake made for the event was Ella Grasso, the country's first female governor elected in her own right and now just weeks into her first term.

The smiling governor was photographed presenting a slice of cake to another noted guest who had been seated at the head table along with, among others, Hartford Mayor George Athanson and former WTIC announcer Allen Ludden, now famous as the host of the game show *Password*. Accepting the plate of dessert from the governor was Bob Steele, also beaming back in delight. Years later, Bob's son Phil noted that in spite of her victory over the eldest Steele son in the gubernatorial campaign, it "never diminished his genuine respect for her, and I think she genuinely respected him."[31] The picture offers clear evidence of exactly this special part of their relationship.

Lost in the excitement of the November 1974 election was an entry in Steele's diary that foretold of a shakeup at the radio station that was surely inevitable following WTIC's separation from The Travelers. On the fourteenth of that month, he sat down with Leonard Patricelli to discuss "our usual, annual topic—but no increase," meaning that his performance review with the company president yielded no raise in his pay. The boss informed him that "WTIC is in the RED—expenses running away with things," and by the next spring, drastic measures were implemented by management to address the financial distress.[32]

The following April, Steele felt downcast not only about the fall of South Vietnam and the real end of the war that created a refugee crisis, but also the economic conditions on the home front that made life increasingly difficult for millions of Americans. Among those affected were members of WTIC, and not just the lower-ranking staff who often become the first victims of corporate cutbacks. Arnold Dean, Lou Palmer, and Ross Miller had their pay reduced, Chuck Renaud took a cut that accompanied the demotion he received, and Steele was informed that another ranking—but as yet unnamed—employee was to be let go. "Things are changing," Steele lamented, and his intuition told him that the "station (despite a tremendous [amount of business] on my program—heaviest ever) is having trouble making payments. Lotta money to pay off."[33]

Almost immediately after learning this bleak news, Steele entered the hospital for a minor surgical procedure, but he was back home in a day. As a celebrity patient, he was amused by the especial attention he was accorded, as many hospital workers found one excuse or another to enter his room to attend to some issue, real or imagined. Steele's uneasy month closed out with a genuinely critical remark he made in his diary about modern music as a result of his youngest son's attendance at a local rock concert. "Steve still having trouble with hearing—one ear—after sitting too close to [the] stage at [the] Civic Center during 'Alice Cooper' exhibition of Idiotics. Volume was idiotically high. Whatsamatta with those damned fools?"[34] He later noted that there was talk of banning rock concerts in Hartford—which would have included those held at Colt Park, an outdoor venue—because "[e]very concert brings disturbances, muggings, rapes, injuries."[35] Steele's opinion of cinematics was further disappointed upon a later viewing of the Clint Eastwood movie *The Enforcer*, which he decried as being among the "junk" productions on offer that were filled with little more than "action—violence—4-letter words."[36]

The genre of rock music was light years from anything that listeners would hear on Steele's program, and the misery of hearing impairment for no seemingly good reason was too much for the father to comprehend. But the autumn of 1975 was marked by a far different Civic Center event more pleasant to the tastes of his audience. Bob Hope made an appearance before a very large crowd, and the legendary entertainer was introduced by Steele, who warmed up the audience by announcing—with the result almost a given—his prediction of a Red Sox victory in the upcoming World Series. When he made known his pick, which "brought the house down," the audience, according to Steele, cheered more loudly than when Hope made his entrance.[37]

Opened in January 1975, the Civic Center was the end product of mixed-use urban development that combined a mall of retail shops with an exhibition hall and an indoor arena capable of hosting basketball and ice hockey games as well as concerts. With a seating capacity of just over ten thousand, the Coliseum portion of the complex now served as the home of the New England Whalers, a franchise granted entry to the new World Hockey Association in 1971 but whose home ice began with two sites in Boston and another pair of venues in Springfield, Massachusetts, and finally now a permanent home in Hartford. When the team skated at a rink in nearby Glastonbury, Steele mugged for the cameras by suiting up to partake in a practice session during which he was checked into the boards to the delight of a *Hartford Courant* photographer.

The Steele family hosted a new on-air personality in the form of Bob's son Phil, who became the news director at Old Saybrook radio station WLIS in early 1976 and also read the sports reports on weekends at WTIC in the fall of 1978. But it was the father who became the clan's first recording artist, of sorts. In conjunction with the annual Eastern States Exposition, better known in New England as "the Big E," a long-playing record was released containing a series of staples culled from Steele's shows. A morning greeting, time check, antenna switch, a reading of "The Lion and Albert," and autobiographical passages were now available for a mere $5.98. In spite of these upbeat events with a personal connection, Steele was dispirited upon learning that the city's afternoon newspaper, the *Hartford Times*, had shuttered its operations in late October.

Steele reached another career milestone when he celebrated his fortieth anniversary at WTIC, and although he enjoyed the honorary reception at the office, he privately remarked about the voluminous well-wishes from co-workers and many listeners, "I don't deserve their plaudits. It's embarrassing. All you have to do is get older."[38] The local press also paid tribute, with a columnist for the *Bristol Press* keeping his fingers crossed that Steele would soldier on with his program: "Happy anniversary, Robert. And for heaven's sake don't let me hear any talk about your possible retirement."[39] Subsequent to this landmark, Steele was named a vice president of The Ten Eighty Corporation at the close of 1977.

A catastrophe of epic proportions shook Hartford in the early morning of January 18, 1978, barely seventy minutes before Bob Steele went on the air. Miraculously there was no loss of life nor were there even any injuries, but the incident and its aftermath became a turning point in the city's history. 4:20 a.m. CIVIC CENTER SPORTS ARENA ROOF COLLAPSES!! was the urgent entry in his diary, and he expressed great relief that nobody was hurt.[40] Occurring about six hours after the conclusion of a University of Connecticut men's basketball game, the certain deaths of perhaps thousands of people was averted by sheer luck of propitious timing. With cleaning and maintenance crews having completed their post-game tasks, only a handful of security personnel remained on site and out of the immediate area of danger.

The collapse was precipitated not by a heavy snowfall on the evening prior, but rather was effected by a fault in the roof's structure inherent from its very beginning. In 1973, the arena's space-truss roof was completed at ground level and then raised for its installation, but this effort at economy led to "the roof [beginning a] progressive failure as soon as it had been installed. Contributing factors included design errors, an underestimation of the weight of the roof, and differences between the design and the actual built structure."[41] Reconstruction of the arena lasted for close to two years, but the new Coliseum allowed for expanded seating that brought it up to the standard that allowed the Whalers to enter the National Hockey League.

In the Christmas classic duet "Peace on Earth/The Little Drummer Boy," recorded in 1977 by Bing Crosby and David Bowie, the two singers meet in a scripted event filmed as part of a holiday television special. In the skit, the generational difference between the aged crooner and a product of 1970s rock and roll is evident not only in their physical appearance but also in their brief chat about older and modern singers. They reach a common ground, however, by singing the title songs in tandem, their harmony thus tempering if not altogether bridging the age gap that actually separated them.

While this sketch was performed as a made-for-TV moment, no such musical meeting of the minds took place between the sixty-six-year-old Bob Steele and WTIC's vice president of operations, Jay Clark, who was young enough to be Steele's son. Clark had been attempting to update the selections of music used on Steele's show, and mere months following the broadcasting of Crosby's "Merrie Olde Christmas," Steele stiffly resisted Clark's bids. "Told Jay Clark what I [thought] of him and his efforts to run my show with his music and innovations. I got, as they say, 'hot.' He really 'bugs' me. I figure he wants me out," Steele confided off-air. "Maybe it will get worse—maybe better.... He said, 'You don't have confidence in me—is it because I'm only 35?' I said, 'I don't care if you're 135, you don't know my show and you're not going to destroy it.'"[42]

Steele's fierce pride had the solid backing of the lengthy track record he had accrued over the preceding decades, but Clark persisted, much to Steele's irritation. The agency charged with tracking the listenership of radio audiences found—according to Steele—that the ratings for the first hour of his show were "down slightly," "even up" for the next two hours, and "up slightly" in the final hour.[43] Despite what appeared to be a zero-sum situation for the program as a whole, Clark insisted that Steele air his (Clark's) modern choices of music in place of Steele's tried-and-true (but dated) recordings. So disgusted was Steele over the wrangling that he actually had a private meeting with Leonard Patricelli and floated the idea of leaving WTIC.

Although he instilled the fear in station management—which had recently endured its series of financial difficulties—that his departure would be a disaster, Steele figuratively if not literally threw up his hands. "Music on my show STINKS," he complained to his diary while fingering the culprit. "Jay Clark has demanded we play modern CRAP instead of my kind of music. He thinks he'll raise our rating (still, though down an insignificant point [in] the latest survey by The Best in Radio) but I'm sure he'll ruin it. If I were [age] 40, I'd worry about it—or fight—but I really don't give a hoot now."[44]

Steele's indifference may have been fueled by his need to direct attention toward a serious medical issue. In late July, he was hospitalized for a partial removal of his prostate gland and thereafter endured suffering that he described as "unbearable" and even worse than injuries from his boxing days or motorcycle accidents.[45] News of his condition prompted an outpouring of support and well-wishes that at least helped his morale through the hundreds of cards sent by concerned listeners and fans. "Not a happy time," he privately noted, "but it could be a lot worse. I'm thankful for everything I have in this world."[46] When he finally returned to work two weeks after the initial surgery, Jay Clark was among a select group who welcomed Steele back, as Clark, Ross Miller, Bob Tyrol, and Perry Ury presented him with a pricey Craig tape recorder with a built-in AM/FM radio.

Steele was most flattered by their thoughtfulness, but the *Hartford Courant* reported in September that Jay Clark's musical dictum had prevailed despite Steele's resistance. Although the Arbitron ratings indicated that Steele remained the undisputed leader at 42.7 percent of the listening audience— versus only 11.8 percent for runner-up Brad Davis, now with WDRC—there was a different way to look at the data, and this change in perspective related directly to the arguments put forth by Clark. Writing for the *Courant*, Stephanie Brown revealed that the ratings told a different story when parsed into age demographics. "Separate the 18- to 34-year-olds listening to morning radio in the Hartford area, and Brad Davis turns up number one."[47] As uncomfortable as this business reality may have been for Steele, it proved the wisdom of Clark's desire to change Steele's musical programming in order to lose fewer audience members who tuned in to a competing station that catered to a younger audience.

Marches, big-band songs, and polkas no longer received air play on Steele's show, their places now taken by a "playlist increasingly [resembling] that of later-in-the-day DJs on this middle-of-the-road station: a mixture of acceptably mellow Top 40 hits, balladeers like Sinatra and Streisand, and soft rock oldies. Bob Steele listeners have, of late, even been exposed to (GASP!) disco."[48] Still working in Steele's favor was the fact that morning was the time when people sought information, be it news from events occurring overnight, sports scores, weather reports, or traffic updates, to start their day. Having long incorporated those features into his show's format, to say nothing of the brand loyalty Steele had cultivated among many in his audience, "music plays second fiddle to information," and according to Steele, "music is just the mayonnaise on the sandwich."[49]

Steele may have thought of music as simply something to fill space on his show, which now began at 5:30 a.m., but the present times called for an awareness that tunes recorded in the early 1960s rather than the 1940s were now considered oldies. Music of the adult contemporary genre would have to find a place on Steele's program in order to keep youthful listeners from seeking alternative radio stations.

The power wielded by Jay Clark took the firmest root possible by the beginning of 1979 when Steele learned that two other radio hosts were told in no uncertain terms that they would be "fired instantly" should they stray from the playlist Clark provided them. "He wants none of my personal selections. Makes me sizzle, of course," Steele complained, but he conceded, "I'll go along for now. The cool head gets the clam chowder."[50] The threat of dismissal extended beyond the hosts: Bob Downes was the engineer for Steele's program for many years, and as the person actually responsible for cuing up the music would have suffered the consequences for errant songs. However, this punishment likely was formulated when Steele selected "something he was forbidden to play ... as much to taunt Clark as anything."[51]

A replay of the gasoline shortage earlier in the decade appeared in the summer of 1979, causing long lines at the pump, increased prices, and implementation of a system by which drivers had to purchase fuel on alternating days according to the last digit or letter on their vehicle's license plate. This latest problem was fallout from the deposing of the Shah of Iran at the beginning of the year, and Steele witnessed the growing unrest in the country as manifest in the strike among truckers who also protested the 55-mile-per-hour speed limit. "Country's in tough shape," he told his diary. "Food and vital materials not being transported."[52] The already difficult year worsened in early November when the U.S. embassy in Tehran was overtaken by supporters of the Iranian Revolution, precipitating a crisis when fifty-two American hostages were taken.

Several items of significance brought Bob Steele's decade of the 1970s to an interesting conclusion. He was honored by the Knights of Columbus, Connecticut State Council, as its recipient of the Father McGiveny Award for "significant humanitarian, civic and social contributions to [his] state and country."[53] Governor Ella Grasso proudly added congratulatory remarks from her office, and in a separate directive she appointed Steele to serve on a state commission to study violence in high school and college sporting events. But it was Jay Clark who had the final word as the 1980s were about to commence.

Replying to a lady in the WTIC audience disappointed with the revised music selections on Bob Steele's show, Clark expressed his sorrow that she felt as she did but informed her that since the introduction of "more contemporary sounds … [the program's] ratings have increased dramatically."[54] Clark further reminded her that Steele was the top-rated radio host in America, and the tangible improvement in market share gave the station little reason to implement any changes, but at least the vice president of operations acknowledged that those in charge "take your criticism to heart."

Less cordial in the first days of the new year were the verbal exchanges Steele had with Clark and Perry Ury, who was soon to become president of The Ten Eighty Corporation, about the pay he received for his "Tiddly Winks" feature—quirky news items that had a comical twist—and for his show on Christmas morning. Looking out for his own best financial interests, Steele vented to his diary, "I'm sure they hate my guts but I know I make [money] for the station."[55] However, the pair of executives placated their top host by giving him plusher office space the very next day.

Steele continued to show concern over the hostage situation in Iran, an international affair that was compounded by the Soviet Union's invasion of Afghanistan in January 1980. His diary contained a litany of summaries on attempts to retrieve the Americans held captive in Tehran, not least of which was what he termed "another 'Bay of Pigs' disaster" that occurred when a U.S. military rescue mission ended in a fatal calamity before even reaching its destination. In mid–May, after noting the hostage crisis, the tens of thousands of Cuban refugees arriving in Florida, rioting in Miami over the killing of a black businessman by a white police officer, the eruption of Mount St. Helen's, and persistent poor reports on the American economy, Steele finally despaired, "Isn't there any good news?"[56]

The publication in late April of *Bob Steele—A Man and His Humor* found an enthusiastic readership that mirrored his on-air popularity. A compilation of his wit, wisdom, biographical information, and outlook on life were packed into a nearly two-hundred-page volume published by Spoonwood Press, whose co-owner was Isaac Epstein, the owner of Hartford's renowned Huntington's Book Store. In support of the book, Steele made numerous promotional appearances around Connecticut to sell and sign copies, which were flying quickly off the shelves of nearly every shop. As thrilled as he was that the book entered a second printing, he was disheartened to learn of the resignation of Governor Ella Grasso in early December due to poor health. She succumbed to the ravages of ovarian cancer just two months later.

Taking a bit of a career turn after spending several years working for various media outlets in the state, Phil Steele graduated from the University of Connecticut's Law School, his commencement in the spring of 1981 attended by his father and younger brother. Steve and Bob continued spending quality father-son time together by taking in first-run movies, among them *Arthur* featuring John Gielgud and Liza Minnelli, but unnamed in his personal notes was the actor playing the title role, Dudley Moore. "I know very few of today's 'stars,'" he confessed, "unless they've been around 15 years or more."[57] This observation was consistent with his resistance to selections of modern music being forced upon him by Jay Clark. At the age of seventy, Bob Steele was a man of his times, but they were of an era now gone by, and the world to him seemed to belong to the generation of Baby Boomers coming into their own.

Steele ended his forty-fifth year at WTIC by signing a two-year contract that would run through 1983 and include an option for a third year, which in early 1984 became an agreement for three more years. He was pleased with the initial deal, as he was with his eldest son taking a position as CEO and chairman of Dry Dock Savings Bank in New York, as well as Phil passing the bar exam that allowed him to join the law firm of Rogin, Nassau, Caplan, Lassman, and Hirtle. Following on the success of his book, Steele released a "Connecticut Calendar and Almanac" that featured trivia, historical facts, local attractions, and a "Word for the Day" for each Wednesday.

By early 1982, with little surprise, *USA Today* reported in its "USA Snapshots" that for radio markets across the country, Bob Steele was the top-rated host at 35.9 percent, ahead of Don Cole (Omaha, Nebraska—31.7), Bob Sievers (Fort Wayne, Indiana—30.6), and Jorge Guillen/Hugo De La Cruz (Harlingen, Texas—30.4).[58] An indication of Steele's star power and how his attraction translated into profits for businesses who paid to use his voice were manifest in a pair of commercials that he read on the air for Connecticut National Bank. Within just a couple of days, the bank claimed that new "Connecticut accounts" totaling $2.2 million had been opened while $16.5 million in new money-market business had been initiated.[59]

Steele's discomfiture with war was never far from the surface of his emotions. In 1982 he hoped that war would not come in the Falkland Islands between Britain and Argentina—but it did—while Israel was bombing Beirut in an effort to thwart the Palestine Liberation Organization. Steele was humbled by the wretched condition of the Lebanese civilian population, even at that time, and he evinced woe over another unsettling domestic scare as tainted over-the-counter medicines began taking the lives of innocent consumers.

> 7 deaths attributed to Tylenol laced with cyanide…. Speculation is that a madman (or woman) is responsible—tampering with capsules—killing people indiscriminately….

Now Excedrin capsules are found to be lethal.... How many "sickies" are among us? And who are they? Candies, medicines, packaged foods—contaminated in various parts of U.S. It's an epidemic. Some incidents, I think, are exaggerated or even imagined but many are real—poisons found in candies, etc. in lab tests. It's big news every day. Sick minds copy others.[60]

As difficult to accept the earlier changes to Steele's musical selections had been, he was also vexed by other gimmickry added to his program when station management decided to include phone-in contests as part of the format. In an effort to retain the existing audience as well as entice new listeners to tune in, WTIC now offered games with prizes, but Steele's son Phil noted years later, "[I]t wasn't the kind of contact with his audience that he enjoyed. He felt that most callers in such a spontaneous format spoke poorly or were uninteresting, making for poor quality radio."[61]

Upon the occasion of the cancellation of the Walt Disney television show, which was actually several long-running series on several networks under the Disney brand, Steele commented on an unfortunate trend found not only in the world of radio. The demise of family-oriented TV programs had claimed its latest victim, with their replacements now "containing a little more sex, a little more garbage, and a little less originality are vying with each other in the ratings."[62]

Steele celebrated his seventy-second birthday on July 13, 1983, and "was flabbergasted" when an entourage of several dozen WTIC staff members and associates "barged into his studio and started singing 'Happy Birthday'" in the middle of his show, but his real present—of sorts—did not arrive for another two months when his perennial baseball pick, the Chicago White Sox, clinched the West Division of the American League.[63] The White Sox, however, would not reach the World Series, losing the league championship playoff to the Baltimore Orioles. Weeks later, Steele was disturbed by a far more serious matter when the United States Marine Corps barracks in Beirut, Lebanon, were bombed, resulting in over two hundred deaths. "Bigger trouble a constant possibility," he later commented in his diary, adding, "Damn war! It's stupid but will never end. It pauses but doesn't end."[64]

Although he was growing bored with lengthy luncheon appearances and was limiting his attendance at such engagements, Steele's show schedule continued as the mainstay for WTIC, which in 1985 celebrated its sixtieth anniversary of broadcasting. But the aging process for both the radio host and the station were in transition, unmistakably so. Just as The Travelers had divested itself of its radio and television enterprises a decade earlier, the insurance giant shed its Travelers Weather Service by closing the operation down, and WTIC segued to using information from AccuWeather, a syndicated meteorological service. One notable personality, weatherman Charlie Bagley, found employment at another Hartford-area station and siphoned some of his loyal listeners from WTIC to his new home at WRCQ.

While WTIC tried to retain its overwhelming market share, that percentage was slowly but discernably eroding as the 1980s continued, and a burning issue that could not be avoided began to gain ever-increasing currency. "Steele's eventual retirement is bound to accelerate that trend [of reduced market share]," opined David Klemm, a renowned media consultant.[65] FM radio's general popularity meant that even more listeners would be drawn away from AM stations, so WTIC would not be alone among such outlets in seeing a reduced audience.

By Steele's seventy-fourth birthday, speculation was beginning to rise as to who would replace him in the all-important early-morning time slot, but honors and recognition were bestowed upon him as his tenure at WTIC reached an amazing fifty years. Citations from Broadcast Music, Incorporated (BMI), the Connecticut Broadcasters Association, the state's chapter of the Associated Press, and the Connecticut General Assembly added further tributes to his career that was highlighted in various newspapers and trade publications. The 1986 release of another book, *Bob Steele's 50th Anniversary: An Affectionate Memoir* by Jane Moskowitz and Jane Gillard, added to the cavalcade of encomiums, not least of which came from the mayor of the town of Wethersfield, Connecticut, Governor Bill O'Neill, President Ronald Reagan, the Boy Scouts of America, and the United States Power Squadrons.

The virtuous endeavors of charity that found favor with Bob Steele culminated in the adding of his name to an enterprise that, given his many years on the air and his attention to language, would be a most appropriate tribute. To commemorate his half-century with WTIC, The Ten Eighty Corporation donated fifty thousand dollars to the Literacy Volunteers of Connecticut, this grant to be used in conjunction with contributions from the Hartford Insurance Group, the Ensworth Charitable Foundation, and the Jodik Foundation to expand the existing Moylan Alternative Learning Center. Steele was most flattered to learn that the new name for the facility would be the Literacy Volunteers/Bob Steele Reading Center.[66]

Steele prided himself on the consistency of his program and its contents, all of which were decades in the making, and the cultivation of this style that endeared him to countless thousands of people retained its grip even as the tastes of listeners across the broad spectrum of audiences reflected a gravitation toward radio outlets with more modern music, freer expression of opinions regarding politics as well as societal and cultural issues, or—very ominously, in Steele's view—the burgeoning employment of crass, provocative material whose purpose was only to draw listeners to a program because of its shock value.

During a 1986 interview with the International Radio and Television Society (IRTS), Steele defended a radio host's programming if it brought about success—"I think [management] ought to let a guy do what comes naturally"—but he quickly qualified his statement when asked what he thought of the "morning zoos and shock jocks that are now predominant coast-to-coast in Top 40 radio of the 1980s."[67] Bristling at this disquieting evolution, Steele said, "Now if he's going to be risqué or offensive, that's different.... I don't like them. I think it's a disgrace." At this point in time, Steele undoubtedly was referring to the antics of personalities such as Don Imus and Howard Stern, whose penchant for deliberately outrageous statements signaled a decline in decorum and the eventual creation of the Broadcast Decency Enforcement Act by the Federal Communications Commission.

Bob Steele's attitude certainly mirrored his age but more importantly it was a reflection of the moral values he deemed to be a pillar of broadcasting propriety. There was no delineation of radio audiences in the way that moviegoers could be restricted entry to a theater by their age, or at least accompanied by an adult. Although a rating system for movies had been in place only since 1968, radio stations for the most part had been self-censors of the content of their shows.

But as the slippery slope of permissiveness allowed a greater degree of off-color programming to find air time, standards of etiquette diminished. "I could drop my pants right in the middle of Hartford right now and the papers would be full of it—everybody would be talking about it, but it wouldn't take any talent," Steele told IRTS. "It would just take a little nerve. I don't believe in that sort of thing."[68] Comments that Steele made about trashy movies that he had seen in recent years—filled with more and more gratuitous violence, foul language, sex, or any combination of the three— mark him as consistent in his low opinion about what was transpiring to the detriment of mass media.

8

Lasting Recognition

America's "only" Radio Hall of Fame is pleased to add your name to its distinguished list of inductees.
—Letter from Bruce DuMont to Bob Steele,
August 7, 1995

The addition of Bob Steele's name to a learning and reading institution was a wonderful tribute as well as a different yet fitting way to put his name in the public eye. But to solidify his place in the pantheon of radio legends, there could be no higher honor than to be chosen for induction into the National Radio Hall of Fame. In December 1986, Perry Ury, the president of The Ten Eighty Corporation, initiated the process to have radio broadcasting's highest honor bestowed on Steele.

"A few weeks ago, you received a 1987 ballot from the [National Association of Broadcasters] for nomination of an individual who has made an outstanding contribution to the radio industry," Ury wrote in a letter to various media associates, and he requested that "you nominate Bob Steele of WTIC AM 1080, Hartford, Connecticut, to the NAB Radio Hall of Fame."[1]

Steele's importance to his radio audience and to the community in general, as manifest in his charitable work, was well known for decades, but one aspect of his career that drew little notice pertained to the financial clout he wielded on behalf of his employer. As his advancing age became a more pressing issue and begged an answer to the question surrounding his inevitable retirement, management at WTIC took stock of what Steele meant to the station's revenue-generating capacity and how the bottom line would be affected when he would leave broadcasting.

Steele tried to soften the blow of his departure by offering a comparison to Walter Cronkite's passing of his anchor position with CBS News to Dan Rather. In their own way, Steele and Cronkite were both unsurpassed in their respective fields, and Steele implied that people did not cease watching the *CBS Evening News* simply because Cronkite was no longer the primary attraction. In a similar fashion, Steele thought that WTIC would be able to maintain continuity of its large market share even after he chose to step away from the microphone. Resorting to a bit of self-deprecating humor, he even said that maybe there was a segment of the population that would be encouraged to tune in because they would *not* have to listen to him.

As was pointed out in a previous chapter, however, Steele had an idea of his financial value to WTIC, but considering the strength of his top market share, one informed source indicates that he accounted for 74 percent of the station's revenue during the peak of his career.[2] Another reconciliation of data was published in early 1987 by *New England Monthly*, and although this estimate was lower, it nonetheless speaks volumes about the power wielded by this champion of the airwaves. "Bob Steele has jollied the Insurance City through the commuting hours, and in the process has built an audience that makes it possible for WTIC to earn roughly forty percent of all its advertising revenue from one four-and-a-half-hour, six-day-a-week radio show."[3] In any case, one may be hard-pressed to think of another corporation as dependent on a single employee—as opposed to a company owner or founder—as WTIC was on their singular star.[4]

If power of popularity can speak to profits, *The Bob Steele Show* was the apotheosis of the ability of a radio station to make money. "[Steele's] recent 31.5 share, although a comedown from his 1984 mark of 37.1 percent, still leaves the competition in the dust. And with the clout of his ratings, WTIC can demand as much as $525 for a single commercial during morning drive time…. No other Hartford station dares charge such rates."[5] Indeed, the next highest rate was $210 at WDRC for an advertisement on Brad Davis's show, and of a total market area thought to comprise $31 million in annual ad revenue, "in theory [Steele's] show could bring in as much as $6 million a year."[6]

But with WTIC's golden goose nearing the cusp of retirement, it was a foregone conclusion that this revenue stream would diminish, quite likely in the near future. And the unavoidable question loomed larger with each passing day: Who would replace the voice with whom millions of listeners awoke for decades? Popularity was an absolutely important factor, but gaining the trust of an audience was another tangible asset that could be years in the making. That Bob Steele had achieved both with stunning success made him unique in radio broadcasting, and while the old saw has it that no one is irreplaceable, the inevitable task of finding a new, attractive morning host would be an imposing challenge for the station's management.

As the search for that fresh voice commenced, Steele's separation due to retirement was not likely to be a sudden halt to his appearances on the air. In the early summer of 1987, Steele met with WTIC senior vice president

Tom Barsanti to discuss a transition away from the studio, whereby he would do a one-hour segment beginning at 9 a.m. Monday through Friday and a typical full show on Saturday. He also gave the manager a figure he deemed to be appropriate compensation for this revised schedule, but when his request was denied just days before his seventy-sixth birthday, Steele was resigned to the verdict: "OK by me. I have decided I've gone far enough. [I will] retire, as agreed, Dec. 31 this year."[7]

Yet, stepping away would not be as cut-and-dried as first believed. Less than a month after he admitted that he was ready to leave, "Steele confirmed … that he's having second thoughts," possibly because the notion of ending his lengthy run was too much to bear.[8] Steele and Barsanti had reopened negotiations, but in the meantime, other stations in the Hartford area were trying to formulate business strategies in reaction to what might lay in Steele's future.

WTIC's competition was also plotting ways to gain listeners who were presumed to be looking for other stations to tune in to once their longtime favorite ultimately departed. The head of a local media consortium, Warren Schroeger, said that "his stations have been preparing several program additions, especially on the FM side, which has been third in the ratings after the two WTIC stations. 'But we're not doing anything until Bob Steele is off the air. Otherwise, it's too much of a gamble.'"[9]

And wait was exactly what competitors had to do. At an extravaganza celebrating his fifty-one years on the air, Bob Steele did his show live from Westfarms Mall before an estimated crowd of two thousand admirers and announced his decision to remain at his traditional post for one more year, his retirement now delayed until the end of 1988. Claiming to be swayed by the correspondence from over a hundred listeners who did not want to see him leave, Steele cited the advice imparted by one gentleman who told him, "You get a lot of aches and pains when you retire…. Don't retire. You feel it physically, and you feel it mentally. You won't be happy."[10]

Steele's segue into his post-radio life was not going to include an abundance of time sitting still. This point was made emphatically when he entered into a partnership with WTIC senior vice president Bob Dunn that would capitalize on his equally famous reputation and skill as a speaker that Steele had crafted at all manner of public and private events. Dunn took a 25 percent commission for handling the arrangements and produced a slick marketing brochure that established the basic ground rules—and fees—as to how sponsors could enliven their occasion with the addition of an appearance by Bob Steele. "Credibility and believability with great humor for successful meetings, ceremonies, roasts, conventions, audio/visual narratives, [and] TV commercials" were to be had for prices ranging from $500 to be charged to non-profit organizations within fifty miles of Hartford up to $6,250 for three thirty-second television announcements.[11] Steele's first gig under the agreement netted $450 for him and $150 for Dunn courtesy of his mid–October appearance at a food show at the annual "Big E" in West Springfield, Massachusetts.

Inchoate retirement plans did not stop the intermittent honor from coming Steele's way, such as when the Connecticut State Dental Association presented him with the Horace Hayden Award for his contribution to good public health, and the Greater Hartford Jaycees recognized him as their "Outstanding Individual of the Year" for 1988. Steele also lent his voice to the political campaign of his son Phil, who was seeking the mayoralty of Hartford (but whose bid fell short).

One momentous gathering of the family occurred in mid–April 1988 when Bob and Shirley's sons and their spouses treated the couple by joining them in New York at the Waldorf-Astoria Hotel to commemorate their fiftieth wedding anniversary. A splendid time was had by all, and the paterfamilias noted that their morning brunch was "sumptuous … even Mama ate more than usual" and ended the festive occasion by extending "thanks to all our sons!"[12]

Boxer Muhammad Ali became renowned for winning the heavyweight crown several times during his storied career, and beginning in the early 1970s he always seemed to be making a comeback or coming out of retirement to face another ring opponent. Whether by accident or design, that pattern was being mimicked by Bob Steele, and the latest version of his plans to leave WTIC were brought to light as the summer of 1988 was about to commence.

THE TEN EIGHTY CORPORATION
WTIC AM & FM
MEMORANDUM

TO: THE STAFF
FROM: TOM BARSANTI
DATE: JUNE 20, 1988

I am delighted to be able to inform you that BOB STEELE has decided to continue his morning program on WTIC AM 1080 thru 1989.

Bob continues to be one of the highest rated air personalities in America and an integral part of WTIC programming.

The retirement postponement, which now was becoming an annual occurrence akin to the blossoming of the cherry trees in the nation's capital, also served as fodder for another celebrity roast that fall, this one sponsored by the Hartford Civitan Club to benefit Connecticut Special Olympics. With the counter on Steele's anniversary at WTIC now at fifty-two years, Hartford Mayor Carrie Saxon Perry entertained the crowd of over four hundred guests at Valle's Steak House by relating a fictitious encounter she had with someone upon entering the restaurant.

> "Hi, mayor, how are you? Where are you going?"
> I said, "I'm going to the Steele roast."
> They said, "Not *again*? He's retiring *again*?"
> I said, "Every year, if he can."[13]

As if his audience needed any reminder of what they would miss about him when he at last would call it quits, the honored guest concluded the affair with a story bejeweled with a signature pun. "When I do retire, though, I want to open a little shop, I want to have a bookstore," he said, leading the attendees down the garden path as only he could. "At Westfarms Mall there's a vacant store that is just perfect. On one side there's a store that sells fishing equipment, and on the other side is a pawnshop. My wife doesn't want me to go into it because she says it's between a hock and a rod place."[14]

Still lurking in the background was the need to find Bob Steele's heir to the studio. The degree of difficulty of the search was ameliorated somewhat by program director David Bernstein's connection to the eventual successor. On April 4, 1989, Steele was informed by Bernstein that he had hired one of his former employees from AM station WDBO in Orlando, Florida. Born in Iowa and moving to Hartford with two decades' worth of experience in broadcasting, Tom McCarthy was inked to a five-year contract and planned on easing into his new position in Hartford by summer.

At the tender age of thirty-six, McCarthy had reached his own pinnacle as "morning host of a top-rated full-service radio show" when he was hired away from central Florida.[15] Working in the replacement's favor was what Bernstein noted as McCarthy's "unaccented, distinct and natural voice," a quality that would be pleasant—or at least less irritating—to the ears of many listeners.[16]

For his part, Steele was cut out of the decision-making process as to who would be assuming his place, telling his diary, "Never heard a word from upper brass—Dunn, Ury, Barsanti."[17] Steele may have been kept in the dark because McCarthy's actual role was presented to the media in late April as being loosely defined: "Whether he'll be host, partner or understudy is up in the air," station executives—including Steele—were quoted as saying.[18] McCarthy claimed that the deal he secured was for five years, so it is hard to imagine that WTIC would have made that kind of commitment for the sake of securing the services of an "understudy," even though it would be natural for him to apprentice under and directly observe Steele for a short period of time to better acclimate the newcomer to the milieu long solidified by the master of his craft.

By early May, McCarthy had found his way to Hartford as had his new mentor fifty-three years prior. McCarthy had better accommodations than when Steele arrived, residing temporarily at the Park-Hilton a few blocks from the Gold Building but intending to take up more permanent residence in Bolton, Connecticut. McCarthy joined Steele as a silent observer in the studio for the last hour of his May 8 program but two weeks later he became an active participant for a quartet of shows at an hour per program. At the end of the test runs, the main players gave McCarthy a thumbs-up: "Sounds OK to me. Barsanti + Bernstein seem to like it," Steele noted.[19] A more definitive if unintended trial occurred in early July when Steele was felled by great discomfort at the base of his spine, and his inability to go to the studio forced McCarthy to do the entire show himself.

Steele may have been growing accustomed to a competent companion sharing the microphone and studio with him, but the presence also of management at the same time was another issue. Two weeks after McCarthy's solo program, Steele made known his displeasure that Bernstein being in the studio constituted a "three's a crowd" scenario. "I suddenly spoke my mind at 6:50 a.m.—about Dave sitting in on the program—he took it pretty well—calmly, but losing color in his face; finally [he] said, 'Well, I'll listen somewhere else and left. Didn't come back. I saw him after ten o'clock—in the corridor—he didn't speak. [I] had to say it. Tom McC and Arnold [Dean] seemed to agree with me."[20]

That Bernstein would intrude—in person—this late in the game on Steele and McCarthy, who seemed to have passed his metaphorical screen test, was too much for Steele to countenance, yet the very next day Bob Dunn called both hosts into his office for a "talking to," much to Steele's dismay. Then as if everything had been normal right along, Bernstein was "'directing' program as though we'd never had [a] disagreement."[21] Whether station executives had heard something previously on the air not to their liking cannot be known, but perhaps this was management's attempt at a passive-aggressive show of force to indicate who was going to maintain an upper hand in the running of Steele's program.

A pair of milestones in Bob Steele's storied career were achieved in September 1989. The first of them was notification that he would receive—one year hence—the Masonic Thirty-third degree, an honor that his son Phil said "was a commendation he had long hoped for" and one that filled him with "huge gratitude and pride."[22] One past master of a Masonic lodge explained that while not all members receive each of the first thirty-two degrees, the thirty-second is always given; however, the Thirty-third degree "is an honorary degree bestowed upon Members who perform exceptional service ... the thirty-third degree is simply a Scottish rite honor, albeit a prestigious one."[23] Steele was to be joined by three titans of the business world in being "coroneted a 33rd Degree Member of the Supreme Council of the [Ancient and Accepted Scottish Rite of Freemasonry] for the Northern Masonic District of the United States."[24]

The second commendation came in tandem with another earned by WTIC. Steele was personally honored with the Marconi Radio Award as "Personality of the Year" presented by the National Association of Broadcasters, this coming at virtually the same time that the station was named the recipient of the Edward R. Murrow Award for Investigative Reporting given by the Radio and Television News Directors Association. Although Steele was proud to accept the Marconi Award, he declined to attend the presentation ceremony in New Orleans "because I don't like to fly."[25] Perry Ury, who was less squeamish about air travel, filled in on his behalf, but Steele was willing to use Amtrak to make his later trip to Milwaukee for the Masons' white-tie ceremony.

By the middle of October, the issue of Steele's retirement had been definitively settled despite rumblings of yet another one-year extension that emerged earlier that month. He retained his full show on Saturday from 5:30 a.m. to 10 a.m., but Monday through Friday would have him on the air only from 9 a.m. to 10 a.m. His new sidekick, Tom McCarthy, confessed that rising at three fifteen in the morning to be in the studio each business day would take a bit getting used to, but he enthused about the chance to be in the company of a radio icon because he had "learned more in five months co-hosting with [Steele] than in the two decades before."[26] One of Steele's associates who would not be following him into semi-retirement was longtime engineer Bob Downes, who produced Steele's program for many years but had chosen to retire in December.

When the new era began on New Year's Day 1990 without Bob Steele as the lead voice during the week, McCarthy still was not alone in the studio. Veteran sports director Arnold Dean joined him to handle the program for the allotted three-and-a-half hours before Steele took over for the final sixty minutes. Although Steele lost his preferred parking spot in the Gold Building garage except for his early Saturday arrival, there was a weekday benefit he loved: "Slept 'til 7:30!"[27] With new promotional material WTIC AM introduced the new McCarthy–Dean pairing while reminding listeners that Steele was still part of the team to convey "Birthdays, TiddlyWinks, the Musical Oldie and those incomparable Steele witticisms and prognostications."[28] His loyal listeners would not desert him: six months into his new routine, he learned that his Saturday program was drawing a remarkable rating of 45 percent of the audience.

Hardly gone and certainly not forgotten, Steele found himself the recipient of another sporting laurel, this one from the Connecticut Sports Writers Alliance, who presented him with its Gold Key Award in February. But his diminished role at the station induced management to reduce the office space he previously enjoyed, and he was forced to move in with Ross Miller, vice president of programming. Other expense trimming took place to his dismay when his personal subscription to *USA Today* was eliminated. In a decision he took by his own initiative, Steele stepped away from the presidency of the Crocodile Club, a luncheon organization that encouraged political japes with a humorous twist. Steele handed the reins of the group to a longtime member who for seventeen years served as the club's president, Channel 3 newsman Gerry Brooks.

Steele's social calendar appeared to remain busy enough to occupy his time, as dinners, visits to hospitals, and other events let him savor a more relaxed pace of life. This change was facilitated further by his "pre-recording a lot of commentary, quips for inclusion on the program" when he was not at the studio.[29] In April 1991, he was thrilled to receive a gift in the form of a ringside seat—at the astounding cost of $1,000—and limousine transportation for the George Foreman–Evander Holyfield heavyweight boxing match in Atlantic City.

Another gala in the form of a live radio show was staged that summer at the Shoppes at Buckland Mall in Manchester, Connecticut, to commemorate Steele's eightieth birthday, a black-tie occasion—at least for the dignitaries seated at the head table—that drew a reported two thousand people. Steele himself was goaded by Tom McCarthy into reading his own name when the time came to cite those people celebrating their eightieth (or greater) birthdays. Among the hundreds of cards he received were best wishes from President George H. W. Bush, and Connecticut's senior U.S. Senator, Chris Dodd, authored a tribute that was printed in the *Congressional Record*.

The year 1991 was not medically kind to Bob Steele, who suffered a number of terrible colds and several bouts of fatigue, was troubled by his prostate gland as well as a spot on the skin of his left wrist, and underwent a laser treatment for his left eye. As active as he had been for so many years, age was catching up with him, and the true end of his six-days-a-week schedule became official after fifty-five years.

On September 30, the day before his fifty-fifth anniversary at WTIC, he announced that he was stepping away for good with the exception of serving as a "consultant" for one year. As had been the case a few years earlier, editorials and columns in the local press sang the praises of Steele, all that he had accomplished on the air, and the ways in which he had touched the lives of countless people. One week later, a retirement party—"He really means it this time," read the invitation—was held at the J. P. Morgan Hotel, two blocks west of the radio studio.[30] When WTIC sports director Arnold Dean signed the guest book for the affair, he may have best captured the sentiments of not only the attendees but also Steele's well-wishers far and wide: "I hope you enjoy your retirement as much as we've enjoyed your work!"[31]

When Tom McCarthy was brought to Hartford, he expressed a desire to "stay here fifty-plus years not only because WTIC is one of America's premier stations, but we're tired of moving."[32] His Iowa upbringing was followed by stints at three radio stations in Florida as well as Schenectady, New York, so with a bit of relief he was happy to have found a place where he and his family could plant firmer roots.

As giddy as his half-century optimism was, McCarthy's stint in Connecticut was even shorter than the average stay at his other employers, and by the end of April 1992 he was off to the Pacific Northwest for a position with station KOMO in Seattle. In place of McCarthy, WTIC hired Ray Dunaway, who, like Bob Steele, was a native of Kansas City, and the coincidence of two Kansas Citians having been a part of the early-morning weekday timeslot at the same radio station for most years since 1936 is admittedly uncanny.

The retirement that Steele was enjoying included personal visitations to Chatfield, a senior assisted living center in West Hartford, his appearances courtesy of a contract he had with the facility. He collected a quarterly stipend from WTIC for the consulting work he did for the station, and he also could be hired for speaking engagements through his association with Landerman & Jarvis of East Hartford. But as Steele luxuriated in his freedom from radio, his latest on-air replacement was currying little favor with long-time listeners who had long grown accustomed to the pace, rhythm, and timing of *The Bob Steele Show.*

"What's happened to WTIC?," carped a letter sent to station management a mere three weeks after Ray Dunaway took to the air. "Where's the reliability and dependability[?] I used to know when Scott Gray came on at 8:15 that I had exactly three minutes to leave my house to catch my bus for work. Also, the other day at 7:35 Angela [Dias] and Ray were bantering back and forth—

Always nattily attired, Bob Steele holds forth at one of his countless speaking engagements (Hartford History Center, Hartford Public Library).

what happened to 10 mins. of news? [You] assured me WTIC would continue to have the same consistent and reliable quality as we were used to. What happened?" The distraught listener closed by pleadingly stating the obvious: HOW I MISS BOB STEELE!!![33]

The above complaint certainly was not the only such missive submitted. It should be noted, however, that at the time of WTIC's original quest for Steele's replacement, which yielded Tom McCarthy, and then the subsequent hiring of Dunaway, Steele had been complimentary to both men during the respective search processes.[34] The weight of Steele's opinions certainly influenced management's decisions to bring McCarthy and Dunaway to the station. Nonetheless, WTIC took action to address the latest tempest in a subtle yet definitive way to placate old-time listeners without compromising the commitment it had made to Ray Dunaway and the latitude afforded his program.

A week before the Fourth of July holiday, Steele was approached to do his show on that day as a one-time event, the timing such that it would occur when Dunaway was not scheduled to be in the studio. There was no advance

warning of Steele's brief comeback, and needless to say, the results were pre-
dictable. "Had many calls from people claiming to be delighted. Will, no doubt,
get [a] ton of mail," Steele proudly noted, and the letter writer who voiced her
earlier displeasure about Dunaway's poor reliability sent a note directly to
Steele—at his residence—expressing her enthusiasm for his reprise.[35]

Other similar before-and-after letters were sent to WTIC and/or Steele,
and an effort was begun to revive *The Bob Steele Show* in very limited form.
The station brokered a deal in mid–August to bring him back for one Saturday
each month to do his regular show. Steele had a mild case of pre-air jitters
with a poor night of sleep, but after waking earlier than he would have liked,
he was back at the microphone at 5:30 a.m. on September 26 for a show that
he believed "went well."[36] There would be no consistency to what particular
Saturday he chose, as if to playfully keep his audience guessing, although
WTIC's promotional advertisements indicated the third or fourth Saturday.
Sponsorship deals were available beginning at $150 for a sixty-second com-
mercial.

The fan mail attending the Steele renaissance brought undisputed relief
to many listeners, and recognizing its success, WTIC signed him for a second
year of Saturday shows. A number of ailments failed to deter him from those
flexible engagements, but a terrible scare came in July 1993 when Shirley suffered a horrific bout of salmonella which caused a significant weight loss and
forced her to be hospitalized and endure a lengthy recovery.

Entering the spring of 1994, the Connecticut Sports Hall of Fame had
but two informally named members, boxer Willie Pep and Bob Steele. However, neither had been officially inducted until a charter group of fourteen
notable figures—including former baseball commissioner Fay Vincent and
past Olympians Lindy Remigino, Dorothy Hamill, and Bruce Jenner—was
recognized and enshrined on May 24 at the Aqua Turf in Southington. A
local sports editor, with tongue just a bit in cheek, commented that Steele
"was our state's first and best-known TV sportscaster [who] entertained millions for a million years on radio with unmatched style and wit."[37]

Birthdays and Saturday shows rolled on but with accompanying medical
issues that vexed the now eighty-three-year-old host, whose Saturday show
was now trimmed to nine annual appearances, again due to WTIC's quest to
limit expenses. After an extended, management-imposed recess, Steele was
back on the air just days after he lost a very dear friend. Bill Savitt, the jeweler
whose "Peace of Mind Guarantee" had been the most enduring label associated with his business and philanthropic endeavors, passed away at the age
of ninety-four.

The letter distributed by Perry Ury to various colleagues in order to encourage them to nominate Bob Steele for the Radio Hall of Fame paid the ultimate dividend in the summer of 1995. In a note mailed to his studio address in Hartford, Steele was informed by Bruce Dumont, the Hall's founder and president, that in the wake of tabulation of "[b]allots sent to over 6,000 radio executives, historians, academicians, and members of the Radio Hall of Fame from across the nation," he would be joining the likes of Orson Welles, Paul Harvey, and Edward R. Murrow as recipients of the media's highest honor.[38] A second inductee with ties to Connecticut, Edward McLaughlin, would join Steele thanks to his work in bringing Harvey and Rush Limbaugh into the national spotlight.

Although pleased to receive complimentary hotel accommodations and first-class air passage to Chicago for the Hall's ceremony, Steele was skittish about having to fly, but conceded that it was the most expedient means to get there. Apart from being aghast at his out-of-pocket cost for room-service breakfast the morning of his departure—"$14.98 plus tip. EGAD!" he observed with shock—Steele appeared to enjoy his time at the black-tie gala.[39]

As that year was drawing to a close, Steele made a private note regarding a new economic trend that was infused with no small measure of political overtones. In the early 1990s, the issue of casino gambling in Connecticut became rooted in the southeastern part of the state on tribal land owned by the Mashantucket Pequot and Mohegan Indians, and following federal recognition by the Bureau of Indian Affairs, the high-stakes Bingo parlors that had been sponsored by the tribes were supplanted by a pair of new resort casinos. As the first of their kind in the region, they generated fantastic amounts of money for the tribes, and deals were brokered in which a percentage of slot machine revenue was collected by the state.

Although the casinos grew in popularity and their coffers swelled with cash through the 1990s, not all observers viewed the boon with enthusiasm, and some conjoined the tribes' new economic situation with other disturbing commercial trends in Connecticut. "Big news every day is about Indian gambling—or 'gaming' as it is usually called—and casinos that are planned—Ledyard [Mashantucket Pequots] is so massively successful 'everybody wants to get into the act' (as Jimmy Durante used to say).... Soon there will be so many, nobody will make any money," Steele told his diary.[40]

His vision was prescient, however, regarding what the future might hold for such enterprises, which were later proposed to be built in neighboring states as well as in other parts of Connecticut. "In time, all the people will be broke and because of excessive competition, the casinos will be bankrupt," and he pointed out the extant peril already affecting the Hartford region: "In sports—the Whalers are terrible…. Crowds are 8,000 to 11,000. Should be 15,000 every time to make a profit. Downtown stores, shops, restaurants are disappearing—hotels are suffering—as in most cities malls are the cause. Parking is a big factor."[41] The suburbs of Hartford had long been bedroom communities for workers who commuted into the capital, yet through the 1980s the downtown area continued to hold its own, and plans for large sky-scrapers were drawn up. But as conditions changed negatively toward the end of the decade, some of those proposals fell by the wayside, not least of which was the construction of what would have been New England's tallest building, the 878-foot-tall Cutter Financial Center, and a later effort to relo-cate the New England Patriots football team to a new stadium to be built in Hartford.

The problems of reasonably priced parking in Hartford lingers to this day, but more importantly, inherent in Steele's opinion of the overbuilding of casinos is the inescapable fact that the general public can support only so much gaming trade, and in tough economic times when people have a reduced—or in some cases little or no—discretionary income to spend at gambling establishments, the harsh reality will, or should, dictate that trying to pay one's bills through money made at a casino is a formula for personal financial disaster. Realizing gambling's adverse effects, Steele's eldest son Robert became an advocate in the effort to stem the propagation of casinos and their related businesses.

Time never stood still for Bob Steele, and in October 1996, he marked sixty years with WTIC by giving an interview to *Northeast Magazine*, the *Hartford Courant*'s Sunday supplement, and while the resulting story did not reveal anything new about him, it served as a reminder of the indefatigable spirit that kept him returning to the studio if even for his occasional monthly show. He devoted ninety minutes of his time to an appearance on Ray Dun-away's program of October 1 that drew the notice of media notables and Gov-ernor John Rowland. Even Tom McCarthy, recently let go from his Seattle radio station, called him the following day to chat.

The Steele name acquired a certain cachet over the years, and it resonated with businesses that sought to use it to their benefit. At his advanced age, he recorded advertisements for Peter L. Brown, a company offering windows, siding, and roofing; Miracle Ear hearing aids, by which time at the age of eighty-five Steele was an appropriate pitchman; and Maxim Medical Supply Company. An occasion that brought back fond memories for Steele was the dedication of a monument in the south end of Hartford to mark the location of the former Bulkeley Stadium at 210 George Street. Having fallen into disrepair by the beginning of the 1960s, the facility was razed and seemingly forgotten until late 1997 when an effort was made to place a commemorative marker at the site. Steele was among the guests in early March 1998 who participated in the unveiling ceremony which, for Steele, recalled his reason for coming to Hartford more than six decades prior.

The bugbear accompanying the aging process are the aches and pains that make life for the elderly uncomfortable if not downright miserable. Not immune to these woes, Steele left a trail of these ills in his diary, yet because his sense of humor never deserted him, he was not above embellishing some of these entries with a touch of whimsy. Near the end of June 1998, he stated the obvious: "I'm getting old. Hope to make it to 87 [in] 3 weeks. I'm sore at just about every point—hands, back, neck—stiff and sore—takes me 2 minutes to bend over far enough to pick up a dropped coin."[42]

One curious aspect to Steele's aging process, which appears to be backed up by copious photographic evidence, is his lack of need for everyday eyeglasses. His retirement, however, allowed him to put his reading glasses, which he had employed for many years, to very good use for the enjoyment of many books. He unquestionably continued to relish the time he spent with his youngest son, as evidenced by the many first-run movies he and Steve attended as well as boxing-related events, whether they were matches at the Hartford Civic Center, testimonials, or dinners.

In the spring of 1999, Steele was pressed into action as chef when Shirley took a fall in the family kitchen, of all places. "Mama's back not good," he privately noted, and then explained the subsequent aftereffect due to his poor culinary skills: "Lousy dinner. I fixed it. Ham sandwiches + soup. But many poor souls in this world would have thought it a BANQUET."[43] Try as he might, his preparations were simply no substitute for the wonders that he long knew Shirley was capable of creating. Later in the year, he commented that he had lost twenty-two pounds, his weight now in the mid–180s.

Another glowing profile of him also appeared at this time in the *Hartford Courant* in which he admitted that perhaps he would give up his monthly Saturday program and retire definitively and completely. The reason was lodged in another decision taken by the management of the radio station and served as a sobering reminder of the economic conditions the city was enduring. The departure of the Whalers, the failure to cement the deal that was supposed to deliver the Patriots to Hartford, and the abundant amounts of vacant office space in a number of large downtown buildings painted a bleak outlook, all of which were augmented by the departure of another institution. "[A]s WTIC prepares to move its studios from downtown Hartford to Farmington, it appears Steele's days of presiding over this reeling town may also be dwindling down to a precious few."[44] The relocation occurred in August 1999, and Steele, now at the age of eighty-eight, did his first show from a studio beyond the Hartford city limits on Labor Day weekend. But even the limousine transportation he was provided did little to soothe the fatigue he endured just to be on the air, and he opined privately that perhaps it was time to step away from the studio permanently.

A major milestone in the lives of Bob and Shirley came via the birth of their first great-grandchild in October 1999, a son to Jeff and Brenda Steele, the new father being the son of Steele's eldest son Robert. By the turn of the new century, Steele was part of WTIC's 75th anniversary commemoration and his eighty-ninth birthday occasioned a thoughtful—and delicious—gift in the form of weekly take-out dinners from Carbone's, Hartford's renowned Italian eatery. This fancy cuisine was juxtaposed by the banal hot dogs and B&M baked beans that he and Shirley often had for Saturday night supper.

In a reprise of his days as a motorcycle columnist, Steele took pen to paper to contribute an introduction to a book published in the spring of 2001, *Hartford: New England Renaissance* featuring photography by Enrique Espinosa. Steele's paean to the former Insurance Capital of the World was an intersection of the place he recalled from the days of his Depression-era arrival and "the change that still strikes me [as] how much Hartford now resembles a big city, with all the big buildings and all the hustle and traffic."[45]

Soldiering on despite his increasingly failing health, Steele labored to continue his monthly Saturday radio show, and the evidence he left in his diary indicates that the chore of doing the program was mitigated to a great degree by the engineer who now worked with him, Glenn Colligan. Another birthday for Steele, his ninetieth, elicited the deserved outpouring of cards and well-wishes in the summer of 2001, just two months before the world-changing catastrophe of September 11. "Day of Terror—in NY and Washington planes crash into World Trade Center—destroy both towers.... Damage immense," he noted as America plunged ahead contemplating "what to do (or not to do) for revenge."[46]

More pleasurable for Steele was his participation in the thirtieth anniversary of the Connecticut Lottery in February 2002, when he received a certificate of appreciation for the work he did on the agency's behalf in its earliest days. Availing himself of the opportunity to collect material for one of the most famous legacies of his radio career, Steele began working that spring with his son Phil on the fittingly titled book *The Word for the Day*, which was published in September. Coming two months after his ninety-first birthday, the volume contained a trove of information from one of the staple segments of his show, which he earnestly used to improve the vocabulary of his listeners in this small but important way.

An entry in Bob Steele's diary contained straightforward information concerning a piece of business that he helped his youngest son tend to on December 4, 2002. Steve had a tooth extracted by Dr. William Marco, a dentist in Wethersfield, the late-morning procedure costing $275. This was an issue obviously requiring professional attention, but the perfunctory note made about it by Steele indicated no reason for concern, to say nothing of being consistent with countless entries he had written over the years that included some sort of financial data. What draws attention, however, is the fact that this would be the final private comment he made, thereby closing out the thousands of such notes he had made over most of the previous eight decades.

The voice of Robert Lee Steele was silenced two days later, the legend having passed away in his sleep. There may have been some surprise expressed by those who indicated that he had been feeling as well as a ninety-one-year-old man could expect to, his schedule just the previous month having seen him in the studio for his monthly Saturday show and also at a local market where he greeted fans and signed copies of his latest book. Photographs of the affair offer proof not only of his ever-present cheerful spirit but also of his physical well-being at a very advanced age.

But just as the passing of many of Steele's associates and friends in recent years took him to their funerals, the tables were now turned, and the loved ones he left behind grieved the loss of an extraordinary man. As praise and remembrances of the WTIC star poured in to area newspapers, the most moving of these expressions was delivered by his son Robert at a memorial service held on December 12 in Wethersfield (see Appendix).

The local press devoted many pages to retell the highlights of Steele's life, and the single, six-inch column that comprised his obituary in the *Hartford Courant* belies the tributes paid to him by newspaper columnists and editorial writers. Listeners of his program, bereft in their own way, penned letters to the editor recalling memories of what Steele meant to them, anecdotes about personal encounters with him, and the like. As the internet became ever firmly rooted and indispensable to society, the website for WTIC alumni gathered accolades and reminiscences of Steele, and Connecticut Public Television broadcast a series of interviews with a number of Steele's colleagues, all of whom contributed memories of what, in their view, made Bob Steele unique.

His voice does live on in the literal sense thanks to compilations of compact disks that capture recordings of past Bob Steele programs, and for those with internet access, the YouTube website contains a collection of audio and video clips that are easily accessible. As pleasant as these artifacts may be, they provide only a substitute for the real McCoy, and there certainly will never be another radio personality like him.

A coda of sorts to the story of Bob Steele came nearly two years after he passed away. On October 11, 2004, the love of his life—whether she was known as Astrid, Shirley, or Mama—died, generating much sorrow for her family and friends but also reuniting her with her late husband. Their unflinching devotion to each other could easily serve as an object lesson in that most elusive quality of the human condition—love.

9

"The sleepless but amusing life of a radio announcer"

The name "Bob Steele" resonates with anyone who lived or grew up in southern New England—Connecticut in particular—any time after 1936 when this book's subject made his debut at WTIC. These first eight chapters relate the story of Steele's life in typical biographical fashion, enumerating the course of events and people influencing him through his journey from youth to adulthood to old age.

However, hidden in plain sight in Steele's life story are various sub-themes, the appearances of which persisted during the writing of this book. As material was gathered and vetted by the author, it became necessary to create a separate document to keep track of those motifs, yet doing so accomplished two purposes: it removed the risk of dragging down the pace of the text while at the same time allowing for a closer look at Steele's home and professional life as well as other personal characteristics that made Bob Steele who he was. Isolating them to be dealt with here allows for exactly that kind of inspection.

Every attempt was made to avoid repetition between material covered previously while retaining the essence of the topics visited below, each intended to provide greater detail and answer questions the reader might have regarding facets of Steele's life thought to be overlooked. One observation can be made with surety: inescapable through all this is the salient fact that the public image and persona of Bob Steele were consistent with those of his private life. Steele distinctly lacked any tendency to a "Jekyll and Hyde" syndrome, so there can be no speculation that he portrayed himself on the air as a punctilious but lovable punster yet once off the property of the radio station would transform into an irascible ogre. The traits manifest in his life at home were simply an extension of the work he did for WTIC, and vice versa.

This probing view of Bob Steele will place him in a context not beholden to a chronological timeline, and therefore allow for a bit more analysis of certain topics that are not constrained by a limited number of years. The quotation used as the title of this chapter is most fitting because it is imbued with a touch of humor, yet the word "sleepless" is an especially appropriate adjective.[1] Steele was a man constantly on the move, his schedule including not only his time on the air but his many speaking engagements, work for charities, attendance at sporting events, time spent on household chores, and, not least, devotion to his family. Taken in total, these abundant activities make one wonder if Steele ever did get a good night's rest, and in more than a few instances sleep was a rare commodity for him. But such was the cost that Bob Steele was willing to bear in order to remain in perpetual motion, thankfully doing things that he loved to do.

The hidden life of Bob Steele is revealed in the diaries he kept and the ephemera he collected for decades. The entries that comprise the diaries were not necessarily written every single day, but there is a remarkable consistency manifest in the discipline he invoked to make an effort to write at least several times each week. At the onset of this book project, Phil Steele mildly cautioned the author that the diaries contained a generous quantity of mundane information. "A lot of entries merely noted what went on that day, or what the family had for dinner," he related, but Phil's assessment understates their real content and significance.[2]

However, the copious amount of information contained therein furnishes an intimate portrait of the man when he was away from the studio. As Phil pointed out, "The diary was a place where he could set forth some of his complaints without having others hear them. In a way that's what the diary shows—how much he kept his complaints to himself."[3] Phil also expressed concern that with his father's personal writings available to the public at the Hartford History Center and now used as source material for this book, some readers might divine that Bob Steele complained frequently about a variety of topics. In the human experience, it is only natural to show degrees of all range of emotion and reaction to the world around us, and to this end, Steele was no different than anyone else.

Although Phil believed that his father would be appalled if he knew that his private observations would one day be laid bare, the revelations of his personal world show him to be an unabashed everyman rather than someone who had something to hide. "Dad was curiously private about his past life, the scrapbooks notwithstanding," noted Phil in late 2017. "Probably it was part of his genuine humility. His self-effacing sense of humor came right out of his essential personality. He would talk about himself, but only when pushed a bit, and I think for his sons the present was busy enough, not to delve into the past."[4]

Bob Steele never intended to log so much personal information over many years in order to provide historians—or anyone else, for that matter—a glimpse into his personal life or that of his family. What is so compelling, however, is that his private thoughts are earnest, are most often lacking in criticism of others, and prove that there was little difference between Bob Steele the radio celebrity and Bob Steele the family man. His diaries thus are open books—both figuratively and literally—into the world of this man who gained the confidence of his audience as well as the people he met in person.

Given Steele's exposure to people ranging from the man in the street to celebrities, his oft-pleasant demeanor was accommodating to many people most of the time, although his son Paul observed that there were times when he could grow less than cordial. "Was Dad a grouch? He sure could be. But the salient point for me is his uncanny ability to keep his hostilities in check in public…. His anger was channeled in proper language. I always wondered how such a stickler of a man could be unoffending on the radio nearly 100 percent of the time. He had an awful lot of talents, but that instinct for decorum was genius."[5]

The consistency of Steele's private and on-air personas can be demonstrated through an analogy to an all-American family depicted in the early years of television. Popular in its day, *The Adventures of Ozzie and Harriet* was a situation comedy whose success was derived from its cloying depiction of the Nelson family, and the show, emblematic of its era and critiqued by the historian David Halberstam, "reflected a world of warm-hearted, sensitive, tolerant Americans, a world devoid of anger and meanness of spirit and, of course, failure."[6] Off-camera, however, the head of the clan, Ozzie Nelson, was the show's primary writer, director, and producer who displayed "an authoritarian, almost dictatorial presence on the set [and] monitored every aspect of his children's lives" in an effort to maintain "their squeaky-clean images" that had been cultivated for the viewing audience.[7]

To be sure, Bob Steele was also demanding in the studio in an effort to deliver as perfect a program as possible, but as will be explored below, life in his household paralleled the folksy quality so characteristic of his radio show. Unlike Ozzie Nelson's split personality, Steele enjoyed the camaraderie of both his listeners and family without the veneer of disingenuousness.

Even as success and fame accrued to him as his career at WTIC deepened, Bob Steele was the embodiment of what it was to be a member of comfortable middle class America. He was not elliptical in his personal or professional conduct, hewing to a line of getting straight to the point in his dealings. "A common theme expressed by Bob's listeners is their feeling that he spoke directly to them, that he came right into their homes as if he were a member of the family."[8] Such forthrightness found favor with many people, while the rich quality of his voice enhanced the smoothness of his delivery, and the volume of it was balanced to better evince a calmness that fostered trust between him and his listeners.

Bob Steele's birth in Missouri and passing in Connecticut are coincidental with those of another former resident of Hartford, the great American writer Mark Twain. While the latter's contribution to this country's literature underpins some of our most enduring writing, Steele in no small way was also a pioneer who ascended to the top of his profession, frequently using a vernacular that Twain would have found comfortable to listen to had their paths been able to cross.

The relentless ambition of Steele's youth carried into adulthood and never deserted him until he was well into his eighties, by which point his diary contained increasingly frequent notes indicating that he would finally retire. His attendance at a multitude of extracurricular events kept him constantly on the go, and some of these activities, such as baseball games and boxing matches, took place in Boston or New York, thereby requiring extensive travel time—especially before the advent of interstate highways—that allowed him little time to sleep before going into the studio.

While many adults, especially men, smoked in mid-twentieth-century America, Steele was not fanatical about the habit, nor was he much of a drinker. It can be argued that keeping these vices at bay contributed to the longevity of both he and his wife, and although they would partake in a preprandial cocktail and cigarette when out on the town, smoking dissipated from Steele's routine by the 1960s while Shirley remained a light smoker. The sponsorship of Steele's *Strictly Sports* by Camel cigarettes in the program's early years did nothing to encourage him to increase his consumption of tobacco.

We have seen that while some of Bob Steele's humor poked fun at women, it is necessary to view this in the context of the times. Described as "a lovely gentleman" by a former staff member, she also said that she excused "his generation-inflicted chauvinism," whereby many men who grew up in the earlier part of the twentieth century were imbued with a superiority complex based on gender stereotypes.[9] For his part, Steele never abandoned his respect for women in earnestly assuming the role of a gentleman.

Further, Steele evinced no racial prejudice in public or private. The crowd of celebrities that he was exposed to contained a rich diversity of ethnicities, whether they were Italian (Willie Pep), Irish (Jack Dempsey), Jewish (Bill Savitt), or black (Joe Frazier), and such contact enhanced his appreciation for the countless thousands who tuned in to his show. Steele's ability to at least pronounce correctly many foreign names and phrases on the air certainly allowed him to connect with audience members whose native tongue was one other than English.

Other aspects of Steele's enjoyment of language and humor will be explored later, but the subjects presented here provide a description of the cornerstone of his existence: his domestic life, and the undying love he had for the woman who became his wife.

Life on the Steele Home Front

The daily routine for Bob and Shirley changed from the time they were married and over the years as their sons were born. Because of his occupation as a morning man on the radio, he was an early riser, yet his long days did little to slow him down. Steele's typical routine of the mid–1940s was described in a profile published by The Travelers' inhouse organ.

> Mr. Steele's life is not easy. His day begins at 5:15. His breakfast consists of one glass of orange juice diluted with water (because of an intestinal weakness…). If there's time, he has a poached egg, which he explains is one cooked well on the outside. At 5:50, Mr. Bill Powers, who drives the Middletown–Hartford route, pauses on the Silas Deane Highway, whistles shrilly and Mr. Steele sprints from Buckland Road to board the bus. At 6:20 he is at the studio preparing his "Morning Watch" script, and at 7:00, he's on the air with gags, whistles, bells and glockenspiel.
>
> From 8:00 to 1:15 he tends his regular announcing duties, then has lunch at Mickey's Villanova, which boasts of his patronage on signboards, street car cards and The Bridgeport Herald. The afternoon he devotes either to shooting pool at the Wooster or doing odd jobs demanded at home by the Little Woman…. Late in the afternoon he returns to the studios to deliver "Strictly Sports" at 6:30. Ten minutes after the broadcast he boards a bus at Grove Street, arriving home at 7:13…. Comes then the family meal, in the kitchen and on a maple dining set. The *paterfamilias* usually helps with the dishes. If he doesn't, he leaves a crisp, new dollar bill under his plate for the children. This custom he calls the Little Steele Wage Formula.[10]

There were afternoons when Steele was occupied by interviews with sports figures, with this fresh material to be used early that same evening, and he kept an active, artistic hand in his notebook by drawing cartoons that he submitted to syndicated cartoonists and national magazines. He also employed the U.S. Postal Service to send impromptu, humorous love notes to Shirley.

As sons entered the household, Steele was most conscious about his fatherly obligations and was decidedly confident about their future. Rhapsodizing about his three sons in the fall of 1944, he noted, "I like those boys. I'll bet they grow up to be great men."[11] Besides acknowledgment for helping to clear the dinner table, the boys also received small financial rewards for good report cards at school, and the proud father extended that system to their participation in Little League baseball: pitching a shutout earned $1.35, a home run was worth two dollars, and even the act of drawing a walk brought

The Steele family in 1951. Standing from left are Phil, Robert, and Paul; Shirley is seated with Steve on her lap (Hartford History Center, Hartford Public Library).

a nickel. Certain times there was no money that changed hands, only consolation offered by father to son: "Robert hits first Little [League] homerun but Exchange loses 2–1 on dropped fly ball with bases loaded and two out. Despair!," Steele lamented, yet he philosophically concluded, "But that's life and baseball."[12] Trips he took with the boys to Fenway Park and Yankee Stadium rounded out their exposure to the national pastime even at the cost of lengthy days spent at a traditional doubleheader that could make the youngsters a bit cranky.

Vacations, such as one the family took in October 1944, could provide fodder for Steele's show. That autumn they spent several days at a primitive cabin in the Berkshire Mountains, and Steele was able to joke about the adventures they endured with inadequate plumbing, wood fires, and backwoods chores. Not divulged on the air, however, was a later episode endured by parents in the process of raising youngsters. "Mama's trying to train Steven for the 'potty.' [Robert] is playing piano; Mama's in [the] kitchen, Steve is in bathroom trying to 'go.' Mama shouts to Robert: 'Robert! Stop playing for a minute—I want to hear Steven in case he grunts!'"[13] Steele and Shirley disagreed about a topic that would eventually affect each of their sons in the normalcy of growing up, but the father won out in this case: "I made Robert shave today—his first—he's 14¾—I don't like to see heavy fuzz on a boy's face. Besides, he has a dark mustache—got to start sometime. Mama didn't like it—but Mamas don't like to see their boys grow into men, it seems."[14]

Bob and Shirley enjoyed the popular programs featured in the early years of television, *Gunsmoke, The Ed Sullivan Show*, and *The Honeymooners* among their favorites as were history-related shows such as *Victory at Sea* and *You Are There* in addition to variety offerings hosted by Steve Allen and Milton Berle. With little surprise, life in the Steele household included tuning the radio to the region's most popular radio program, as the family "literally grew up with WTIC in the background in the morning."[15]

Shortly before Christmas 1954, Steele took the time to pen a status of what each of his sons was involved in, providing a look into the mind and observations of a proud father.

> Steve coming to my chair in nite clothes to put his arms around me. He's a great one! So are Phil, Paul, & Robert.... Robert's my height—looks good. Does barbells in basement—arms look good—he worked a few Saturdays at auto wash after turning 16. Paul grinds out a 6 or 7 spot a week on TIMES [newspaper] route—has saved nearly [$]400 in about a year. He's a thrifty one. Getting bigger every day. Phil's a cartoonist—with jokes! He's a smart boy.[16]

Christmas was a special time for the family, but Steele's obligations to his program also meant that except in years when the holiday fell on a Sunday, he would be on the air that morning. To adjust to his work commitments, Steele prerecorded Christmas greetings from his sons to be aired on his holiday show, and the family opened gifts on Christmas Eve to accommodate the absent father.

Contrary to the chauvinistic division of chores in many households, the Steele home pulsated from the willing assistance supplied by the paterfamilias. Famous for his window-cleaning concoction—½ cup of ammonia, ½ cup of white vinegar, 2 tablespoons of corn starch (or Bon Ami), and one bucket of warm water—that he passed on to his listeners, he practiced what he preached because he personally used it.[17] Steele was no stranger to the cleansing of panes—which also once cost him a nasty fall from a ladder at the age of eighty-six!—nor was he averse to handling the other manly duties such as yardwork or painting the floor of the garage. The lady of the house was a bit more agile, as Steele comically noted in the summer of 1954: "Mosquitoes are wicked! Shirley spends about an [hour] each nite before retiring [from] killing 'em—smashes 'em against the ceiling with a damp Turkish towel. She stands on chairs, tables, bathtub—anything & everything goes Thud! Thud! Thud!"[18]

When Shirley was indisposed with a case of the mumps and another time needed hospitalization, Steele took care of laundry and prepared meals, which likely would have included a breakfast offering for which he became renowned. His "eggs à la Steele" were a hit with listeners—as well as the Connecticut Dairy and Food Council—and he divulged the recipe to a friend at the *Hartford Times*, who, in turn, shared it with readers.

> Break two eggs in a bowl, add a generous teaspoon of cottage cheese and a dash of heavy cream and whip with a fork.... Pour into a hot buttered skillet and finish off to your liking. Sometimes I use a good flame [on a gas stove] and push the mixture around constantly while it's cooking. Other times I put a lid on the thing and let it cook slowly. Don't worry about how to cook it. This is such a smart dish it knows what to do once you get it in the pan. P.S.—This is a good portion for one but you might as well make double the recipe to begin with because everyone isn't going to want to share![19]

The separation of tasks between husband and wife meant that Shirley had to assume the role of dinner chef, but she "was such a good cook that Bob was content to be her faithful dishwasher (with help from the boys)."[20] This part of KP had Steele working overtime at the kitchen sink on special occasions, making already long days even longer. "I did dishes," he said late Christmas Day in 1968, "took me 1½ hours and my dogs were barking at the finish line!"[21] His personal notes indicate repeat performances of this duty through the early 1990s, although son Steve furnished welcome assistance at times.

Back in Connecticut after finishing school in Pennsylvania, Steve had taken a job at the Hartford Civic Center, where he was employed for over twenty years. A resident of Wethersfield, he developed a bond with his father whereby the two spent much time going to see first-run movies, dining out, and—an apparent favorite activity for both—attending prize fights. Steve even assisted on occasions when his father served as the ring announcer at the Civic Center, and the many diary entries Steele recorded about these ventures are filled with the kindred spirit and warm relationship between father and son.

Despite the addition of pounds to his frame over the years, Steele remained physically active by walks and bicycle rides, even at an advanced age. In the early 1970s he rode to work when the spring weather was favorable, although he took a tumble in the summer of 1985 that resulted in cuts and a broken rib. Biking was far more favorable than another form of transportation in which he partook to promote the just-arrived Ringling Brothers circus in Hartford: "I rode ½ mile—got off—never to ride an elephant again! Never!"[22] Photographic evidence of this misadventure clearly indicates Steele's uncomfortable countenance and supports his renunciation of further such stunts.

Due to his work schedule and many speaking appearances, Steele's relaxation around the house was limited mainly to Sundays, but he relished the tranquility of that morning. "Up 6-ish (as usual)," he once noted, "Washed Skylark, drove to Viking [Bakery]—bread + pastry—always enjoy Sunday a.m.—best morning in [the] week—nobody around—world is quiet—and seems so peaceful—UNTIL MORNING PAPER ARRIVES!!"[23]

Steele's employment in radio naturally exposed him to news and current events, yet he also paid attention to the print media to further inform his world view. Some of these happenings prompted him to express his opinions privately, but as tumultuous as some instances were, especially in the 1960s, he remained very patriotic toward his country while always openly hoping for a peaceful resolution to any strife that arose domestically or abroad. "Flag burning is legal! Believe it or don't…. Freedom of speech bunk, etc.," he complained bitterly in the wake of the 1989 decision by the United States Supreme Court that supported the First Amendment, and he tersely revealed his thoughts about the seemingly unending conflict in parts of the globe: "War— Mankind's most senseless activity."[24]

In the Steele home, worldwide discord was left better addressed on the board of the popular game of Risk, a favorite of the Steele sons, who played it even as adults at family gatherings with their father. The bonding of family remained at the forefront of Steele's mindset, and that trait was manifest most strongly in the relationship he had with the woman he first encountered in an elevator at The Travelers back in the 1930s.

"Mama"

"Smitten by the love bug" is as trite an expression as can be employed when describing the romantic emotion that one person is feeling toward another. In the case of Bob Steele, it is compelling to note the incredible and genuine love he felt for Shirley not just when he first met her but also consistently throughout the decades that they were married. "'Til death us do part" was unquestionably another saying that proved prophetically true for this very special couple whose separation was brought about only by his passing in 2002. Even though Shirley did not leave a paper trail of evidence the way that Bob did to substantiate their relationship, there is no question that his love was not unrequited. Years later the couple's oldest son observed that their romance was as strong "as if they had just met."[25]

Steele's quick wit and his cartooning ability were conjoined in the missives he sent to Shirley, and such artistry and whimsy were not necessarily kept out of sight of the postman. The envelopes themselves were often graced with the drawings and elaborate fonts he created, sometimes employing a rainbow of colors to enhance his latest expression of love, and special delivery stamps were commonly affixed to ensure prompt delivery.

The messages contained therein, both handwritten and typed on Travelers letterhead, were spiced with heavy doses of comical phonetics—"H'lo.... Shoiley," he greeted her on one postcard—that conveyed the impression that his sense of humor was not ever likely to desert him.[26] One note he sent several months prior to their marriage even drew attention with purposeful errors: "To the Sweetest Girl in ~~The Travelers City of Hartford State of Connecticut United States~~ Whole Wide World."[27] At times he even adopted the role of an historic figure such as Thomas Edison or a cleverly named fictitious character to burnish the message of the moment.

When business took Steele away from Hartford, Western Union was trusted with delivering telegrams that lacked his drawings but nonetheless conveyed brief messages of devotion, often tinged with a poetic slant. Detained in New York longer than expected on one trip, "Robert L" alerted her with the following ditty: HEY HEY HAD TO STAY I SAY LOTS OF LOVE ANYWAY WHAT DO YOU SAY?[28]

This puppy love was as durable as the two people who cherished it, and although the volume of letters and telegrams diminished once the Steeles were wed, one-way correspondence, as it were, continued through the seemingly countless entries Steele penned in his diary throughout the rest of his life. Photographs in his scrapbooks further attest to the quality time he savored with the entire family as the years progressed, and also as the Steeles' household demographics changed from newlyweds to parents to empty-nesters.

While their sons grew up and began to lead their own lives, the spark of Bob and Shirley's love never diminished. On the eve of their trip to Maine for Paul's commencement from Bates College in 1962, Steele left her a typed noted informing her that even after two decades of marriage, "Honey: You were never more beautiful or more terrific than last night. I just had to tell you again that I LOVE you."[29] Just weeks later, she returned the sentiment in her own cursive and added phonetic touches that he was sure to enjoy.

Honey:

If I don't waken before you go to work I'll be in [son] Robert's room sleeping. I came to bed at 10:30 but you were sound asleep on my side even tho you held my hand as I put my hand on yours. You squeezed my fingers as is your habit. I think that's why I love you so much. You are still a little boy.

I love you, I love you, I love you,
U-no-hoo
xxxxxx[30]

Steele had been referring to Shirley as "Mama" in his private writings for quite some time, and still infatuated with her good looks, he used his diary to remind himself, "I love Mama. She's like 23—No change."[31] She, however, was a bit less impressed by her husband's physical appearance, which prompted her to leave this playful yet chiding note inside the refrigerator.

Are you eating again[?]
Shame on you
No wonder you look the way you do
Ha ha ha
You'll be sorry[,] fatty
Do yourself a favor and shut the door.[32]

While Shirley retained her svelte figure through the years, leading her husband to observe that she "looks like a young model—make that *younger* model," her splendid culinary talents were no doubt a contributing factor to Steele's caloric woes.[33] Not only were her aforementioned Swedish pancakes a treat but she had a deft hand with all manner of dishes that made their way to the dinner table, including leg of lamb and pork chops prepared using Shake 'n' Bake products. But the woman Steele declared to be the "greatest cook in [the] Universe" seemed to be most guilty of exacerbating the size of his waistline due to her production of fresh-baked pies.[34] "Weight now 205. Dang! I can't lose an ounce," he lovingly complained in the autumn of 1990. "Mama makes too many delicious, wonderful apple pies—and everything else."[35]

Steele's feelings were still unflinching as he approached his eighty-fifth birthday: "Mama is in [the] kitchen most of [the] time—right now baking pineapple upside-down cake. I weigh 203 stripped. Tomorrow: 204½. I love what she bakes—and I love her."[36] The conflation of outstanding homemade food and intimacy provides an apotheosized portrait of a happy home able to stand the test of time.

Shirley was not confined to the interior of the homestead, drawing praise from her husband for clearing the driveway and walks in the aftermath of a snowfall while he was at work. And her birthday each February 5 provided another excuse for him to dote on her with gifts, but he also took pleasure from the return on his investment. "Enjoyed shopping, eating, drinking + each other," he made note of a shopping spree they went on in 1969 for her birthday.[37]

By the end of a typical day, it was time to finally unwind. "7:30. I'm sitting in leather chair in den waiting for Mama to come in to sit on my lap, as is our custom for about an hour," Steele wrote in the spring of 1975. "We watch TV until I get too sleepy to stay up—which is about 8:30."[38] By that hour, it would be time for him to retire so that he could rise early the next morning and head to the studio for his next program. When Steele made this particular entry in his diary, *The Adventures of Ozzie and Harriet* had been off the air for nearly a decade, and as television programming moved away from its 1950s-inspired depictions of the roseate life of America's middle class, it is comforting to learn that some households actually retained a genuine spirit that was in the Nelsons' case only made for TV.

The love and respect that Bob and Shirley Steele mutually held for each other certainly was not unique to them. However, the sincerity and endurance of their relationship were what set them apart from couples who merely existed or lived together for the sake of maintaining appearances. Commenting years later in regard to his father's feminine-related gibes, son Paul stated, "The main butt of his jokes about women was my mother. Yet, his love for my mother was solid gold."[39] Such was the intimacy that formed the bedrock of the Steeles' marriage.

There is only a remote chance that Steele would have selected a particular adjective for a "Word for the Day" feature because even though that word accurately describes his relationship with Shirley, he may have been too reluctant to admit publicly it. According to the *Oxford English Dictionary*, *uxorious* means "greatly or excessively fond of one's wife, doting," which is most appropriate to Bob Steele, not pejoratively but in the most positive sense one can imagine.[40]

The Figure Filbert

In addition to the pillars of affection that buttressed the Steeles, another cornerstone that played a vital role in the life of the family was Bob's attention to finances and his capacity to be a "figure filbert" with a multitude of various forms of data. There is no question that he was a numbers man with regard to the cost of consumer goods and services, and because he was cognizant of where the pennies were going, he had a firm grasp of how the household budget could be managed. Phil Steele observed of his father, "Bob hated being in debt and would pay his bills as soon as he received them," a proud testament of the prudent stewardship that ensured security for his family, not least of which was the joy he expressed on October 15, 1953: "Paid off house—[$]2179.07. It's all ours!"[41]

The epitome of aging gracefully: Bob and Shirley Steele, circa 1983 (Steele Family Collection).

Many amounts Steele posted in his diary show exact dollars and cents, indicating his foible for attention to detail, although it is curious that he used his daily log to record such information rather than an accountant's ledger book. In any case, this trail of financial and other personal information offers yet another aspect of the interesting life that he led.

Although his physical weight had nothing to do with money management, Steele over the course of most of his adult years was very conscious of how much he tipped the scales. In 1948, Steele complained in one of his radio program scripts, "Boy am I getting fat ... 22 pounds overweight the doctor told me. I'm 5–10, weigh 200 even."[42] He fixed the blame for this condition, according to his narrative at the time, on Shirley, whose bread pudding was too delicious to pass up. As noted previously, Steele's weight dropped into the 180-pound range as he reached his nineties.

But Mama's mastery in the kitchen was not solely to blame for her husband's caloric intake. Dining outside the home also took its toll, and the eateries visited by Steele ran the gamut, although there were some in a higher price range that he liked to patronize. Yet, just because Steele had an income that allowed entry to better restaurants did not mean he was ignorant of value. "I ate at Hearthstone—they have a new wrinkle!" he complained in the spring of 1967. "Lunch is all à la carte—what used to cost 2.00 is now 3.00. That's progress? Always improving!?"[43]

Steele had an active hand in helping establish his younger sons with a portfolio to build their future holdings. "Bank acc[oun]ts + stocks at today's prices total 38 big ones," was Steele's 1956 year-end status of his composite holdings. "Most stock in Glen[n] Martin (41) + Balt[imore] & Ohio [Railroad] (45). Phil has [New Britain] Machine (36). Paul has Gen[eral] Motors (44)."[44] This was an impressive accumulation considering that eight years earlier there was $8,700 in the family bank account, and Steele was earning just over $300 per week, still tidy sums relative to the era immediately following World War II.[45]

Whether he invested in gold is not known, but at least he was aware that one ounce of the precious metal sold for $845 in mid–January 1980. And certificates of deposit offered by many savings institutions were paying double-digit interest rates, some as high as 20 percent. But as old age crept in, Steele penned entries that longed for a simpler, which is to say cheaper, time.

> Today's prices are something. Gas 1.35 for 93 octane unleaded; 1.26 regular 87 octane unleaded. 7-stick chewing gum—25¢ (+2¢ tax).... Many places get 2.95 for a cup of soup—$2 and more for a dish of ice cream! And a good shirt that used to cost $3.00 is now $25 and usually made in Hong Kong, Taiwan, Czechoslovakia, etc. with name brand label Hathaway, Arrow, etc.[46]

Prices for just about anything were less of an issue in Steele's household than most others because of the income he derived from his vocation as well as the ready cash he earned from speaking engagements. The demand for his after-dinner appearances prompted him to charge what he believed to be high fees in the hope of discouraging such invitations, but there was always an organization willing to foot the bill to ensure that Bob Steele would be on hand to entertain the gathering. "Got.... C-note [$100] from CMPA [Connecticut Milk Producers Association] for cott[age] ch[eese] recipe w/ eggs," he recorded, and there was a cool $800 he received from the commencement address he delivered at Tunxis Community College in 1976.[47]

These are but two examples of the hundreds of such engagements he had over the decades of his career, so the supplemental income accumulated in that time was significant to Steele's coffers. Yet in 1988, Steele also cleverly demonstrated a degree of shrewdness by flipping neckties, of all things: after landing a true bargain by purchasing eight ties at a dollar apiece while running errands, he "sold all for $5 each 30 minutes later at oil change station on Maple Ave. while having Buick serviced. Profit: $32."[48]

Aside from the loves of his life, which were his wife and family, what brought Steele the most joy was a new automobile. When coupled with the generous income he earned, this long-running fixation with cars meant that his purchases could include those of better makes and models, such as a new 1947 Oldsmobile or his 1949 Cadillac. And consistent with his philosophy of making sure that he got his dollar's worth, Steele made this observation in early 1971: "I went to Cadillac [dealer] to look—they want 7000 [dollars] for a Calais 2 door with air [conditioning]—that's the cheapie—no vinyl roof. 3000 + the Buick [on a trade-in]! Nope. Will wait for Buick. Been waiting 3 months now! But I'm in no hurry."[49]

In their later years Bob and Shirley shared the same sentiment for a good value, as he gave a playful nod to their shopping habits at the end of 1997: "Mama + I don't give [gifts] to each other—bargains after Christmas!"[50] The only way to understand the worth of anything is to know the numbers associated with it, and upon Steele's passing in 2002, even close family members were unaware of the sizable estate he had accumulated.

To the end, Steele was a master of mathematics. Perhaps the only thing he had a better grasp of was the language that he used—and loved.

The Wordsmith

As fastidious as Bob Steele was about language and pronunciation, he absolutely delighted in the colloquial and phonetic aspects of speech and very often included these on the air and in his personal correspondence. Such usage gave weight to the endless puns that were a staple of his programs and private life. He sometimes employed affected accents to add authenticity to his presentation but never for purposes of mocking or ridiculing someone or something, a trait that stands in sharp contrast to the manners of many twenty-first century media personalities.

Steele was probably influenced at a younger age by the way in which print media treated language, especially in cartoons, where an artist might transform "let go" into "leggo," "don't you" could become "doncha," and "is that so" might appear as "zasso."[51] This style of writing and captioning had its provenance before Steele was even born, yet the whimsy inherent in it found obvious favor with him, and he was only too happy to adopt it for his own creative purposes. Bouts of plebeian speech endeared Steele to the masses while at the same time his tendency to invoke precise pronunciation in other instances appealed to learned listeners, thus balancing humor with an educational quality that offered something for everyone in his audience. Steele's eldest son very perspicaciously described his father's on-air persona that was the very essence of the man: "I'm not sure exactly how to define it myself, but I do know that it involves the rare quality of being able to appeal to both the college professor and the moving van driver."[52]

If given a choice between the two, Steele by far favored lowbrow rather than elitist, thus his private and public remarks could be peppered with expressions and pronunciations heavily invested with phonetics such as "gotta go to woik," "hearing people say HAWG and Uncle TAMW agin," and "I dint pick da Reds dis year! I pickt da Dodgers. But tanx."[53] Straddling the fine line between informal speech and proper English opened the possibility of offending someone—"Whattaya tryin' to do, show off?" was a reaction he sought to avoid from his audience—so in the spring of 1948 he wrote a newspaper column in an attempt to explain the difficulties of trying to please everyone.

> Only recently I found myself stranded in a long, involved sentence and needing only one word to get out of it. Suddenly a slang expression came to mind and it saved the day. But then it occurred to me that some listener might resent my use of slang. So, I apologized, and assured my audience that I hadn't intended to spoil the speech habits of any children who might be listening but that slang did, in my opinion, have a place in U.S. language.[54]

Steele enjoyed the reputation he had cultivated as a wordsmith and was proud of the huge, unabridged dictionary that G & C Merriam sent to him in 1951, the better to learn from and then pass on his knowledge to his audience. "Bob never hesitated to correct or improve the grammar, usage or style of anything he shared with his audience.... [He understood] the great importance he always placed on using emphasis to convey the sense of the message."[55] The Merriam edition was one of four such books, as well as a thesaurus, that Steele owned and used as his personal reference library.

Steele's "Word for the Day"—sometimes anthologized as "woids fudda daye" or "words furdaweek"—that dated to at least late 1950 was his trademark, and many years later his son Paul observed, "Dad would have tons of criticism for announcers who mispronounced words. We'd be listening together and he'd almost seethe at others' miscues. It seemed he was the natural born guardian of the English language."[56] Phil Steele concurred, opining that his father "felt a pride, or an investment, in knowing the right way to pronounce names like Giovanni, and the 'Word for the Day' feature became a kind of mini-crusade to steer the majority [of listeners] to what, at least once, had been the standard."[57]

There were rare occasions when Steele got his comeuppance, as was the case with Jerry Wilson, a meteorologist with The Travelers Weather Service whose North Carolinian speech mannerisms never left him completely. During a live weather segment, Wilson mentioned the Appalachian Mountains, which Steele used for a subsequent Word for the Day to tell his audience that the range's name was pronounced "Ap-uh-LAY-chee-uns." Wilson, a Tarheel, parried Steele's unwanted correction with the following live rejoinder: "Bob, whatever you may say here, where I come from it's Ap-uh-LATCH-uns."[58]

Variations in dialect notwithstanding, Steele could be "audibly disgusted" on the air when he was handed poorly written copy pockmarked with gaffes, redundant terms, and the like. He depended on other staff members to properly vet and edit material given to him because he had no chance to preview anything that had to be read on the spot. When given a script containing the two-noun phrase "a fun activity"—nouns cannot be used to modify other nouns—he immediately followed this with a mocking commentary: "Let's have a 'fun' time check, then maybe some 'fun' sports." As one commentator put it, "His revulsion was clear," because not only was the text incorrect, but listeners would think that Steele, having read the faux pas, was solely responsible for it.[59]

Lapses on the part of continuity writers could elicit a burst of temper from Steele, who, for better or worse, expected the same level of perfection that he himself strove to achieve. But Steele also realized the large degree of truth to the axiom "To err is human," and he collected newspaper headlines containing typos that found their way into print. According to his son Phil, "It astounded him that editors writing headlines could so frequently be so sloppy."[60]

Although Bob Steele's pedantry with words might have seemed overarching, his chief desire was to "[balance] his witty commentary with a serious concern for good language," thus allowing him to be sensitive to the effects and influences of modernity, as in 1987 when he observed that "no problem" had become a common phrase used in place of "okay."[61] By any standard, the remarkable attention Steele paid to the ebb and flow of the English language turned him from a humble but proud high school graduate into a master of linguistics, and he was only too happy to inculcate his audience.

Integrity

Besides the immutable love of family and spouse that was the mainstay of Bob Steele's life, another innate property of his persona was an unflinching predisposition for high standards of probity and rectitude. Honesty is the best policy, as the saying goes, yet few people were as able as Steele to uphold impeccable degrees of virtue and truthfulness.

Not wanting to risk embarrassment to WTIC, an adoring public, private associates, friends, or family, the moral bar was set quite high for this star of the airwaves. In addition to his show of righteousness, Steele significantly demonstrated a sense of loyalty to his employer when one realizes that he could have fulfilled any contractual obligations and then sold his services to the highest bidder at another radio station, a move that certainly would have yielded a financial windfall for him. Conscious of the image he spent years cultivating and the attendant rewards he had received because of his hard work, Steele admitted during an interview in 1980 that he was content to maintain his employment with WTIC while at once expressing a fear that changing jobs for the sake of more money could lead to personal disappointment.

> I've always been fortunate in making enough to raise a family and have enough food on the table. That's one reason I've stayed where I am. I had a chance to make a little more in other cities.... After I'd been on the air about fifteen years I had a couple of good offers, but I thought if I go someplace else, I might not catch on as well as I have [at WTIC].... What if I go there and in a year I've got to leave? I'm gonna stay right where I am, and it worked out.[62]

Steele's desire to play a sure thing took to heart the catch phrase used for years by his friend, the jeweler Bill Savitt, who promulgated a "peace of mind guarantee" that kept uncertainty at bay. Better for Steele to not uproot his family while chasing more dollars—including an astounding fifty thousand dollars from an outlet in Philadelphia in 1964—because he was aware that the grass was not necessarily greener on the other side of the fence.

The fame that Steele garnered also brought temptations that were not available to commoners, especially in times of need. The privations of World War II, by which time Steele had firmly established himself in the public eye, meant a shortage of new automobiles created by the prioritization of manufacturing industries to support American armed forces. The lingering effects remained as the United States transitioned to a peacetime economy, and at the end of 1946, Steele noted in his diary, "20 million people wanting new cars and I [could have bought] 3 in one day if I chose. Could have sold 2 and made $2,000 without trying—in 30 minutes. But [I] couldn't do it. Dealers, who were doing me a favor in each case, would have figured I was a heel— and I would have been."[63] Keeping his conscience clean, Steele elected to pass up a quick buck rather than face the opprobrium of an ill-gotten profit.

Steele was a man's man, and his popularity prompted invitations to more than just events sponsored by civic organizations. Appearances at men's-only gatherings such as bachelor parties furnished latitude for him to show the ribald side of his sense of humor, and he was happy to oblige attendees with jokes that could never be used on the air. He kept a little memo book of off-color material, but even a mildly suggestive wisecrack such as "old bankers never die, they just lose interest" was apt to go unused because "as the radio spokesman for Hartford National Bank, it just didn't feel right to him." In this case, the hint of a swipe at an unnamed financier was enough to restrain Steele from eliciting titters from even a limited audience.[64]

But with regard to Bob Steele's favorable appeal to his everyday G-rated audience, he often indulged in using fan mail as fodder for his radio schtick, but not in the self-flattering sense. Rather than stroking his ego by reading laudatory correspondence from his admirers, Steele preferred to use missives that skewered him, criticized features of his show, or otherwise found fault. Although he did save mail that was complimentary, "Bob carefully avoided reading on the air the many letters from listeners that praised him, while airing anything that knocked him," Phil Steele commented, this ploy being a perfect fit for the self-deprecatory humor that Bob Steele knew was good for a laugh.[65]

In 1967, the serious side of Steele led him to read an old letter written from President Harry Truman to his daughter, parts of which served as humble inspiration: "Keep your balance, and display all the Truman–Wallace mulishness where right and wrong are in the balance. Right must always prevail…"[66] A bit preachy in its tone, this note nevertheless imparted a moral lesson worth the attention of all members of Steele's audience, and he was only too happy to share it.

As that year drew to a close, Steele committed a miscue that played out over the course of several days, its origin stemming from his reference to shares of stock he owned in a film production company incorporated in Delaware. Once Steele let slip his initial mistake during his show, the drama unfolded away from the public as station management quickly recognized the gravity of the situation, and he recorded the steps taken to resolve the issue and allow his virtue to come to the fore with no damage to his reputation.

> December 27, 1967—A blunder! I mentioned Pathé Industries stock on the air at 9:15 or so—shouldn't have. Against regulations. Source of great concern to me now. Can only hope no serious consequences. [WTIC vice president Bob] Tyrol called me in afternoon for explanation. Also Henry Sapia and George Parker of Walston. Idiotic thing to do—I should have known better.
> December 29, 1967—[WTIC president Leonard] Patricelli calls—3:45 p.m.—sez they've talked it over (Roy Wilkens et al.) + decide I should sell 5500 Pathé at once (must wait now till Tues). To play it safe. If any profit—give to charity. I say OK.
> January 2, 1968—Sold 5500 Pathé @ 1⅝ [bought] 1000 [shares] at 1⁷⁄₁₆, 4500 @ 1½ Made $3125 after paying comm[ission] of 660–330 in + 330 out! But glad to be out.[67]

Steele's self-flagellating comment on the day he misspoke, his willingness to donate any earnings realized from the sale of his stock to charity, and the speed with which he addressed the problem—in a matter of days over a holiday period—all speak highly of his desire to atone for an error that would likely have resulted in the station's firing of a lesser personality. In like fashion, he was firm to stand his ground when he knew he was in the right, as on an occasion when he took umbrage at his insurance carrier, who was pressing him over a disputed payment. "Miserable, impersonal people in that office," he complained to his diary. "They assume everybody is trying to beat them."[68]

Courtesy and proper demeanor on air and in public were inherent in Steele's actions, and he expected that respect to be returned in kind. When civility was lacking, it did not go unnoticed, as he privately commented of one of his speaking engagements, a black-tie affair, no less: "Rather rude group—several talked aloud as I spoke—some left."[69]

As the decade of the 1960s progressed, the flaunting of older traditions and proper comportment became degraded as did cultural standards, notably in the motion pictures that Steele attended. His low opinion of the movie *The Boston Strangler*, for which actor Tony Curtis was nominated for a Golden Globe Award, reflected an undesirable change in the quality of films and the venues in which they were screened: "E.M. Loew's … theatre almost empty—loud kids—dirty, dusty atmosphere. Disgusting. Shows aren't what they used to be when all the family could enjoy."[70] While he thought Barbra Streisand in *Funny Girl* was terrific, he deemed *Sam Whiskey*, originally produced with a scene featuring a topless Angie Dickinson that was then cut from the released version, the "worst [movie] I ever saw in my life."[71]

Honesty was a policy that Bob Steele did his best to uphold, and upon the occasion of one of his later birthdays, "Someone said, 'You look 65. How do you feel?' I said, 'I feel like 65.' I'm honest, myself. I admit it. And I admire honesty in others."[72] This quality was on full display a few years later when he "[r]ealized I hadn't reported CD dividend" for his 1986 income tax return, and elaborated, "[I] have to change return. Costs more $ but has to be."[73] Whether the Internal Revenue Service would have discovered his omission can only be left to speculation, but the guilty conscience that was Steele's moral compass dictated that amends had to be made. And in this case, Steele discovered the oversight before submitting the return, thereby saving himself a further penalty.

On another occasion, Steele filled in for his eldest son at a speaking engagement when he otherwise should have been bedridden. With Robert needing to travel to West Germany as a member of the U.S. congressional House Foreign Relations Committee in January 1973, Steele soldiered on despite suffering with an awful cold. "Miserable—How am I going to fulfill my promise to speak at Ellington High School soccer banquet tonite—as a sub for [my son]—at no fee? How? Just DOING it. I promised. I'm going."[74]

Steele's sensitivity to the needs and tastes of the general public, whether on the air or off, endeared him to his many admirers. For entertainment purposes, he felt that offensive jokes were simply used as a poor substitute for the virtue of true creativity, and just as foul language was forbidden on the radio, so too was it not used in the Steele home. Over the decades of his experience, Steele was able to gauge the pulse of his listeners and tailor his show's content accordingly, thus drawing them deeper into his expansive comfort zone. The remarkable consistency of his public and private lives kept hypocrisy at bay, and by catering to his audience with humor and his sensible, apolitical perspectives rather than preachy or condescending lectures, Steele led by example.

Charity

Another point on Bob Steele's moral compass was his engagement with charitable endeavors of many stripes. Fulfilling part of his unending restless ambition, Steele lent his voice to events staged for the benefit of youth groups, civic organizations, and fundraisers, and although his advancing age forced him to cut back on these appearances, the record shows that his desire to help worthy causes extended into his eighties. The list of those who benefited from Steele's presence and willingness to assist is lengthy, but his favorite beneficiaries were the American Red Cross, whose blood drives Steele could easily promote on his show, and the Literacy Volunteers of Connecticut. Again leading by example, Steele rolled up his sleeve many times to donate blood, not just simply encourage others to do so.

Drives to purchase United States Savings Bonds had their place on Steele's calendar, but helping to raise money for people who suffered from various maladies or accidents drew his attention. When a football player at Wesleyan College was paralyzed, Steele sold more tickets than anyone to a show at Bushnell Auditorium in the effort to defray the young man's medical expenses. Appearing on the CBS game show *Strike It Rich*, he won $500 on behalf of a person afflicted with multiple sclerosis, and Steele supported funds established to aid several people injured in automobile accidents. Other health-related causes included awareness of the work done for Easter Seals, the American Cancer Society, the United Cerebral Palsy Association of Greater Hartford, the Hemophilia Association, a bicycle safety crusade, and

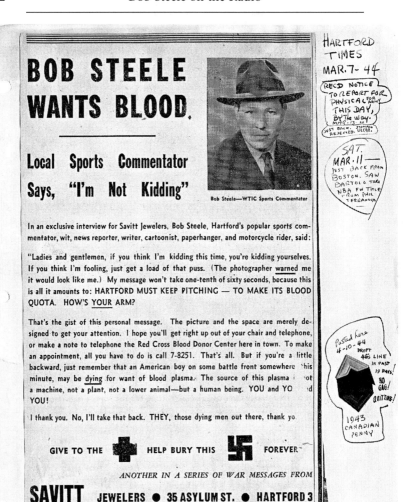

Blood drives were foremost among Bob Steele's charitable interests. Note the marginalia of this page from one of his scrapbooks, which also served as a diary of sorts. (Hartford History Center, Hartford Public Library).

the American Heart Association, and he served as a celebrity waiter for the Leukemia Society of America while also chairing a similar event for the American Lung Association of Connecticut. Steele's visits to the Shriners Hospital in Springfield, Massachusetts, were augmented by similar appearances at the Newington Veterans Hospital near his home.

As a lifelong avid sportsman, Steele relished the work he did for sports award banquets held at prisons in Wethersfield and Somers; the Men's Brotherhood of St. John's Congregational Church in Springfield, Massachusetts; the Meriden Boys' Club softball jamboree; and The Neutral Corner, Inc., a Hartford boxing organization. He also partook in a charity roast for Connecticut Special Olympics, which he enjoyed greatly. Municipal groups— New Haven Community Chest, Hartford City Spring Clean-Up Campaign, United Council and Fund of Greater Waterbury, and the YMCA of Westfield, Massachusetts—successfully sought him out, and the Greater Hartford Chamber of Commerce noted his work for the Martin Luther King, Jr., Youth Fund. A Channel 30 telethon to raise money for Catholic schools in the Hartford area as well as a one-hundredth birthday celebration to benefit the Capitol Region of Churches indicated Steele's willingness to help religious endeavors.

Despite his difficulties in transitioning the musical selections on his show to more modern tunes, Steele was the honorary chairman of the 1980–1981 Rock 'n' Roll Jamboree that ultimately benefited the Connecticut Heart Fund. He was no stranger to auctions at Connecticut Public Television, and his chairmanship for the Mark Twain Memorial's 1987 Annual Appeal as well as the work he did for the Individual Giving Campaign for the Science Museum of Connecticut added more to the coffers of those efforts. Even Steele's unofficial public service reminders drew the notice of the commissioner of Connecticut's Department of Motor Vehicles, who presented him with copies of a poster that the DMV created based on Steele's "reminder to drivers always to take their car keys with them to help prevent automobile thefts."[75]

Taken in total, this dizzying array of charitable causes demonstrates the diverse appeal Steele possessed as well as the sincere compassion he felt for others. Engagements were often booked at a cost to the promoters because of the appearance fees he charged in an effort to dissuade requests for his time, but there were instances when he reduced or eliminated these charges. If anything, Bob Steele was a victim of his own popularity, but that so much good was derived from his association with those causes made for better organizations and the communities they served.

Sporting Figures

Clearly evident from an early age was Bob Steele's love of athletes and the sphere in which they moved. Motorcycling and boxing were his stock-in-trade during his formative years, but as adulthood beckoned and his radio career took flight, Steele found the circle of celebrity sporting figures to which he was exposed growing each year. The work he did with his *Strictly Sports* program enabled him to connect with many legendary athletes.

From the world of pugilism, Jack Dempsey and Willie Pep were among his favorites, but he also interviewed Gene Tunney, Floyd Patterson, Rocky Graziano, Jack Sharkey, Rocky Marciano, Tony Galento, Sugar Ray Leonard, Primo Carnera, Tommy Loughran, and a notable pair of modern-day heavy-weights, Joe Frazier and Muhammad Ali. And from nearby Glastonbury came Bob Backlund, a professional wrestler whose legitimacy ran counter to the general inanity of that so-called sport.

Golfers Tommy Armour, Gary Player, Arnold Palmer, and Jack Nicklaus spoke with Steele, as did hockey's Eddie Shore and the pole vaulter Bob Richards. From the gridiron came New York Giants coach Steve Owen, Frank Gifford, Sam Huff, and the legendary Vince Lombardi. Auto racing's Wilbur Shaw, Innes Ireland, Lee Wallard, and Cale Yarborough were among Steele's interviewees, as was basketball star John Havlicek of the Boston Celtics. But the national pastime furnished the largest bevy of talent whose conversations with Steele gave him the opportunity to share with his audience his love of baseball.

Many players and coaches associated with the Hartford Chiefs, the city's minor-league affiliate of the Boston/Milwaukee Braves, were easily accessible to Steele, as were others who had a link to the state of Connecticut: Al Schacht, known as the "Clown Prince of Baseball," Dick McAuliffe, Walt Dropo, and Jimmy Piersall. Old-timers Ty Cobb, Cy Young, Connie Mack, and Pie Traynor were interviewed, as were front-office executives Red Patterson and Fresco Thompson. At least one baseball commissioner, Happy Chandler, spoke with Steele as did the longtime voice of the New York Yankees, Mel Allen.

Several solid performers on the major-league scene such as Rip Collins, Tommy Holmes, Charlie "King Kong" Keller, Snuffy Stirnweiss, Yankee pitchers Tom Ferrick, Bobby Shantz, and Roland Sheldon and their teammate Bill Skowron, found time to answer questions posed by Steele. Managers Ralph Houk and Johnny Keane added to a Steele lineup that leaned heavily toward the Bronx, but the luster of that roster glowed when a passel of baseball Hall-of-Famers is taken into account. Frankie Frisch, Joe McCarthy, Mickey Cochrane, Johnny Mize, Dizzy Dean, Bob Feller, Ted Williams, Satchel Paige, Rabbit Maranville, Lefty Gomez, Phil Rizzuto, and Yogi Berra appeared with Steele.

But three baseball luminaries who stand out highest are the "Yankee Clipper," the "Sultan of Swat," and a baseball pioneer who became a leader in the civil rights movement of the mid-twentieth century. Joe DiMaggio, Babe Ruth, and Jackie Robinson were all-time greats who forged distinctive careers and became fixtures in the firmament of American culture. Although Steele's athlete interviews occurred as their playing days were nearing the end or were, in fact, over, it is nonetheless significant that he was able to speak with them and bring their stories to his listeners.

These lists are certainly incomplete given the hundreds of people Steele encountered during his lengthy career, but the reputation he made for himself facilitated his ability to speak with so many stars in the world of sports. One exception stands out, however, and it would have been entirely appropriate for Steele to have had the chance to speak with a man who became a baseball Hall-of-Famer, not as a player but as an executive.

Bill Veeck owned the Cleveland Indians when they won the World Series in 1948, and when he bought the Chicago White Sox a decade later, Steele rooted for them as a perennial underdog. Besides the zany promotions for which Veeck was well known, he was also a "champion for the little guy," as commemorated on his plaque in Cooperstown. Through these traits of genuine character and forthrightness, Steele could have easily bonded with Veeck because he also understood the plight of common people.

As a team owner, winning and profits were important to Veeck, but he derived more pleasure from knowing that fans placed a value on the entertainment provided by baseball and appreciated it when they could walk away from a Sox game satisfied from the experience. In like fashion, Bob Steele's voice resonated in the broadcasting range of WTIC in the same manner that people went to Comiskey Park expecting to have a good time. Both Veeck's and Steele's audiences, replete with many "little guys," were the better for it.

The above review of several facets of Bob Steele's life is intended to focus on the more private side of his persona. By putting the man in historical context, describing a snapshot of what transpired in his household, framing the relationship he had with Shirley, and highlighting his penchant for numbers and love of language, we see the characteristics driving Steele as he lived on a day-to-day basis, all of which was guided by his moral compass that pointed toward a high degree of integrity.

That Steele was involved in so many charitable ventures over the decades he spent at WTIC emphasizes his willingness to help others, and the sporting personalities he met in the course of his career serve as a reflection of the company he kept. It was unquestionably a charmed life that Bob Steele led, but one that was well deserved.

10

The Comedian
in the Studio

A funny man's greatest source of humor is himself. Bob has certainly proven this to be true.
—*Jane Moskowitz and Jane Gillard*[1]

Once stationed behind WTIC's microphone, Bob Steele became ensconced in the inner sanctum that was his studio. If Steele could be considered a president of the airwaves, then the workspace he occupied was transformed into an Oval Office of sorts, at least for the hours he was there. Upon the completion of his show on any given day, Steele would cede the desk to the next host scheduled to go on the air, so in that sense there was nothing sacred about the space itself. Rather, Steele's presence was the aspect that bestowed it with a special aura, allowing him to deliver for the benefit of his audience a program worthy of their time and crafted in Steele's unique style.

The humor that infused his content and the precision of the timing in its deployment during each show were components critical to his mission. Equally important was the work of WTIC staff to furnish Steele with information that was composed to the standards of how he himself would have written it, which is to say with correct grammar, spelling, punctuation, and word usage. When errors occasionally seeped in, they were the source of great irritation because Steele always sought a blemish-free show. As unpleasant as his off-air reaction was to these gaffes, it demonstrates the unflagging gravity of Steele's approach and ethic.

As a man seemingly born into comedy, Steele was never at a loss for words or the ability to view any situation from a lighthearted point of view. The only child from a marriage broken when he was just a boy, Steele showed no outward manifestation resulting from this. Preoccupied with schooling and various jobs he took to support his mother, he could have turned inward and traveled a narrow path in his life's course. But Steele scarcely concealed the jocularity of his soul, and a case can easily be made that humor was exactly the diversion that shaped his future actions and attitude toward life. Sharing this *joie de vivre* became Steele's motivation and the most salient characteristic of his personality, and his approach on the air was to inform and entertain, not pontificate.

In their "affectionate memoir" commemorating Bob Steele's fiftieth anniversary at WTIC in 1986, Jane Moskowitz and Jane Gillard published a magnificent compendium of material that Steele used on the air.[2] The authors blended their narrative by combining Steele's humor along with comments and feedback that derived from members of his audience, lending a huge degree of credibility to this aspect of the book by citing the names of the listeners and their towns of residence.

Bursting with Steele's jokes and groan-inducing puns, the book covers a full range of topics that influenced and informed Bob Steele up to the date of its release. Whether by accident or design, the cover of their work puts a bit of slapstick in plain sight: an inspection of the photograph of Steele in his studio reveals it to be a reverse-negative print, as proven by the backward lettering on the microphone.

That so much fan material comprises this book testifies to the close relationship that Steele nurtured with his audience. People wrote in to comment on something that Steele said on the air or to provide him with a new joke or a story of their own personal experience that Steele would, in turn, use in a future script. Steele's give-and-take with listeners thus evolved into a seemingly unending source of new material for him and provided a reason for individuals to stay tuned to see if something they shared with him would eventually find its way into a program.

Aided by Steele's cooperation through the correspondence and artifacts he shared with them, Moskowitz and Gillard reproduced a dialogue of sorts, carried on between radio host and the listeners he not only reached but who were inspired to write back to express their thoughts on any given subject. For example, related to Steele's difficulty in having management dictate changes to his musical selections, one lady, about to celebrate her eightieth birthday, made a poignant observation in the form of a witty poem.

> While waiting to hear my birthday
> With ears all full of cotton.
> That crazy music you have on
> I think is really rotten.
>
> Isn't there a decent record
> That we seniors would enjoy

While we wait to hear our birthdays?
Please get one, Bob old boy!
—Francine Towers, Waterbury, CT[3]

No subject escaped Steele's notice if any measure of humor could be extracted from it, but it was always done without the pejorative, hostile, or ribald edge that has been the stock-in-trade of shock jocks for decades. Phil Steele penned a remarkable analysis of his father's humor, which, when distilled to its most basic form, could be any—or all—of the following adjectives: clean, cute, folksy, outrageous, ridiculous, wholesome. Although Bob Steele acquired a reputation for lowbrow humor, Phil refuted this perceived quality of character.

The many puns in Steele's ostensibly endless collection could elicit—depending on the listener—one sort of incredulous reaction or another, but in many cases one had to glowingly admire the cleverness he employed to create a bon mot. Jokes that some people described as corny were, to Steele, "sophisticated," an adjective he deemed most appropriate because when he died "he wanted to be remembered … not [as an] entertainer or comedian or radio announcer but [as a] 'wordsmith.'"[4]

Besides demonstrating his wit at the events he attended as the featured guest speaker, Steele could also inject impromptu humor into the mundane errands he had to run, such as the time he commandeered the public address system at an automobile dealer and asked the owner of a car with a fictitious seventeen-digit tag number to move the vehicle. "The car is not blocking anyone but the license plate is," he announced to customers and workers alike.[5] Pranks like this also bring to mind his frequently used announcement on April 1 in which he made known his intention to leave WTIC, just to see if anyone was paying attention to the fact that it was April Fool's Day.

While Bob Steele may have eschewed psychological interpretations of his comic outlook on life, there was "a philosophical stance" he was taking, not in the name of comedy but rather for the purpose of innovation, as Phil adeptly explained.

> Going through the thousands of jokes Bob invented and the thousands more he culled, crafted and honed from wherever he could find them, the zany names he concocted, the cartoons he doodled, the scripts and routines he spun out of his fertile imagination from the vagaries of life, and the unending shenanigans he pulled on his public, one has to conclude that the word that really captures the spirit of Bob Steele is not corny but *creative*.[6]

Steele relished taking brash criticism directed toward him and adding humorous twists that he knew would be even more delightful to the audience. Where one person may have spotted ill will, Steele saw an opportunity for a laugh. "Your bus leaves in an hour," said one letter he received, which concluded tartly, "Be under it."[7] Snide items like this, rather than being viewed as offensive and tossed in the wastebasket, found their way into a script for Steele's program. "Far from throwing out [a] nasty diatribe, Bob used it to entertain his listeners, even honing the message," noted Phil.[8] With red pen in hand, Steele would make appropriate edits to prepare these remarks for his show, tailoring it for his manner of presentation to best effect. If there was a lull in fan mail critical of him, Steele might concoct a phony postcard or a simple slip of paper full of "deliciously self-deprecating humor" that he would use as part of his "spiel" on the air or for speaking engagements.[9]

The total number of jokes employed by Steele, who jotted them down on virtually anything made of paper or whatever was handy at the moment, is staggering. According to one reliable estimate, "If he used just seven gags on every show, that would add up to over 100,000 jokes," and Steele recycled many of them over the years, filing jokes away marked with a "used date" so that he knew how long to keep them in reserve before breaking them out again, sometimes years later.[10]

Steele also made sure his name was available for skewering: on occasion he altered "Bob" into "Boob," and for times when he announced his proper full name of Robert L. Steele, he reminded listeners that the "L." stood for "Elmer." June 1956 marked the debut of Sassafras O'Sullivan Steele—note that the initials are S.O.S.—which was "the earliest reference among all of Bob's archives to the fictitious metallic family he made famous."[11] Although Sassafras falls short of the imagery of metals, future characters such as Uncle Stainless and Uncle (Cold) Rolled were infused with exactly this quality and became part of this merry clan.

Serving as president of his self-created "100 Per Cent Wrong Club," Steele was not disturbed by his lackluster forecasting reputation. "If his overall rate was under 50 percent, that was undoubtedly because he liked long shots, liked going with the underdog," Phil Steele later noted, adding, "Anybody can pick a winner. [His father] loved bringing in a longshot."[12] Thus, Steele's persistent selection of the Chicago White Sox to win the American League pennant.

Speaking of sports, he might spice up his otherwise straight reporting of game scores—for example, saying "Yale over Dartmouth"—by tacking on "a few extras like Eggs over Easy, Burberry over Coat, or Man over Board" because "his audience encouraged his wordplay."[13] One prominent listener was the writer James Thurber, who corresponded with Steele in the 1940s and is credited by Phil with furnishing the "Eggs over Easy" puns.[14]

Steele's famous "Tiddlywinks" were not material original to him but were brief news items taken from the wire services that had a humorous twist or concerned celebrity gossip. Not content to read these passages verbatim as they spewed from the teletype, Steele performed careful editing "to make [them] sound less stilted and more colloquial" without changing the meaning of the message.[15]

Comedy notwithstanding, it is important to understand that this aspect of Steele's persona was not manufactured solely for the benefit of the listening public. His humor was merely an extension of the demeanor he cultivated during his youth, and given the difficulties of the circumstances in which he grew up, it is also remarkable that there were no visible traces of bitterness in him. Steele could find a lighter side to every situation. If an argument could be made that laughter—especially of the self-deprecating variety—contributes to longevity, then Bob Steele would be the unquestionable example to follow.

For all the amusement in which Steele reveled, it was but one strand in the fabric that was woven into his show. Programs consisted of news and sports, traffic and weather reports, time checks, antenna switches, to say nothing of music, and all these elements required their own choreography to ensure that they fit into their appropriate format and time slots. Activity occurring behind the scenes in the studio that contributed to the production of each show was out of public view and earshot, just as there is much taking place behind the camera on the set of a movie production. Taken for granted by listeners, these hidden machinations supported thousands of Steele's offerings, and in their own way were the technical repeat performances that necessarily went hand in hand with every action taken by Steele in the studio.

When the time came for Bob Steele to go on the air, the serious business of delivering a smooth-running and mistake-free show assumed the highest priority imaginable. That Steele had arrived at the pinnacle of radio broadcasters was no accident, and the careful crafting of the scripts he used were placed into his program's schedule in order that its flow and continuity moved along with assembly-line precision. The more time listeners spent tuned in to Steele's show, the more ingrained they would become to the routine, the segments of which were dictated by the clock with no allowance for slippage.

A day in the life of the iconic host was profiled by Joel Lang in 1982, his story appearing in the *Hartford Courant*'s Sunday supplement, *Northeast Magazine*.[16] Lang's observations were fixed at the particular time in which he wrote his story, and they obviously did not take into account past variations in Steele's routine that were the result of changes in broadcasting technology that took place over the many years since Steele began his career at WTIC in

1936. Nevertheless, the essay captures the contemporaneous ebb and flow of the elements and activities that comprised a typical workday for Steele.

No movement by Steele seemed to elude the journalist's notice as he accompanied him from the Steele household to the WTIC studio. Departing home to head into downtown Hartford, parking the car in the Gold Building garage, disposing of old newspapers in a trash bin before entering the facility, and fixing the morning's first cup of coffee in the station's kitchenette were part of the routine that Steele had performed thousands of times over the years, although One Financial Plaza was only the station's most recent venue.

By 5:30 a.m., Steele is seated not in the oversized executive chair at the studio's table but rather at a plain swivel chair positioned so that he can easily interact with the engineer in the control room. Following an antenna switch consuming a matter of seconds, Steele's theme song, "A Hunt in the Black Forest," opens the program, and the host greets his audience by indicating

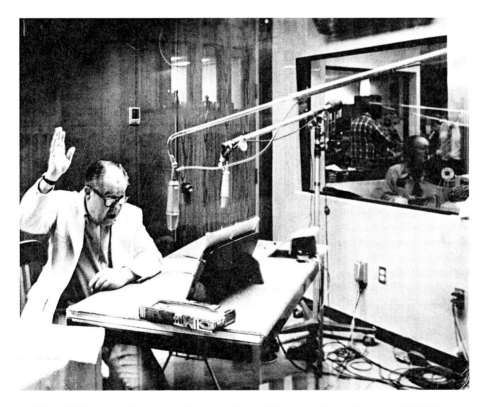

After WTIC vacated Broadcast House, Bob Steele's new studio was in the Gold Building. In 1976, this was his temporary workspace, used while renovations were in progress (Hartford History Center, Hartford Public Library).

the current day and month. His banter with unseen listeners is interspersed with a musical selection leading up to the first sports report, which is segued into promptly at quarter of (and quarter past) each hour and read by Scott Gray. With the proceedings turned back to Steele, the host ensues with a summary of financial information and the lottery numbers drawn the previous evening before moving to his selection for "The Word for the Day."

Flavoring this narrative are jokes both subtle and broad, all inserted with the exact timing that could have landed Steele in the world of comedy had he opted to do so. During breaks when he is not actively on the air, Steele might be found tending to a bit of personal grooming, reciting copy handed to him to be read shortly, or editing such copy if its wording does not feel comfortable to him.

Lang adeptly described the remoteness in which Steele operated, a condition starkly contrasted by the 200,000 or so members of the audience tuned in to his show. Yet, for all the vacuity attending Steele during the hours of his program, the *Courant* reporter observed "[a] pale man, in a pale blue suit, hunched over his work, moving very little, outlined against the sky [seen through the studio windows]. If a media superstar has to have presence, Steele's is not visible, you think. It's all from the inside, from his voice."[17]

Fluid yet ephemeral, the content of a given day's program was a script for Steele in much the same way that sheet music is for a musician, that is, the written, black-and-white version of the material to be performed. And the voice of Bob Steele was what resonated figuratively and literally with his audience, bringing to them in reliable fashion the content they had come to expect in the same manner that a song comes to life when musicians begin to play. His long tenure even informed his judgment about instrumental tunes he preferred playing as a news segment approached: "I hate to fade out a vocal [track]. It's not good radio."[18]

Steele would whistle or use his chime to signal the exact time, such as 7:21 a.m. And the exactitude he delivered on the air was enhanced by his physical appearance, which no listener could see. Dressed in a suit and neck tie even though he was out of public sight, Steele was attired not just as a matter of professional pride: in many instances he was merely being ready to move on to a speaking engagement or business luncheon at the conclusion of his program. At times during long breaks in the studio, he availed himself of an electric razor to ward off any five-o'clock shadow that may have crept in by late morning.

Although his program's format was well known to loyal followers, Steele was nebulous when asked to characterize the workmanship he applied to his show. His lengthy tenure, however, contributed to that which became second nature to him and afforded the flexibility to tailor his presentation on the spot. "I do whatever comes naturally to me," he explained to *Northeast Magazine*. "If I think of a joke in the middle of a commercial, it might not work, but I'll do it right there without preparing. I don't want to wait."[19] Such quick judgment could only be formulated through years of experience behind the microphone and an awareness of the tastes and sensibilities of his audience.

Yet, Steele revealed a subtle technique that kept him mentally focused while addressing the listeners. "When [I'm] doing a joke or something, I feel like I'm talking to one person or a few people, never to 150,000 or whatever the audience is. And when I'm doing the commercials, I think [only] about the commercial."[20] The inflection of his voice, the timing of his unhurried delivery, when combined with a voice colored by a raspy hint, were the traits that invested the sonorous Steele style.

The warm adulation showered upon Bob Steele by his faithful listeners belies the drama that took place in the offices of WTIC as scripts and other material were prepared for him. One young assistant, a senior at Bulkeley High School, recalled her time in the late 1950s when she worked in the pool of stenographers at The Travelers, and she was also offered a part-time job typing for Steele. "I typed his [scripts] the day before he was on the air," said Joyce Mainelli years later. "He wanted no spelling mistakes. The [scripts] had the time for each commercial and event. If he had a nine o'clock commercial, it [had] better be [the] right commercial. If it said coffee it better be coffee, not soap. That would upset him."[21]

Yet Ms. Mainelli further disclosed a softer side of Steele, which was surely an extension of the respect he had for women. "I had no problem with Bob," she noted. "He said, 'Good afternoon, Joyce' every day, [and] one event stood out for me. [Someone at the station] got donuts one afternoon. I was never aggressive and stayed at my desk. He came over with a donut and said, 'I hope you like jelly.' He made my day."[22] In addition to sharing donuts, Steele would offer extra coffee—mixed with lots of cream and sugar—from his thermos that he filled at Dunkin' Donuts on his way into Hartford.

Steele was far less kind when news items, weather reports, and the like were not presented to him in a timely manner. "These early-morning tirades were loud and graphic," remembered Sue Leroux, another programming assistant, but they "end[ed] abruptly if a woman was spotted. With a genuine blush, he would take pains to personally apologize for his unseemly outburst."[23]

The Radio Continuity department was comprised of staff members, including Mlles. Mainelli and Leroux, who were charged with creating scripts, commercials, public service announcements, and copy material other than news. During the mid–1970s, when Sue worked at WTIC, she noted that this group

> worked with salesmen and advertisers to prepare and get approval of all the commercials and even reviewed and brought into compliance those sent to us by ad agencies. WTIC had a lot of live commercials because we had "personalities" to read them, kind of a passive endorsement.... The staff had special typewriters that had large eighteen-point type so the copy was easier to read.[24]

To maximize the value that an advertiser could extract from a given ad to be read on the air, there were instances when too many words would be crammed into the allotted time space, thereby forcing the Radio Continuity members to note how long it took to read an ad at a comfortable pace and make any necessary edits. "And then for every show," Sue explained, "we would have to assemble the copy in the order presented on The Log and put it in the studio for each announcer."[25]

The Log was a manifesto of the items to be used for each program, and it offered proof of advertisements being read and music played, the latter to ensure that royalties were properly paid. These were the pre-packaged scripts that Steele demanded be perfect in every instance because, reading them live, he had no opportunity to vet them in advance for errors. Steele was completely dependent on the staff to be as flawless in their creations as *he* needed to be on the air.

Ms. Leroux offered her insight of how detailed Steele could be about his pursuit of perfection when it came to language.

> Bob loved a grammar debate and he would occasionally come in to discuss our writing. What I remember most is his opinion on the serial comma. Now note this is RADIO. Bob would always question the writer who did not include the serial comma, although Strunk and White, as I recall, said it was optional. So if Copaco in Bloomfield was selling "apples, pears, and bananas," Bob would come in to question if we wrote "apples, pears and bananas."
>
> As a young writer, he provided great experience because you knew 1) you needed to be grammatically correct. (All of us carefully proofread our copy with each other to try to head off any issues.) But you also knew 2) you needed to be able to defend your position. In the end 3) you needed to know when to back off. He was the boss, and if he felt he was right, you just had to let it go.[26]

Isolated in the studio behind soundproof glass, Steele had no opportunity to experience the immediate reaction of his audience to a joke he told, so sometimes he would visit the Radio Continuity staff during a break and retell it in order to "get the laugh that he couldn't hear while on the air."[27]

Sue Leroux, whose maiden name was Kretzmann, was an unwitting source of fodder for Steele's trove of humor before *and* after her marriage: Steele took her first name and slurred it into a truncated version of her prenuptial last name, thus forming "SueKretz," a clever play on Sucrets, the old brand of throat lozenges. After her wedding, Steele switched to quickly saying her first and new last name into a sing-song admixture pronounced SOO-le-ROO, the mere utterance of which assuredly was delightful to his ears.

Even more crucial to the operation that girded Steele's program were the engineers who worked in tandem with him. Occupying this position from 1963 to 1977 was Bob Scherago, who performed tasks on the Monday edition of the show, and he wrote a vignette of the typical studio environs during one of his shifts.

> I would arrive at five o'clock a.m. and, using the program log, would get all the commercials from the commercial library ready, in order of time played. At first they were all on transcription discs, either directly from the ad agencies, or cut in our studios. Eventually, they were on tape cartridges; continuous lengths of tape in plastic cases which allowed them to be played instantly from tape cartridge players at the press of a button. I would also pick up the stack of records selected by the record librarians.
>
> I would take the commercials and records into the control room around ten minutes before six and make sure all was in order. Meanwhile, Bob had also arrived long before six and was in his office preparing for the show. He would usually arrive in the studio as his theme was being played.[28]

Scherago related the beginning sequence of Steele's program, conjuring an image of the petals of a closed flower opening up to sunlight.

> The table in the studio was covered with papers, clippings, and his always-full coffee cup. Sometime after six o'clock he would press the button to turn on his microphone; this was the signal to me to fade down the theme music so he could be heard. He would greet the audience, give a time check, and signal me to start the first record. This went on for the next four hours. We played very little music; he spent the bulk of the time talking. Sometimes he'd read and comment on a newspaper article, sometimes he'd tell a joke, give sports results, weather, and, always, the time. Sometimes he'd tell stories. He looked as though he was very disorganized, but in fact he was in full control of the program.
>
> In the meantime, I would keep track of the commercials and when they had to be played, or read live, I would communicate that to him through the "squawk box," or intercom. I also noted when a half-hour segment of the program was nearing the end so that the news could be read, usually by a staff announcer, on the hours and half-hours. I would back-time, or, as we called it, *dead-pot* an instrumental record so it would end right at the end of the segment. As Bob closed out the segment, I'd sneak in the music, and bring it up to full [volume] as he finished talking.[29]

Over countless thousands of hours on the air, day in and day out, for more than sixty years, Bob Steele repeated this routine with the copy writers and engineers who performed the duties of support hidden from his listeners, who simply tuned in to WTIC and savored the product of all that effort. Cer-

The Bob Steele commemorative plaque, affixed to the Grove Street Building of The Travelers downtown campus in Hartford, can be found at the intersection of Prospect Street and Grove Street, renamed Bob Steele Street. However, Steele would have found fault with it: he was inducted into the Radio Hall of Fame in October 1995, not 1996, and the Oxford commas that should have appeared after the words "cartoonist" and "humor" are missing. His cartoon self-portrait is in the lower right corner (Steele Family Collection).

tainly the technology evolved since Steele's first day in 1936, his program hours varied, and the faces of the staff members and other personnel changed over time. But through it all, remaining fastidiously in place: the voice, persona, and wit of Bob Steele.

Bob Steele Street was posthumously dedicated in early 2013 thanks to the efforts of a committee that included Phil Steele and several prominent members of the local media who worked in conjunction with the office of Mayor Pedro Segarra. The section of Grove Street running from Prospect Street to Columbus Boulevard was renamed as a tribute to a man whose actions—and especially his voice—touched the lives of millions of people over the course of the sixty-six years that he was the most integral part of the most powerful radio station in the state of Connecticut. However, if one strolls down this wide thoroughfare, it is impossible not to notice that no doorways exist that provide access for pedestrians, motor vehicles being the only traffic allowed into and out of the few buildings lining this city-block stretch of asphalt and sidewalks.

In a surreal sense, this seems appropriate, as if the configuration is a firm nod to the automobiles that Bob Steele loved. Yet when traversing this one-way street, those vehicles move in an easterly direction, and facing *ad orientem* holds much significance for purposes of praying, thus offering a religious connotation to the honorific. The true reason for selecting this particular passage to honor Steele was the fact that this was the address of the original WTIC studios, so the street's orientation is merely a coincidence. Nevertheless, this symbolism cannot be ignored, however contrived it may seem.

The naming of streets in tribute to historic figures has long been part of many cultures, and Hartford, Connecticut, has done its part as well, Ann Uccello, Ben Franklin, and George Washington being but a few examples. By the creation of Bob Steele Street, a degree of permanence has been conferred to the man's legend and reminds both passersby and motorists of the fame and status he achieved and the place where his legacy began.

And what a legacy Bob Steele created. After all, he seemed to have done well as a high school graduate. Very well, indeed.

Appendix:
Remembering Dad

"Goodbye. Adios. Sayonara. Hasta la vista.
Pip, pip, cheerio, and all that other stuff."

The chapters of this book have been written in a traditional biographical narrative, and as they relate the story of Bob Steele's extraordinary life, no attempt will be made to elaborate further. However, presented here unedited is *the* final word on the man himself, which has been reserved for the eldest son of Bob and Shirley Steele, who delivered this beautiful and compelling eulogy shortly after the passing of WTIC's most famous personality.[1]

Memorial Service for Robert L. Steele
Wethersfield Congregational Church
Wethersfield, Connecticut
December 12, 2002
Robert H. Steele

Last Saturday night there were almost two hundred emails on the *Hartford Courant* website in which people were sharing their memories of Dad. There was one person, however, who was baffled by all the outpourings. She wrote simply: "Who is Bob Steele?"

Well, I guess that depends on your perspective.

If you were a reporter, you'd probably start by saying that he was a Radio Hall of Fame broadcaster who for many years had the highest rated morning radio show in America.

You'd recount that he was a single child, born in 1911 in Kansas City, Missouri. That his parents divorced five years later. That he dropped out of school several times to work and help support his mother. And that before he turned twenty he had become a veteran motorcycle hill climber and racer, a columnist for a national motorcycle magazine, and an amateur and then professional welterweight boxer, a sport his mother and his own good sense finally talked him out of.

In 1930, with the Great Depression underway, you'd continue, Dad moved to Los Angeles, where he worked as a motorcycle salesman, continued to write about motorcycles, got a taste of Hollywood working as a movie motorcycle stuntman, and began announcing motorcycle races over the radio, all of which eventually brought him to Connecticut for what was supposed to be a temporary assignment doing the track announcing for the motorcycle racing season at Bulkeley Stadium in Hartford.

That opportunity, you'd note, changed Dad's life. He arrived in Hartford in May of 1936 with twenty cents in pocket, entertained the stadium crowds for the next five months, and then hours before leaving to return to Los Angeles, made a spur of the moment decision to audition for a radio announcing job at WTIC, one of the premier radio stations in the country.

Long story short, he got the job, met and fell in love with a beautiful girl, raised a family of four boys, and built a storied career as WTIC's morning man and evening sports show host.

In trying to explain Dad's success, you'd probably point out that he was blessed with a rich, baritone speaking voice, had a folksy erudition about him, and was an accomplished raconteur and humorist with a quick wit and the timing of a standup comedian. And you might add that he had an extraordinary ear for language, which led him to become one of radio's leading authorities on pronunciation and grammar and enabled him to pick up accents, inflections and intonations of native foreign language speakers and rattle off names and phrases in their native tongues.

As a result, Dad was one of a kind, and he dominated southern New England radio. He forged bonds with hundreds of thousands of people whom he never met, becoming an integral part of their mornings and practically a member of their families. He helped ease them into their day with a relaxed combination of music, news, weather, and sports interspersed with personal stories and observations, generous dollops of humor that made them laugh and smile, and special features ranging from "The Word for the Day," to a children's segment including classics like "Jack and the Beanstalk" and "Puss in Boots" narrated by The Great Gildersleeve. Not only did he entertain, as one writer noted, but "he taught more about the English language than an army of English teachers." And in the process he did almost the impossible for an entertainer: he appealed not to just one or two, but to four generations.

Now that wouldn't be a bad description to give the woman who asked

"Who is Bob Steele?" But if I were answering the question, I'd probably answer it from a different perspective.

Growing up during the 1940s and '50s, I always thought of Dad in three parts—morning radio personality, evening sportscaster, and father. And to understand my thinking, you've really got to understand his schedule.

To begin with, he got up at four thirty in the morning six days a week to do his morning show. He then worked until noon Monday through Friday as a staff announcer, after which he'd spend the afternoon preparing for his 6:15 p.m. radio sports show, gathering material for his next morning show, answering the hundreds of letters he received each week, and attending to other tasks like visiting sponsors and making public appearances in support of various causes. In addition, he was in high demand as an after-dinner speaker, which had him out many nights speaking somewhere in Connecticut or western Massachusetts.

Dad would get home by 7 p.m. when he wasn't out speaking, but since both he and the family had usually already eaten based on our own schedules, it turned out that we didn't have either breakfast *or* dinner with him during most of the week. Nevertheless, while I didn't see him much during the week, I heard him, because Mom always had the radio on in the morning and early evening. So, in a way, I had more contact with my father than most kids have with theirs, in that, in a sense, I could go to work with him every day and get to know him the way others knew him.

And as I listened to the radio, I grew to increasingly appreciate these first two parts of the man—the morning part and the evening part.

In the morning, Dad was this wonderfully entertaining radio host who might one moment be delivering the news about some major event in Europe or Asia, and the next leisurely retelling a joke he'd heard the previous night at a banquet. Then in the evening, he was this award-winning sportscaster with his fast-paced show *Strictly Sports*. A man's man who, to me, knew more about sports than anybody; who interviewed all the sports stars who came through Connecticut; who did the blow-by-blow broadcasts of Willie Pep's championship fights; who was photographed with everyone from Jack Dempsey to Joe DiMaggio; and who introduced us kids to a parade of sports figures who came through his life.

Now, as a kid, I liked Dad's sportscaster part the best, simply because it was the most exciting and interesting role to a young boy. But as a got older, I came to realize that his morning role defined him best and gave him by far the biggest stage to perform on.

But the part of him I liked the very best was the third part—the father part we saw on weekends and on some weekday evenings.

There were the family rides in the country after World War II when people could finally buy cars, followed by a stop at the Lincoln Dairy for milk shakes or ice cream sundaes. On Saturday, he carved out as much of the day as possible for the family when we were young, coming home after his morning show and taking us kids to the Y to swim, to the movies, and maybe to play miniature golf—anything to give Mom a partial day off. He'd then bring us home for an afternoon family dinner before he went back to the station for his evening radio sports show, and beginning in 1957, the TV sports show he added that year. As we got older, he took us to as many sporting events as we could possibly fit in. To the auto races in Thompson and Avon, to UConn basketball games, to Yale Bowl for football, to the Hartford Coliseum for boxing, to Bulkeley Stadium to see the Hartford Chiefs play baseball, and—even better—to Stillman Field in Wethersfield, where he hit Paul and me long, high fly balls which we'd track down and catch.

On Sunday, he'd usually take us to Sunday school and once in a while he'd even attend church. In fact, I remember sitting with him one morning in one of the balcony pews up there over to the left, and his leaning over and suggesting that I might want to stop being so restless and pay closer attention to what the minister was saying. And then on most Sunday afternoons he'd take the family out to dinner at the Hearthstone in Hartford, which was his favorite restaurant.

So that's how I remember him—in those three parts, morning radio personality, sportsman, and father, and all three parts blended together to make him the remarkable person he was in my eyes. Oh, and I also remember some of the times he disciplined me, but it's funny how most of those memories fade. What I will always remember is the way he managed to balance our family and his demanding career, and his love and devotion to all of us.

There is also another important thing that I will always remember about Dad, and that is the way he treated the public. Over my lifetime, I must have seen him meet and interact with at least a couple of thousand people, and it never made any difference who they were. What race, creed, religion or station in life. He was always friendly, respectful, interested, never curt or abrupt, and always ready to give a little piece of himself. And people loved him for it.

People from all walks of life would stop him on the street, wanting to shake hands, pat him on the back, chat, tell him a story, and most of all hear one of his. And amazingly, in a business of huge egos, it never went to his head. He was one of the most humble men I ever knew and, although not an outwardly religious person, I know that he thanked God every night for his blessings.

There's a scene in *The Lion King*—both the Broadway production and the animated movie—which I think speaks to all of us who are related to Dad. The young Lion Cub is grieving for his father, who has died. The Cub's advisor tries to comfort him by assuring him that his father will always be with him, whereupon the Cub asks how that can be. His advisor answers that all he need do is look at his own reflection in the lake they are standing by.

As the Lion Cub looks down, his tears ruffle the water, and the image that forms looks strikingly like his father. You see, the advisor says, your father lives in you.

This morning is meant to be a celebration of Dad's life, and an opportunity to remind ourselves that he lives in all of his children, his eight grandchildren, his two great grandchildren, his two new great grandchildren who are on the way, and all that follow.

I know that if Dad were standing here now, he would say this growing, thriving family is by far the most important part of his life.

Chapter Notes

Chapter 1

1. Phil Steele, *Bob Steele's Century*, hereafter referred to as BSC, Vol. 1, 10.

2. Hog and cattle powder was an "antibiotic-vitamin mixture for use as an aid in prevention and treatment of bacterial diarrhea and the like in poultry, cattle." See https://trademarks.justia.com/owners/columbian-hog-and-cattle-powder-co-96673/. Viewed December 28, 2017.

3. Phil Steele email to author August 31, 2017; Robert H. Steele telephone interview September 6, 2017; Robert H. Steele interview, November 2, 2017; Paul Steele email to author September 26, 2017.

4. Letter from Bob Steele to Hampton Steele, November 14, 1917, Bob Steele Collection, Box 3, Folder 9, Hartford History Center, hereafter referred to as HHC, Hartford Public Library, Hartford, CT.

5. BSC, Vol. 1, 31. Such loyalty later kept Steele in the employ of WTIC in spite of temptations to leave for higher paying jobs with other radio stations.

6. BSC, Vol. 1, 27.

7. BSC, Vol. 1, 27, 30.

8. Bulkeley Stadium program, September 29, 1936, BSC, Vol. 1, 155.

9. BSC, Vol. 1, 29.

10. BSC, Vol. 1, 30. Steele claimed in 1936 that his fascination was rooted in an incident that occurred in 1916, when he was only five years old. His father "came home one day all bruised up" from having been "knocked for a loop by a hit and run motorcyclist. I immediately got the urge to buy a motorcycle, mingle with the riders and hunt down my man." See BSC, Vol. 1, 155.

11. Robert H. Steele telephone interview, September 6, 2017.

12. BSC, Vol. 1, 32.

13. *Ibid.*

14. "Steele—Sathoff Win Hill Climb," *Kansas City Post*, 1926, BSC, Vol. 1, 34.

15. BSC, Vol. 1, 44.

16. Bob Steele, "Latest from Kansas City," *MotorCycling*, 1927, BSC, Vol. 1, 49.

17. Bob Steele, "Krazy Kracks from K.C.," *MotorCycling*, 1927, BSC, Vol. 1, 51.

18. 1928 Diary, Bob Steele Collection, Box 11, Item 1, HHC. Other quotations that follow are from this same source. Regarding the three states he mentions, Delaware could not possibly been in his sight from the Allegheny Mountains. The third state Steele likely espied was the northernmost portion of Virginia or eastern West Virginia that lay to the south of western Maryland.

19. BSC, Vol. 1, 84.

20. Ray King, "Bob Steele—Announcer," *The Open Road*, June 1932, BSC, Vol. 1, 111.

21. BSC, Vol. 1, 87.

22. Bob Steele, "Krazy Kracks from K.C.," *MotorCycling*, 1930, BSC, Vol. 1, 94–95.

23. BSC, Vol. 1, 99.

24. Glen Gendzel, "1914–1929," in Stephen J. Whitfield, ed., *A Companion to 20th Century America* (Malden, MA: Blackwell Publishing, 2004), 31.

25. David M. Kennedy, *Freedom From Fear: The American People in Depression and War* (New York: Oxford University Press, 1999), 38.

26. Bob Steele, "Krazy Kracks from K.C.," *MotorCycling*, December 1930, BSC, Vol. 1, 100. Marginalia indicates that this column was Steele's "last one before leaving K.C. for Cal[ifornia]—Dec. 1930."

Chapter 2

1. Robert H. Steele telephone interview, September 6, 2017.

2. Paul Steele email to author September 26, 2017.

3. BSC, Vol. 1, 105.

4. *National Speed Weekly*, 1932, BSC, Vol. 1, 109.

5. *Coast Auto Racing*, 1932, BSC, Vol. 1, 111.

6. BSC, Vol. 1, 119.

7. BSC, Vol. 1, 123. Gambling was a nagging issue for Steele. However, when he passed away in 2002, he did so having accumulated a very large estate, thus indicating that he had never been in serious financial difficulty.

8. Bob Steele, "I'll Say It Looks Like a Big Season!" 1934, BSC, Vol. 1, 127. Emphasis in original. Between 1931 and 1950, Los Angeles alone boasted ten different venues for motorcycling events. A full list of speedway motorcycle tracks for the state of California is available at speedwaybikes.com. Viewed September 17, 2017.

9. Bob Steele, "Poppings of the Day," *The Motorcyclist*, February 1936, BSC, Vol. 1, 146.

10. Jess Zimmerman, "Dot Robinson, 'First Lady of Motorcycling," www. historybyzim/ 2013/10/dot-robinson-first-lady-of-motorcycling/. Viewed September 24, 2017. Covering such a distance in that amount of time calculates to a sustained rate of about 33 miles per hour.

11. Letter from George Lannom to Bob Steele, April 13, 1936, BSC, Vol. 1, 150.

12. *Ibid*. Emphasis added.

Chapter 3

1. BSC, Vol. 1, 151. Phil Steele also refuted a myth that Bob literally rode into Hartford on a motorcycle. "Bob's story was that he was riding in a truck with Hills and Hills' wife, with a couple of motorcycles in the back. Just outside of Hartford, one of the cycles was coming loose from its tethers and, since they were so close to their destination, Cliff asked Bob to simply sit on the cycle to hold it down." Email from Phil Steele to author, December 4, 2017.

2. Ellsworth Strong Grant and Marion Hepburn Grant, *The City of Hartford, 1784–1984: An Illustrated History* (Hartford, CT: Connecticut Historical Society, 1986), 43–44.

3. Bob Steele, "Bob Steele," Bulkeley Stadium Program, September 1936, BSC, Vol. 1, 155.

4. *Hartford Courant*, July 28, 1936, BSC, Vol. 1, 154.

5. BSC, Vol. 1, 158.

6. Donald L. Miller, *Supreme City: How Jazz Age Manhattan Gave Birth to Modern America* (New York: Simon & Schuster, 2014), 298.

7. Miller, *Supreme City*, 301–302.

8. Donna Halper email correspondence with author, November 12, 2017. An expert in the history of early radio, Donna has graciously provided an account of the beginnings of broadcasting in Connecticut, for which the author is most grateful.

9. "WTIC Radio to Remember," wti-calumni.com/history.htm. This website contains an excellent trove of information that lives up to the opening comment on its History page: "The story of the station reads like a history of broadcasting...." Viewed October 12, 2017.

10. The author had the experience of listening to WTIC in distant Williamsburg, Virginia, early on a Saturday morning in October 1988. Phil Steele also noted that at the time of Bob Steele's hiring, the station had a world map with places marked to indicate where its signal was being received. "There were so few stations in the [1930s] and even beyond that WTIC's strong signal was sometimes picked up in such faraway places as Norway, even Australia." Phil Steele email to author, December 4, 2017. Radio historian Donna Halper supports this notion by explaining that under certain ionospheric conditions the phenomenon known as "sky wave propagation" could allow even low-wattage broadcasts to travel across the Atlantic Ocean to England. Donna Halper email to author, December 9, 2017. In the station identifications he said on the air, Bob Steele would intone, "Hartford, Connecticut, *USA*," the country's three initials serving notice of the complete geographic origin of his broadcast, even long after WTIC's signal failed to extend beyond greater southern New England.

11. "WTIC Radio to Remember," wti-calumni.com/history.htm. Viewed October 12, 2017.

12. *Ibid*.

13. *Ibid*. Five deaths were also attributed to the flood.

14. Bob Steele employment application, BSC, Vol. 1, 159.

15. BSC, Vol. 1, 158.

16. "Robert L. Steele," in *WTIC Radio to Remember*, The Ten Eighty Corporation, n.d., 15. This publication commemorates the station's 60th anniversary, so it likely was published in 1985.

17. Bob Steele, "Bob Steele," Bulkeley Stadium Program, September 1936, BSC, Vol. 1, 155.

18. BSC, Vol. 1, 158.

19. David M. Roth, ed., *Connecticut History and Culture: An Historical Overview and Resource Guide for Teachers* (Hartford, CT: Connecticut Historical Commission, 1985), 179.

20. Even when Steele assumed his role as a regular announcer years later, he still wrote

"Stalling Around... with Steele." The column was so popular that he was once paid $7.50 for his monthly essay despite the fact the editor neglected to print it, an omission that prompted an outcry from readers of *Motorcyclist*. Letter to Bob Steele, November 1947, BSC, Vol. 3, 116.

21. She also switched her first and middle names in a demonstration of her preference for "Shirley," but Phil Steele later noted that "Bob loved [Astrid] and it took him years to go along with her and call her Shirley instead of Astrid." Phil Steele email to author, December 4, 2017.

22. *Ibid.*

23. BSC, Vol. 1, 166.

24. Letter from Bob Steele to Astrid Hanson, August 31, 1937, BSC, Vol. 1, 174.

25. Telegram from Bob Steele to Astrid Hanson, September 16, 1937, BSC, Vol. 1, 175.

26. Letter from Bob Steele to Astrid Hanson, October 13, 1937, BSC, Vol. 1, 176.

27. Letter from Bob Steele to Astrid Hanson, October 20, 1937, BSC, Vol. 1, 177.

28. Telegram from Bob Steele to Astrid Hanson, HHC, Letters to Astrid Shirley Hanson, Box 3, Folder 11.

29. BSC, Vol. 1, 188.

30. Marriage certificate of Robert Steele and Astrid Hanson, BSC, Vol. 1, 188. At least there was consistency in the error: Astrid's last name appears as "Hansom" in both entries on the certificate.

31. Bob Steele, "Poppings of the Day," *The Motorcyclist*, June 1939, BSC, Vol. 2, 8. The police dog may have been an apocryphal embellishment to the story. Phil Steele email to author, December 4, 2017.

32. BSC, Vol. 1, 196.

Chapter 4

1. Stephen Dunn, "Bob Steele, Radio Broadcaster" in "Hartford Legends," *Hartford Courant*, n.d., 9. Although not dated, this special insert to the *Courant* was likely from a 1991 edition of the newspaper.

2. BSC, Vol. 2, 12.

3. Advertisement, *Radio Daily*, April 12, 1940, BSC, Vol. 2, 21.

4. A. B. McGinley, "The Sporting Vista," *Hartford Times*, July 27, 1940, BSC, Vol. 2, 26.

5. A. B. McGinley, "The Sporting Vista," *Hartford Times*, July 27, 1940, BSC, Vol. 2, 26.

6. BSC, Vol. 2, 35.

7. Bob Steele personal notes, BSC, Vol. 2, 33.

8. *WTIC Radio to Remember*, 24. A total of 89,872 dimes were needed to complete one mile.

9. *WTIC Radio to Remember*, 24.

10. Sports editor A.B. McGinley of the *Hartford Times* told readers of his April 29, 1942, column "The Sporting Vista" that "the annual sports dinner at the prison has grown from a small beginning to an event of importance, one that brings down there as guests an imposing array of well-known Connecticut sports figures.... That annual sports dinner and show gives sports a big 'lift' at the institution." BSC, Vol. 2, 53.

11. BSC, Vol. 2, 45.

12. BSC, Vol. 2, 45.

13. *WTIC Radio to Remember*, 23.

14. Advertisement, *Hartford Courant*, January 27, 1942.

15. "From W53H to WTIC," *Bridgeport Herald*, April 26, 1942, BSC, Vol. 2, 50.

16. "Pep To Give Ring Exhibition At Old State House," *Hartford Courant*, June 21, 1942, BSC, Vol. 2, 59. This article may have been from the *Hartford Times*.

17. Letter from Paul Morency to Bob Steele, May 26, 1942, BSC, Vol. 2, 54.

18. BSC, Vol. 2, 61.

19. BSC, Vol. 3, 95.

20. BSC, Vol. 2, 68.

21. J. H. Beaudry, "An Open Letter to Bob Steele," *The Motorcyclist*, January 1943, 6, BSC, Vol. 2, 73.

22. Blood donor card, BSC, Vol. 2, 75. Steele's card indicates that he gave blood five times, from February 1943 to April 1944.

23. Phil Steele email to author, January 2, 2018; interview with Robert H. Steele, January 2, 2018.

24. Bob Steele script, March 11, 1943, BSC, Vol. 2, 79.

25. BSC, Vol. 2, 79.

26. Bob Steele script, March 23, 1943, BSC, Vol. 2, 80.

27. Bob Steele, "Air Waves Bumpy," *Hartford Times*, September 12, 1944, BSC, Vol. 2, 163.

28. Such an extensive book, roughly six inches thick, weighed about sixteen pounds.

29. "Selective Service System Classifications for WWI, WWII, and PWWII through 1976," www.cufon.org/CRG/memo/74911231.html. Viewed December 25, 2017.

30. BSC, Vol. 2, 82. The continent Steele referred to was, of course, Europe. There was much angst between the United States and Britain with regard to the policy of conducting the war as it concerned how best to attack Germany.

31. Bob Steele script, May 31, 1943, BSC, Vol. 2, 83. The figure of 100,000 is derived from

"World War II: A Timeline of American Casualties," ajc.com/news/anniversary-world-war-2/. Viewed December 25, 2017.

32. Bob Steele note, BSC, Vol. 2, 87.

33. Bob Steele script, June 2, 1943, BSC, Vol. 2, 88.

34. Bob Steele, "Willie Pep of Hartford," *Esquire*, August 1943, 151.

35. Letter from Bob Steele to Shirley Steele, July 30, 1943, BSC, Vol. 2, 100.

36. BSC, Vol. 2, 119.

37. *Ibid.*

38. Charles C. Hoffman memo, November 17, 1943, BSC, Vol. 2, 122–123.

39. The full text of the poem can be found in BSC, Vol. 4, 16.

40. Bob Steele script, 1944, BSC, Vol. 2, 131.

41. Frank E. Perley, "Stealing a Day From Bob Steele," *Hartford Courant Magazine*, March 12, 1944.

42. *Ibid.*

43. BSC, Vol. 2, 136.

44. "Keep Baseball Going," https://baseball-hall.org/discover/short-stops/keep-baseball-going. Viewed December 28, 2017.

45. Letter from Franklin Delano Roosevelt to Kenesaw Mountain Landis, January 15, 1942, https://baseballhall.org/discover/short-stops/keep-baseball-going. Viewed December 28, 2017.

46. "On the Air Lanes," *The Sporting News*, April 27, 1944.

47. John Lardner, "Science Took Belated Bow In Ring Squabble," (Baltimore) *Evening Sun*, November 28, 1944.

48. BSC, Vol. 2, 179.

49. Letter from Bob Steele to Shirley Steele, March 13, 1945, BSC, Vol. 2, 195.

Chapter 5

1. Promotional material for Bob Steele, February 15, 1945, BSC, Vol. 3, 2–3. Steele's son Phil suspects that all of this information may not have been written by Steele alone. "Bob Steele had something to do with the WTIC promotional material but I don't know how much, even if the style [of writing] sounds a lot like him.... The 'color' idea, in particular, does not sound to me like Bob Steele but something another WTIC staff member came up with." Phil Steele email to author, February 23, 2018.

2. "Dorian a Devil With Women, Say Folks at Avery," *Hartford Times*, April 20, 1945, BSC, Vol. 3, 6; advertisement, *Hartford Times*, April 27, 1945, BSC, Vol. 3, 6.

3. Bill Lee, "With Malice Toward None," *Hartford Courant*, May 23, 1945, BSC, Vol. 3, 10.

4. BSC, Vol. 3, 10.

5. "50,000 View Airborne Attack Simulating Real 8-Day Action," *Hartford Times*, July 2, 1945, BSC, Vol. 3, 17.

6. WTIC teletype bulletin, August 10, 1945, BSC, Vol. 3, 23.

7. "Rivals Hire WTIC Alumni In Early-Morn Radio War," *Bridgeport Herald*, November 25, 1945, BSC, Vol. 3, 36.

8. BSC, Vol. 3, 36.

9. Scrapbook entry, February 20, 1946, BSC, Vol. 3, 45.

10. Postcard to Bob Steele, 1946, BSC, Vol. 3, 55.

11. Scrapbook entry, July 31, 1946, BSC, Vol. 3, 62. The issue that Jews had been protesting pertained to the small number of refugees being allowed *into* Palestine, not those getting into foreign countries. The news script that Steele used had this point erroneously reversed. In the event, the King David Hotel in Jerusalem "housed the British administrative offices and was a prime symbol of the British presence in Palestine." See Charles D. Smith, *Palestine and the Arab-Israeli Conflict: A History with Documents*, Fourth Edition (Boston: Bedford / St. Martin's, 2001), 186–188.

12. 1947 announcing schedule, Bob Steele 1944 diary, HHC, Box 11, Item 2.

13. Diary entry, January 27, 1947, BSC, Vol. 3, 86; BSC, Vol. 3, 113.

14. Postcard from Bob Steele to his sons, February 28, 1948, BSC, Vol. 3, 123. Steele also would later visit Dempsey at his restaurant in New York City.

15. Letter from Elwood Rigby to Bob Steele, February 9, 1948, BSC, Vol. 3, 123.

16. Diary entry, February 28, 1948, BSC, Vol. 3, 123.

17. Scrapbook entry, May 1948, BSC, Vol. 3, 137.

18. Diary entry, April 24, 1948, Bob Steele 1944 diary, HHC, Box 11, Item 2.

19. The facility, founded in 1898, was originally named the Newington Home for Incurables, and in a far less sensitive era, patients were referred to as "inmates," to say nothing of the site for the hospital having been selected away from the city of Hartford so that "the public would [not] be exposed to the children and their infirmities." It later became renowned as the Newington Children's Hospital and eventually merged with Hartford Hospital in 1996. See opacity.us.site238_newington_home_and_hospital_for_crippled_children.htm. Viewed January 13, 2018.

20. Phil Steele email to author, January 14, 2018.

21. Diary entry, February 20, 1949, BSC, Vol. 3, 163. The $17,000 figure may have included bonuses or other incentives. Steele also briefly had a financial stake in a shoe store, Greene's Footwear in West Hartford.

22. Letter from Shirley Steele to Bob Steele, December 31, 1949, BSC Vol. 4, 2.

23. Letter from Bob Steele to Shirley Steele, January 16, 1950, BSC Vol. 4, 18.

24. Letter from Robert H. Steele to Shirley Steele, January 20, 1950, BSC Vol. 4, 22.

25. Diary entry, December 3, 1950, Bob Steele 1944 diary, HHC, Box 11, Item 2.

26. Letter from Shirley Steele to Grace Stock, December 12, 1950, BSC Vol. 4, 53.

27. Diary entry, January 6, 1951, Bob Steele 1951 diary, HHC, Box 11, Item 5.

28. BSC, Vol. 4, 58.

29. Truman quoted at www.leatherneck.com/forums/archive/index.php/t-49377.html. Viewed January 26, 2018.

30. "The New Marine Corps Hymn," BSC, Vol. 4, 62. Phil Steele speculates that his father did not use this on the air until possibly 1974, but it is included here because of its date of origin.

31. Diary entry, July 12, 1951, Bob Steele 1951 diary, HHC, Box 11, Item 5.

32. "Clients Came in Droves," *Broadcasting*, July 30, 1951, 29.

33. Letter from Ostrom Enders to Bob Steele, quoted in "Clients Came in Droves," *Broadcasting*, July 30, 1951, 29. Phil Steele recounted years later that his father used the services of Hartford National Bank "for his checking account for the rest of his life." Phil Steele email to author, February 23, 2018.

34. Diary entry, May 27, 1952, Bob Steele 1952 diary, HHC, Box 11, Item 6.

35. Diary entries, October 11, 1952; October 26, 1952; Bob Steele 1952 diary, HHC, Box 11, Item 6.

36. Diary entry, November 6, 1952, Bob Steele 1952 diary, HHC, Box 11, Item 6.

37. Diary entry, February 13, 1954, Bob Steele 1953 diary, HHC, Box 11, Item 7.

38. Diary entry, April 18, 1952, BSC, Vol. 4, 98.

39. *WTIC Radio to Remember*, 35.

40. *Ibid*.

41. Diary entry, September 18, 1952, Bob Steele 1952 diary, HHC, Box 11, Item 6.

42. Diary entry, May 15, 1952, Bob Steele 1952 diary, HHC, Box 11, Item 6.

43. Diary entry, May 12, 1953, Bob Steele 1953 diary, HHC, Box 11, Item 7.

44. Diary entry, November 5, 1953, Bob Steele 1953 diary, HHC, Box 11, Item 7.

45. Diary entry, November 22, 1953, Bob Steele 1953 diary, HHC, Box 11, Item 7.

46. Robert D. Byrnes, "Travelers Loses Decision On 'Live' Show Definition," February 1, 1954, BSC, Vol. 4, 165. This story was a newspaper clipping that likely came from the February 2, 1954, edition of the *Hartford Courant*.

47. The figure of $6,200 is based on a comment Steele wrote in his diary in which he mentioned that 1954 year-end bonuses would be paid to all employees of The Travelers Insurance Company. "5 pct of annual salary—Mine should be 310 appx—less about 60.00 tax—net around 250." Therefore, 5 percent of $6,200 equals $310. See diary entry December 14, 1954, Bob Steele 1953 diary, HHC, Box 11, Item 7.

48. Diary entry, July 6, 1954, Bob Steele 1953 diary, HHC, Box 11, Item 7; interview with Robert H. Steele, February 13, 2018.

49. Bob Steele quoted in "Jimmy Jemail's Hotbox," *Sports Illustrated*, November 15, 1954, BSC, Vol. 4, 187.

50. Diary entry, December 14, 1954, Bob Steele 1953 diary, HHC, Box 11, Item 7.

51. *WTIC Radio to Remember*, 38.

52. "Principal Radio Stations and Advertising Rates," 1951 Diary, 401–403, HHC, Box 13. The cover of the diary is embossed *A Personal Book for Executives—1951*.

Chapter 6

1. James T. Patterson, *Grand Expectations: The United States, 1945–1974* (New York: Oxford University Press, 1996), 61.

2. Paul W. Morency, "WTIC-TV Opens—A Community Station Designed for Community Living," *Hartford Times*, September 21, 1957, 34.

3. "WTIC to Air, News, Sports and Weather," *The Billboard*, August 19, 1957, 12. Not until the autumn of 1958 would WTIC become an affiliate of CBS.

4. George Rowe, "WTIC-TV a 'Producer's Dream' in Terms of Its 'Unexcelled Production Facilities," *Hartford Times*, September 21, 1957, 34.

5. Walter C. Johnson, "A New Station and a New Way of Life," *Hartford Times*, September 21, 1957, 35.

6. Bob Steele diary entry, September 13, 1957, BSC, Vol. 5, 58. Steele's relationship with Ehrlich did not pan out and seems to be a very rare instance where Steele developed a distaste for a particular individual. In the spring of 1966, Steele "told [Ehrlich] off in the newsroom before

going on [the air]. Gets me all stirred up. Can't stand the guy." Perhaps Ehrlich was trying to establish himself more firmly in a not-so-subtle competition with Steele: that year, Ehrlich received his second award as Connecticut's top sportscaster, although he was still two short of the number won by Steele. See Bob Steele diary entry, April 26, 1966, BSC, Vol. 6, 82.

7. Bob Steele, "Old Strictly Sums Up WTIC-TV Sports," *Hartford Times*, September 21, 1957, 36.

8. BSC, Vol. 5, 59.

9. *Ibid.*

10. Bob Steele diary entry, January 25, 1966, BSC, Vol. 6, 75.

11. BSC, Vol. 5, 59.

12. Memo from Leonard J. Patricelli to Bob Steele, BSC, Vol. 5, 62.

13. "State Gripped By Multi-Million Dollar Growing Pains Known As Redevelopment," *New Haven Evening Register*, December 10, 1959, 1.

14. "State Gripped By Multi-Million Dollar Growing Pains Known As Redevelopment," *New Haven Evening Register*, December 10, 1959, 1.

15. Peter C. Baldwin, *Domesticating the Street: The Reform of Public Space in Hartford, 1850–1930* (Columbus: Ohio State University Press, 1999), 42.

16. Baldwin, *Domesticating the Street*, 44.

17. Phil Barlow, "Hartford's Constitution Plaza: Potential Still Unfolding," www.sasaki.com/blog/view/357/, October 1, 2013, viewed March 28, 2018. Emphasis added. A lower class of citizens apparently would be welcome as visitors to the new plaza, so long as no one else had to observe their wretched living conditions.

18. Phil Barlow, "Hartford's Constitution Plaza: Potential Still Unfolding," www.sasaki.com/blog/view/357/, October 1, 2013, viewed March 28, 2018.

19. John Peter, "One City's Answer to Downtown Decay," *Look*, September 21, 1965, 46.

20. Bob Steele diary entry, January 10, 1958, BSC, Vol. 5, 73.

21. *Ibid.*

22. Diary entry, November 16, 1958, Bob Steele 1953 diary, HHC, Box 11, Item 7.

23. *Ibid.*

24. Author unknown, "Why Do We Wait?" BSC, Vol. 5, 99.

25. Bob Steele diary entry, July 10, 1960, BSC, Vol. 5, 142.

26. Phil Steele email to author, April 17, 2018. The reason for the surgery remained a mystery for years after it occurred. None of Steele's sons had any recollection of the procedure.

27. Clarence T. Hubbard, "A Breeze from the East," n.d., BSC, Vol. 5, 196. The article is taken from one of Steele's scrapbooks, and there is no indication of the name of the original publication, but it may have been a media trade magazine.

28. Robert Steele interview, May 15, 2018.

29. *Ibid.* Generally speaking, the state of Connecticut would not have fared well had a real war erupted. Pratt & Whitney Aircraft, which manufactured jet engines for commercial and military purposes, was based in East Hartford; the Electric Boat division of General Dynamics in Groton built—and continues to build—submarines for the U.S. Navy; and the Navy's northeastern submarine base is located in New London. A thermonuclear detonation in the greater Hartford area would have laid waste to Pratt & Whitney as well as the Steele homestead just a few miles away to the south.

30. Art McGinley, "Good Afternoon: A Personal Chat with Art McGinley," *Hartford Times*, May 24, 1963, 20.

31. Bob Steele diary entry, November 22, 1963, BSC, Vol. 6, 28–29.

32. BSC, Vol. 6, 43.

33. Bob Steele diary entry, August 2, 1964, BSC, Vol. 6, 42.

34. WTIC NFL promotional flyer, BSC, Vol. 6, 49.

35. *Ibid.* Emphasis in original.

36. *Ibid.*

37. Bob Steele diary entry, July 9, 1966, BSC, Vol. 6, 85.

38. Robert Steele interview, May 15, 2018.

39. Bob Steele diary entry, February 2, 1967, BSC, Vol. 6, 96.

40. Bob Steele diary entry, January 31, 1966, BSC, Vol. 6, 75.

41. BSC, Vol. 6, 95, 99.

42. William Manchester, *The Glory and the Dream: A Narrative of American History, 1932–1972* (New York: Bantam Books, 1975), 1114.

43. "WTIC Drops Show, Outcry Trails Move," *Hartford Courant*, March 15, 1967, 1.

44. *Ibid.*

45. Thomas B. Dawson, "The People Speak—Television Station Commended," *Hartford Times*, March 24, 1967, 10B.

46. Mrs. Myron Weiner, "We Do Not Need A 'Big Brother,'" *Hartford Courant*, March 19, 1967, 2B. Modern-day readers need to keep in mind that this controversy took place nearly one year before the Tet Offensive, two years prior to the revelation of the massacre at My Lai, and three years before the invasion of Cambodia—events that greatly exacerbated the rift on the American home front.

47. Bob Steele diary entry, March 21, 1967, BSC, Vol. 6, 99.
48. Bob Steele diary entry, March 25, 1967, BSC, Vol. 6, 99.
49. Bob Steele diary entry, June 8, 1967, BSC, Vol. 6, 104.
50. Bob Steele scrapbook entry, October 1967, BSC, Vol. 6, 109.
51. Bob Steele diary entries, April 4–5, 1968, BSC, Vol. 6, 125.
52. Bob Steele diary entry, June 5, 1968, BSC, Vol. 6, 130.
53. Bob Steele diary entries, November 6–7, 1968, BSC, Vol. 6, 133. Emphasis added. Nixon actually outpolled Humphrey by over 510,000 popular votes and won the electoral college ballot with 301 votes, the correct margin later noted by Steele in his entry of November 8.
54. Bob Steele diary entry, January 29, 1969, BSC, Vol. 6, 136.
55. Bob Steele diary entry, October 16, 1969, BSC, Vol. 6, 158.

Chapter 7

1. Claude Hall, "Adult-Geared Morning DJs Spur Middle-of-Road Sales," *Billboard Magazine*, January 1970, 1, 38.
2. Arthur B. McGinley, "Bob Steele," program of the 22nd Annual Banquet of the Connecticut Boxing Guild, May 5, 1970, BSC, Vol. 6, 167.
3. Phyliss Hodsdon, "'I really don't know what my rating is. They never told me,'" *AdEast*, May 1972, 20.
4. Letter from Rose Smith to Bob Steele, June 2, 1970, BSC, Vol. 6, 172–173. Emphasis in original.
5. Robert H. Steele letter to author, July 17, 2018.
6. Letter from Rose Smith to Bob Steele, June 2, 1970, BSC, Vol. 6, 172–173. Emphasis in original.
7. Bob Steele script, June 2, 1970, BSC, Vol. 6, 172–173. Emphasis in original.
8. Bob Steele script, November 8, 1971, BSC, Vol. 7, 8.
9. Photograph, *Bristol* (CT) *Press*, September 16, 1970.
10. Joyce Rossignol, "Steele Says Son Got Up Earlier Than He," *Wethersfield* (CT) *Post*, September 30, 1970. Despite keeping distance from his son while on the air, Steele nonetheless was enormously proud of Robert's accomplishment in the political arena. As Phil Steele noted as he was curating the trove of mementoes collected by his fa-

ther, "During the four years Robert served in Congress, Bob filled his scrapbook with dozens of articles on his oldest son." BSC, Vol. 6, 187.
11. Bob Steele diary entry, January 9, 1971, BSC, Vol. 6, 194.
12. BSC, Vol. 6, 195.
13. Bob Steele diary entry, April 22, 1971, BSC, Vol. 6, 196.
14. "The Number Is All That Is Necessary," *Meriden Record*, March 22, 1972.
15. "Steele Terminates Lottery Emcee Job," newspaper article, March 22 or 23, 1972, BSC, Vol. 7, 17.
16. Bob Steele diary entry, March 21, 1972, BSC, Vol. 7, 16.
17. Bob Steele diary entry, April 4, 1972, BSC, Vol. 7, 18.
18. Bob Steele diary entry, September 6, 1972, BSC, Vol. 7, 25.
19. Bob Steele scrapbook entry, November 1972, BSC, Vol. 7, 27.
20. Bob Steele diary entry, January 22, 1973, BSC, Vol. 7, 35. Approval by the Federal Communications Commission was granted at the end of January 1974, and the legal papers effecting the sales were signed in early March.
21. Philip H. Dougherty, "In 1900, Readers in New York Had a Choice of 15 Newspapers," in James Barron, ed., *The New York Times Book of New York* (New York: Black Dog & Leventhal Publishers, Inc., 2009), 221.
22. *WTIC Radio to Remember*, 44.
23. *Ibid.*
24. WTIC "Maximum Traffic Plan" flyer, BSC, Vol. 7, 55.
25. Bob Steele diary entry, May 10, 1973, BSC, Vol. 7, 45.
26. Bob Steele diary entry, April 2, 1973; Bob Steele diary entry, April 30, 1973; Bob Steele diary entry, May 18, 1973, BSC, Vol. 7, 43, 46.
27. Bob Steele diary entry, December 5, 1973, BSC, Vol. 7, 57.
28. Bob Steele diary entry, January 15, 1974, BSC, Vol. 7, 58.
29. Bob Steele diary entry, November 5, 1974, BSC, Vol. 7, 78. Emphasis added.
30. Alan H. Olmstead, "'Old' Bob Steele Applauded," *Bristol Press*, November 1974.
31. Phil Steele email to author, July 12, 2018.
32. Bob Steele diary entry, November 14, 1974, BSC, Vol. 7, 78.
33. Bob Steele diary entry, April 26, 1975, BSC, Vol. 7, 90. Eighteen months would pass, but Steele finally was given a five-year contract—with a pay increase—in the fall of 1976.
34. Bob Steele diary entry, April 30, 1975, BSC, Vol. 7, 90.

35. Bob Steele diary entry, August 4, 1976, BSC, Vol. 7, 106.
36. Bob Steele diary entry, December 25, 1976, BSC, Vol. 7, 116.
37. Bob Steele diary entry, October 9, 1975, BSC, Vol. 7, 96.
38. Bob Steele diary entry, October 1, 1976, BSC, Vol. 7, 112.
39. Lou Bachman, "Downtown," *Bristol Press*, October 1976.
40. Bob Steele diary entry, January 18, 1978, BSC, Vol. 7, 139.
41. Ben Gammell, "Almost a Tragedy: The Collapse of the Hartford Civic Center," connecti-cuthistory.org/almost-a-tragedy-the-collapse-of-the-hartford-civic-center/. Viewed June 28, 2018.
42. Bob Steele diary entry, March 7, 1978, BSC, Vol. 7, 139. The author's own reaction was one of bewilderment that Bob Steele was playing a song by the popular 1980s rock group The Cars. A slow, mellow tune from 1984, "Drive" impressed as being very much out of character compared with Steele's normal selection of tunes.
43. Bob Steele diary entry, June 16, 1978, BSC, Vol. 7, 160.
44. Bob Steele diary entry, June 21, 1978, BSC, Vol. 7, 160.
45. Bob Steele diary entry, July 25, 1978, BSC, Vol. 7, 161.
46. Bob Steele diary entry, July 31, 1978, BSC, Vol. 7, 161.
47. Stephanie M. Brown, 'Meet the Morning Man...," *Hartford Courant*, n.d., BSC, Vol. 7, 167. Although no date or publisher is noted, the typeset is easily recognizable as that of the *Courant*.
48. *Ibid.*
49. *Ibid.*
50. Bob Steele diary entry, January 14, 1979, BSC, Vol. 7, 174.
51. Phil Steele email to author, July 12, 2018.
52. Bob Steele diary entry, June 22, 1979, BSC, Vol. 7, 190.
53. Program of the Father McGiveny Award Ceremony, October 1979, BSC, Vol. 7, 196.
54. Jay Clark to Helen E. Burns, December 31, 1979, BSC, Vol. 7, 204. The ratings had risen to 48 percent, which was five points higher than the time of the Clark-Steele set-to.
55. Bob Steele diary entry, January 2, 1980, BSC, Vol. 8, 2.
56. Bob Steele diary entry, January 2, 1980, BSC, Vol. 8, 13.
57. Bob Steele diary entry, July 18, 1981, BSC, Vol. 8, 54.
58. Heidi Ehrlich, "USA Snapshots," *USA*

Today, n.d., BSC, Vol. 8, 71. This likely appeared in a February 1982 edition of the newspaper.
59. WTIC advertisement, n.d., BSC, Vol. 8, 123. This ad was likely from the summer of 1984.
60. Bob Steele diary entries, October 3, 1982; October 26, 1982; October 30, 1982; BSC, Vol. 8, 95.
61. BSC, Vol. 8, 97.
62. Bob Steele marginalia on Associated Press teletype vignette by Ira Dreyfuss, February 14, 1983, BSC, Vol. 8, 99.
63. Bill Ryan, "Bob Steele, 72, Gets Birthday Greeting," *Hartford Courant*, July 14, 1983.
64. Bob Steele diary entry, December 5, 1983, BSC, Vol. 8, 109.
65. Marc Gunther, "At 60, WTIC Radio Has Reason To Celebrate," *Hartford Courant*, February 9, 1985.
66. The Steele name was later dropped, apparently after the grant money ran out. Phil Steele email to author, July 12, 2018.
67. "Pulse Maker Interview," untitled publication of International Radio and Television Society. n.d., BSC, Vol. 8, 185.
68. "Pulse Maker Interview," untitled publication of International Radio and Television Society. n.d., BSC, Vol. 8, 185.

Chapter 8

1. Perry S. Ury letter, December 2, 1986, BSC, Vol. 9, 34–35.
2. Robert H. Steele interview, November 2, 2017.
3. Joseph B. White, "The $6,000,000 Man Steps Out," *New England Monthly*, February 1987, 16.
4. Robert H. Steele email to author, July 30, 2018.
5. Joseph B. White, "The $6,000,000 Man Steps Out," *New England Monthly*, February 1987, 16–17.
6. Joseph B. White, "The $6,000,000 Man Steps Out," *New England Monthly*, February 1987, 17.
7. Bob Steele diary entry, July 7, 1987, BSC, Vol. 9, 51.
8. Bob King, "Retirement 'not a definite' for Steele," *Journal Inquirer*, August 6, 1987, 38.
9. *Ibid.*
10. James Endrst, "Radio days go on for man of Steele," *Hartford Courant*, October 2, 1987, E1.
11. Bob Steele promotional brochure, n.d., BSC, Vol. 9, 52–53.
12. Bob Steele diary entry, April 17, 1988, BSC, Vol. 9, 88.

13. "Steele, Roasted," *Northeast Magazine/Hartford Courant*, November 20, 1988.

14. *Ibid.*

15. Bob King, "McCarthy to join Bob Steele on morning show," *Journal Inquirer*, April 21, 1989.

16. Bob King, "McCarthy to join Bob Steele on morning show," *Journal Inquirer*, April 21, 1989.

17. Bob Steele diary entry, April 4, 1989, BSC, Vol. 9, 126.

18. Bob King, "McCarthy to join Bob Steele on morning show," *Journal Inquirer*, April 21, 1989.

19. Bob Steele diary entry, May 26, 1989, BSC, Vol. 9, 131.

20. Bob Steele diary entry, July 25, 1989, BSC, Vol. 9, 134. Serving on the air for many years, Arnold Dean was no stranger to WTIC listeners.

21. Bob Steele diary entries, July 26, 1989; July 27, 1989, BSC, Vol. 9, 134.

22. BSC, Vol. 9, 137.

23. Scott Hilsee, "What is a 33 degree Freemason," www.quora.com/What-is-a-33-degree-Freemason. Viewed July 13, 2018.

24. "Hartford 1—Kansas City 0." *Connecticut Square & Compasses*, February/March/April 1990, 11. The title of this article is a playful jab implying that the loss of Kansas City was Hartford's gain when Steele left his home town and ultimately settled in Connecticut.

25. Bob Steele diary entry, September 16, 1989, BSC, Vol. 9, 138.

26. Tom McCarthy, "Bob Steele's Successor—Tom McCarthy," *The Connecticut Yankee*, November/December 1989, 18.

27. Bob Steele diary entry, January 1, 1990, BSC, Vol. 9, 146.

28. WTIC 1080 advertisement, BSC, Vol. 9, 147.

29. Allen M. Widem, "Bob Steele Takes a Breather," *Imprint Newspapers*, n.d.

30. Bob Steele retirement party invitation, BSC, Vol. 9, 200.

31. Bob Steele retirement party guest book, BSC, Vol. 9, 201.

32. Tom McCarthy, "Bob Steele's Successor—Tom McCarthy," *The Connecticut Yankee*, November/December 1989, 18.

33. Evelyn F. Kerlejza letter to Greg Mocheri, May 29, 1992, BSC, Vol. 10, 6–7. Ms. Kerlejza was hardly alone in this unfortunate disruption of routine. The author experienced this same problem with tardy openings of the show at 5:30 a.m.

34. Robert H. Steele interview, November 20, 2018.

35. Bob Steele diary entry, July 4, 1992, BSC, Vol. 10, 9.

36. Bob Steele diary entry, September 26, 1992, BSC, Vol. 10, 14.

37. Randy Smith, "Numbers game in state hall," *Journal Inquirer*, April 21, 1994, 58.

38. Bruce DuMont letter to Bob Steele, August 7, 1995, BSC, Vol. 10, 44–45.

39. Bob Steele diary entry, October 30, 1995, BSC, Vol. 10, 56.

40. Bob Steele diary entry, November 2 and 5, 1995, BSC, Vol. 10, 59.

41. Bob Steele diary entry, November 5, 1995, BSC, Vol. 10, 59.

42. Bob Steele diary entry, June 26, 1998, BSC, Vol. 10, 84.

43. Bob Steele diary entry, March 18, 1999, BSC, Vol. 10, 97. Emphasis in original.

44. Jim Shea, "As Time Goes By," *Hartford Courant*, May 26, 1999, F1.

45. Bob Steele, "Introduction," in Enrique Espinosa, *Hartford: New England Renaissance* (Memphis: Towery Publishers: 2000).

46. Bob Steele diary entries, September 11, 2001; September 13, 2001; BSC, Vol. 10, 128.

Chapter 9

1. "Announcer Kept Busy, Steele Says," *Waterbury Republican*, December 1946, 20.

2. Phil Steele interview, August 4, 2017.

3. Phil Steele email to author, July 12, 2018.

4. Phil Steele email to author, October 15, 2017.

5. Paul Steele email to author, July 12, 2018.

6. David Halberstam, *The Fifties* (New York: Villard Books, 1993), 514.

7. Halberstam, *The Fifties*, 515.

8. BSC, Vol. 3, 41.

9. Sue Leroux, "The Last Word," *Northeast Magazine*, September 12, 1982.

10. George Malcolm-Smith, "Gently Steele Upon the Ears," *The Travelers Beacon*, n.d., 5. This publication is likely from late 1943 or early 1944. However, Steele's eldest son later disputed the "family meal" noted in the story. Because the father did not arrive home until after seven o'clock, Shirley and the boys would have already eaten dinner about an hour earlier. Saturday afternoons were often the first time during the week when the whole family could gather for a meal. Robert H. Steele email to author, September 22, 2018.

11. Diary entry, September 25, 1944, BSC, Vol. 2, 164.

12. Diary entry, August 1, 1951, Bob Steele 1951 diary, HHC, Box 11, Item 5.

13. Diary entry, August 16, 1952, Bob Steele 1952 diary, HHC, Box 11, Item 6.

14. Diary entry, August 9, 1953, Bob Steele 1952 diary, HHC, Box 11, Item 6.

15. Robert H. Steele email to author, March 4, 2018.

16. Diary entry, December 14, 1954, Bob Steele 1953 diary, HHC, Box 11, Item 7.

17. Formula on WTIC memo, BSC, Vol. 7, 99.

18. Diary entry, August 23, 1954, Bob Steele 1953 diary, HHC, Box 11, Item 7.

19. "Good Afternoon," Art McGinley, *Hartford Times*, April 10, 1954.

20. BSC, Vol. 5, 29.

21. Diary entry, December 25, 1968, BSC, Vol. 6, 135.

22. Diary entry, May 18, 1976, BSC, Vol. 7, 104.

23. Diary entry, July 26, 1981, BSC, Vol. 8, 54.

24. Diary entry, June 30, 1989, BSC, Vol. 9, 131; scrapbook note, BSC, Vol. 10, 95.

25. Robert H. Steele interview, May 15, 2018.

26. Bob Steele postcard to Shirley Steele, June 25, 1945, BSC, Vol. 3, 18.

27. Bob Steele letter to Astrid Hanson, November 10, 1937, BSC, Vol. 1, 178.

28. Bob Steele telegram to Astrid Hanson, December 9, 1937, BSC, Vol. 1, 182.

29. Bob Steele note to Shirley Steele, June 1, 1962, BSC, Vol. 5, 190.

30. Shirley Steele note to Bob Steele, August 30, 1962, BSC, Vol. 5, 194.

31. Diary entry, May 20, 1967, BSC, Vol. 6, 103.

32. Shirley Steele note to Bob Steele, May 1968, BSC, Vol. 6, 129.

33. Diary entry, December 26, 1964, BSC, Vol. 6, 55.

34. Diary entry, April 2, 1972, BSC, Vol. 7, 18.

35. Diary entry, November 26, 1990, BSC, Vol. 9, 164.

36. Diary entry, January 3, 1996, BSC, Vol. 10, 61.

37. Diary entry, February 6, 1969, BSC, Vol. 6, 139.

38. Diary entry, April 2, 1975, BSC, Vol. 7, 90.

39. Paul Steele email to author, July 12, 2018.

40. *Shorter Oxford English Dictionary*, Vol. 2, Sixth edition (New York: Oxford University Press, 2007), 3488.

41. BSC, Vol. 4, 154; diary entry, October 15, 1953, BSC, Vol. 4, 154.

42. "Steele's Remarqs," March 21, 1946, BSC, Vol. 3, 167.

43. Diary entry, April 10, 1967, BSC, Vol. 6, 100.

44. Diary entry, December 31, 1956, Bob Steele 1953 diary, HHC, Box 11, Item 7.

45. Diary entries, January 18, 1948, BSC, Vol. 3, 120; September 22, 1947, BSC, Vol. 3, 108. Steele's income at WTIC fluctuated depending on the number of features or programs he did.

46. Diary entry, July 3, 1982, BSC, Vol. 8, 79.

47. Diary entry, February 20, 1954, BSC, Vol. 4, 166.

48. Diary entry, August 10, 1988, BSC, Vol. 9, 99.

49. Diary entry, January 7, 1971, BSC, Vol. 6, 192.

50. Diary entry, December 25, 1997, BSC, Vol. 10, 81.

51. Clare Briggs, "The Western Sea," reprinted in Bill Madden, "Drawing Cards," *Memories and Dreams*, Vol. 40, Number 3 (Summer 2018), 23. This baseball cartoon was a commentary on the National League pennant race of 1914, and the artistic style also was one followed by Steele in his own drawings and sketches.

52. Robert H. Steele note to Bob Steele, February 22, 1964, BSC, Vol. 6, 32.

53. Bob Steele note to Shirley Steele, April 25, 1945, BSC, Vol. 3, 7; Bob Steele note to Shirley Steele, January 17, 1950, BSC, Vol. 4, 19; Bob Steele scrapbook entry, BSC, Vol. 5, 168.

54. Bob Steele, "What Annoys Radio Men? Why, You, Dear Public," *New Britain Herald*, n.d., BSC, Vol. 3, 130–131. The placement of this article on these pages of this particular Vol. puts the timeframe in early 1948. The subtitle of the essay—"Bob Steele Tells His Troubles With People Smart and Not So"—is also revealing.

55. BSC, Vol. 5, 79.

56. Scrapbook items, BSC, Vol. 5, 198–199; Paul Steele email to author, July 12, 2018.

57. BSC, Vol. 10, 59.

58. BSC, Vol. 8, 35.

59. William Haskell, "Hill Country Letter," n.d., BSC, Vol. 7, 172. The dateline indicates Colebrook, Connecticut, as part of an article published in late 1978 in a local newspaper.

60. BSC, Vol. 8, 48.

61. BSC, Vol. 8, 35; diary entry, August 26, 1987, BSC, Vol. 9, 61.

62. Bob Steele interview with Dave Barber, February 1980, BSC, Vol. 4, 113.

63. Diary entry, December 16, 1946, BSC, Vol. 3, 80.

64. BSC, Vol. 4, 172.

65. BSC, Vol. 5, 115.

66. Harry Truman letter to Margaret Truman, January 28, 1952, BSC, Vol. 6, 111.

67. Diary entries, December 27, 1967, December 29, 1967, January 2, 1968, BSC, Vol. 6, 114–115.

68. Diary entry, January 18, 1969, BSC, Vol. 6, 136.

69. Diary entry, November 16, 1968, BSC, Vol. 6, 135.

70. Diary entry, November 22, 1968, BSC, Vol. 6, 135.

71. Diary entry, March 15, 1969, BSC, Vol. 6, 141.

72. Diary entry, July 12, 1976, BSC, Vol. 7, 106.

73. Diary entry, March 13, 1987, BSC, Vol. 9, 44.

74. Diary entry, January 6, 1973, BSC, Vol. 7, 34.

75. John J. Tynan letter to Bob Steele, May 7, 1968, BSC, Vol. 6, 129.

Chapter 10

1. Jane Moskowitz and Jane Gillard, *Bob Steele's 50th Anniversary: An Affectionate Memoir* (Hartford, CT: Spoonwood Press, 1986), 69.

2. Moskowitz and Gillard, *Bob Steele's 50th Anniversary.*

3. *Ibid.*

4. BSC, Vol. 3, 178.

5. BSC, Vol. 3, 179.

6. BSC, Vol. 3, 179. Emphasis added.

7. Moskowitz and Gillard, *Bob Steele's 50th Anniversary*, 68.

8. BSC, Vol. 6, 62.

9. BSC, Vol. 5, 152–153; Phil Steele email to author, October 26, 2018.

10. BSC, Vol. 4, 158.

11. BSC, Vol. 5, 27.

12. Phil Steele email to author, October 26, 2018.

13. BSC, Vol. 3, 155.

14. Phil Steele email to author, October 26, 2018.

15. BSC, Vol. 8, 94.

16. Joel Lang "Our Man in the Morning," *Northeast Magazine*, August 29, 1982, 8–13, 16.

17. Lang, 11.

18. Steele quoted in Lang, 12.

19. Steele quoted in Lang, 15.

20. Steele quoted in Lang, 15–16.

21. Joyce Mainelli email to author, July 15, 2018.

22. Joyce Mainelli email to author, July 15, 2018.

23. Sue Leroux, "The Last Word," *Northeast Magazine*, September 12, 1982.

24. Sue Leroux email to author, August 21, 2017.

25. *Ibid.*

26. *Ibid.*

27. *Ibid.*

28. Bob Scherago email to author, August 30, 2017.

29. Bob Scherago email to author, August 30, 2017.

Appendix

1. Robert H. Steele email to author, July 17, 2018. The title is drawn from the typical way in which Bob Steele signed off his program.

Bibliography

Special Collections

Bob Steele Collection, Hartford History Center, Hartford Public Library, Hartford, Connecticut.

Books

Baldwin, Peter C. *Domesticating the Street: The Reform of Public Space in Hartford, 1850–1930.* Columbus: Ohio State University Press, 1999.

Barron, James, ed. *The New York Times Book of New York.* New York: Black Dog & Leventhal Publishers, Inc., 2009.

Carruth, Gordon. *The Encyclopedia of American Facts and Dates.* New York: HarperCollins, 1993.

Espinosa, Enrique. *Hartford: New England Renaissance.* Memphis: Towery Publishers, 2000.

Grant, Ellsworth Strong, and Marion Hepburn Grant. *The City of Hartford, 1784–1984: An Illustrated History.* Hartford, CT: Connecticut Historical Society, 1986.

Halberstam, David. *The Fifties.* New York: Villard Books, 1993.

Kennedy, David M. *Freedom From Fear: The American People in Depression and War.* New York: Oxford University Press, 1999.

Manchester, William. *The Glory and the Dream: A Narrative of American History, 1932–1972.* New York: Bantam Books, 1975.

Miller, Donald L. *Supreme City: How Jazz Age Manhattan Gave Birth to Modern America.* New York: Simon & Schuster, 2014.

Moskowitz, Jane, and Jane Gillard. *Bob Steele's 50th Anniversary: An Affectionate Memoir.* Hartford, CT: Spoonwood Press, 1986.

Oxford University Press. *Shorter Oxford English Dictionary,* Volume 2, Sixth edition. New York: Oxford University Press, 2007.

Patterson, James T. *Grand Expectations: The United States, 1945–1974.* New York: Oxford University Press, 1996.

Roth, David M., ed. *Connecticut History and Culture: An Historical Overview and Resource Guide for Teachers.* Hartford, CT: Connecticut Historical Commission, 1985.

Smith, Charles D. *Palestine and the Arab-Israeli Conflict: A History with Documents,* Fourth Edition. Boston: Bedford / St. Martin's, 2001.

Steele, Phil. *Bob Steele's Century.* Volumes 1–10. Hartford, CT: Kelly Design Company, 2011.

Weaver, Glenn, and Michael Swift. *Hartford, Connecticut's Capital: An Illustrated History.* Sun Valley, CA: American Historical Press, 2003.

Whitfield, Stephen J., ed. *A Companion to 20th Century America.* Malden, MA: Blackwell Publishing, 2004.

Newspapers

Bridgeport (CT) *Herald*
Bristol (CT) *Press*
Evening Sun (Baltimore)
Hartford Courant
Hartford Times
Imprint Newspapers (Hartford)
Kansas City Post
Meriden (CT) *Record*
New Britain (CT) *Herald*
New Haven Evening Register
New York Enquirer
Waterbury (CT) *Republican*
Wethersfield (CT) *Post*
USA Today

Publications

AdEast
The Billboard
Broadcasting
Coast Auto Racing
Connecticut Square & Compasses (Freemasons)

177

The Connecticut Yankee
Esquire
Look
Memories and Dreams
MotorCycling
Motorcyclist
National Speed Weekly
New England Monthly
Northeast Magazine
Open Road
Radio Best
Radio Daily
The Sporting News
Sports Illustrated
The Travelers Beacon (Company magazine)
WTIC: Radio to Remember. Hartford: Ten Eighty
    Corporation, 1985.

Websites

ajc.com
americanmotorcyclist.com
articles.latimes.com
chs.org
connecticuthistory.org

crockermotorcycleco.com
cufon.org
ebay.com
hartfordhistory.net
historybyzim.com
leatherneck.com
opacity.us
quora.com
radiohof.org
speedwaybikes.com
thepeoplehistory.com
trademarks.justia.com
wikipedia.org
wticalumni.com

Interviews / Correspondence

Donna Halper
Sue Leroux
Joyce Mainelli
Bob Scherago
Paul Steele
Phil Steele
Robert H. Steele

Index

Buckland Mall 111
Bureau of Indian Affairs 115
Burns, George 43, 85
Burns, Joseph 87
Bush, George H.W. 111
Bushnell Memorial Hall 87, 141

Camel cigarettes 57, 124
Camp Courant 60
Capitol Region of Churches 143
Carbone's (restaurant) 118
Carnera, Primo 144
Carter, Boake 6
Carter, Jimmy 74
CBS Evening News (television program) 104
Central Intelligence Agency (CIA) 74
Chandler, Happy 144
Channel 3 (television station) 60–61, 65, 71, 77, 78, 79, 80, 90, 111
Charles Wright School (Wethersfield, CT) 71
Chase, David 90
Chatfield (senior assisted living center) 112
Chicago White Sox 80, 101, 145, 149
Christ Church Cathedral (Harford, CT) 37–38
Churchill, Winston 37
Clark, Jay 96–97, 98–99, 100
Cleveland Browns 66
Cleveland Indians 145
Close-Up on Sports (television program) 66
Clymer, Floyd 16, 25, 75
Coast Auto Racing (magazine) 14, 16
Cobb, Ty 144
Cochrane, Mickey 144
Cole, Don 100
Colligan, Glenn 118
Collins, Rip 144
Colt Firearms 26
Colt Park 94
Columbia Broadcasting System (CBS) 59, 62, 71, 73, 76, 104
Columbia University 73
Columbian Hog and Cattle Powder Company 4
Comiskey Park (Chicago) 145
Congressional Record (publication) 111
Connally, John 75
Connecticut Boxing Commission 45
Connecticut Boxing Guild 83, **84**
Connecticut Broadcasters Association 102
Connecticut Dairy and Food Council 128
Connecticut Dental Association 107
Connecticut Department of Motor Vehicles 143
Connecticut Gaming Commission 87, 88
Connecticut Heart Fund 143
Connecticut lottery 87–88, 118
Connecticut National Bank 100
Connecticut Public Television 119, 143
Connecticut Special Olympics 107, 143
Connecticut Sports Hall of Fame 114
Connecticut Sports Writers Alliance 111

Connecticut State Prison (Somers, CT) 143
Connecticut State Prison (Wethersfield, CT) 31, 34, 36, 143
Connecticut Turnpike 68
Connie (hurricane) 62
Constitution Plaza 69–70, 90
consumer goods tampering (1982) 100–101
consumerism 64–65
Cooper, Alice 94
Copaco Company 154
Corey, Herbert 9
Cousy, Bob 75
Cowles, Walter 23
Crocker, Al 16, 24
Crocker Throttle Krax (publication) 15
Crocodile Club 111
Cronin, Joseph 58
Cronkite, Walter 104
Crosby, Bing 96
Cross, Milton 6
Cross, Wilbur L. 26
Cuban Missile Crisis 73, 74
Curtis, Tony 140
Cutter Financial Center 116

Davis, Brad 97, 105
Daytona 500 77
Deagan chime 37
Dean, Arnold 93, 109, 110
Dean, Dizzy 20, 48, 60, 144
De La Cruz, Hugo 100
Dell, Carl 33
Dell'Orto, Vince 36
Democratic National Convention (Chicago) 81
Dempsey, Jack 33, 48, 53, 124, 144, 161
Dempsey, John 75, 81, 91
DeWitt, J. Doyle 73
Diane (hurricane) 62
Dias, Angela 112
Dickinson, Angie 140
DiMaggio, Joe 144–145, 161
Dio, Tommy 45
Disneyland 72
Disorderly Conduct (movie) 15
Dodd, Chris 111
Dodd, Thomas 75
Dodger Stadium (Los Angeles) 68
Dow Jones Industrial average 92
Downes, Bob 97, 110
Dropo, Walt 144
Dry Dock Savings Bank 100
Dumont, Bruce 115
Dunaway, Ray 112, 113, 116
Dunn, Bob 106–107, 108
Durante, Jimmy 115
Durocher, Leo 20, 48
Dzu, Maj. Gen. Ngo 86

E. J. Korvettes (retailer) 64
Easter Seals 141

Eastern Airlines 53
Eastern States Exposition 95, 107
Eastwood, Clint 94
economic climate (CT) 115–116
economic development 64, 68–69
The Ed Sullivan Show (television program)
    127
Edgar, Marriot 42
Edward R. Murrow Award 110
Ehrlich, George 66, 78
Eisenhower Recession 71
Electric Boat 86
Ellington (CT) High School 141
E.M. Loew's (theater) 140
Empire Restaurant 36
Enders, Ostrom 57
energy crisis (1973) 91–92
energy crisis (1979) 98
The Enforcer (movie) 94
Ensworth Charitable Foundation 102
Epstein, Isaac 99
Equal Rights Amendment 85
Erector Set (toy) 22
Espinosa, Enrique 118

Falkland Islands War 100
Farr, Tommy 29
Father McGiveny Award 98
Federal Communication Commission (FCC)
    22, 60, 61, 62, 65, 75, 89, 103
Feller, Bob 144
Fenway Park 80, 127
Ferkauf, Eugene 64
Ferrick, Tom 144
Flood of March 1936 23–24
Fonda, Jane 91
Foreman, George 111
Foster, Bob 81
Franklin, Ben 157
Frazier, Joe 124, 144
Fresno Speedway Association 16
Frisch, Frank 20, 144
Front Street (Hartford) 69
Funny Girl (movie) 140

G & C Merriam Company 136
G. Fox Department Store 37–38, 54, 60, 70
Galento, Tony 144
gambling 115
Gambling, John, Jr. 83
Garde Hotel (Hartford, CT) 19
General Dynamics Corporation 86
General Motors 134
Gengras Motors 50
Geoghegan, Bud 49
Gielgud, John 100
Gifford, Frank 144
Gillard, Jane 102, 146, 147
Gilmore, Earl 16
Gilmore Stadium (Beverly Hills, CA) 14, 16
Gladwyn, Graham 27

Glenn Martin Corporation 134
Godfrey, Arthur 59
Gold Building (Hartford, CT) 70, 90, 109
Gold Key Award 111
Golden Globe Award 140
Gomez, Lefty 144
Governor's Foot Guard Hall 35
Graham Media Group 90
Grand Canyon 76
Grasso, Ella 92, 93, 98, 99
Gray, Scott 112, 152
Graziano, Rocky 144
Great Depression 11, 12, 13, 19–20
Great New England Hurricane 30–31
Greater Hartford Chamber of Commerce 143
Greater Hartford Open 88
"Green Light Letter" 44
Greene, Ed 60
Guillen, Jorge 100
Gunsmoke (television program) 127

Halberstam, David 123
Hall, Floyd "Red" 10
Hall High School (West Hartford, CT) 28
Hamill, Dorothy 114
Hanna, Martha Susan (Bob Steele's mother)
    see Steele, Martha Susan
Hanna, Mayme 71
Hanna, Robert C. 3
Hansen, Roy 50
Hanson, Astrid Shirley *see* Steele, Astrid
    Shirley
Hanson, Esther 27–28, 55, 90
Hanson, Oscar 27–28, 77
Harley-Davidson motorcycles 7
Hartford Auditorium 35
Hartford Chiefs 74, 144, 162
Hartford City Spring Clean-Up Campaign
    143
Hartford Civic Center 94, 95–96, 117, 128, 129,
    162; roof collapse 95
Hartford Civitan Club 107
Hartford Courant 22, 23, 34, 59, 88, 95, 97,
    119, 150, 159
Hartford Courant Northeast Magazine 43, 116,
    150
Hartford History Center 2
Hartford Hospital 44
Hartford Insurance Group 102
Hartford National Bank and Trust 57, 70, 77
Hartford: New England Renaissance (book)
    118
Hartford Public Library 2
Hartford Senators (baseball team) 20
Hartford Sheraton 93
Hartford Telecasting Company, Inc. 60–61
Hartford Times 23, 33, 39, 49, 59, 74, 83, 88,
    95, 128
Hartford Whalers 96, 116, 117
Harvey, Paul 1, 115
Havlicek, John 144

Steele, Josephine 4
Steele, Kristen 73
Steele, Mark Conrad 81
Steele, Martha Susan (Bob Steele's mother) 11, 16, 50, 53, 61; birth 3; death 71–72; divorce 4; move to California 13
Steele, Orie 10
Steele, Paul Alan 2, 61, 71, 73, 81, 87, **126**, 127, 131, 134; birth 33; marriage 73
Steele, Philip Lee 2, 4, 33, 38, 53, 54, 55, 67, 71, 72, 73, 76, 77, 78, 81, 87, 93, 95, 99, 100, 101, 118, 122, **126**, 127, 134, 136, 137, 138, 139, 141, 144, 148, 149, 157; birth 44
Steele, Robert Hampton 2, 4, 6, 8, 55, 60, 61, 65, 71, 73, 74, 78, 81, 87, 99, 100, 116, **126**, 127; marriage 73; political life 82, 86–87, 88–89, 91–93, 140–141
Steele, Robert Jesse *see* Steele, Robert L.
Steele, Robert L. ("Bob"): advertising spokesman 116; antiwar stance 5, 34–35, 37, 40, 45–46, 49, 55, 56, 78, 80, 93, 100, 101, 129; audition at WTIC 21, 25; awards 37, 73, 74, 83, 91, 98, 102, 107, 110, 111, 114, 115; baseball announcer 20; birth 1, 3, 4; boxing 8, 11, 16; boxing announcer 11, 29, 35, 46, 53; car wash business 58–59; cartoonist **46**, **50**, 130; change of middle name 5; charitable interests 37, 41, 46, 141–143; chauvinist comments 85–86; commemorative plaque 156; competing job offers 54, 59; "Connecticut Calendar and Almanac" 100; courtship of Shirley Hanson 28–29; death 119; departure from WTIC 96, 104, 106, 107, 148; draft classification 40, 42; drawing talent 5, 8, 10; early interest in radio 6; early life 4–5; education 5, 6, 7; "eggs à la Steele" 128; eightieth birthday 111; family life 125–129, 161; as father 125–129, 161–162; fictitious family names 149; fiftieth wedding anniversary 107; financial impact to WTIC 105, 114; flipping cars 15; format of radio program 150, 151–153; fortieth anniversary at WTIC 95; gambling 6, 15–16; grammar 136, 146, 154, 160; health problems 42, 60, 70–71, 73, 94, 97, 111, 117; humor 1, 7, 9, 29, 38, 39, 41, 43, 45, 57, 66–67, 83, 85–86, 99, 105, 106, 117, 122, 124, 130, 135, 138, 139, 146–150, 154, **156**; interest in data 133–135; interest in language 135–137; literacy work 102, 141; love of cars 76; marriage 30; moral character 137–141; motorcycle trip (1928) 9–10; motorcycling 7, 14, 159; motorcycling announcer 14, 16, 18; move to Hartford, CT 18–19; move to Southern California 13; move to Wethersfield, CT 34, 73; music selections 87, 96–98; National Radio Hall of Fame 1, 104; National Radio Hall of Fame induction 115; no-school announcements 77; on-air indecency 102–103; patriotism 37, 129; promotions 78, 95; rapport with audience 1, 5, 6, 9, 37, 38, 39, 42, 44, 53, 83, 85–86, 87, 97–98;

99, 101, 102–103, 105, 108, 111, 114, 123, 125, 135–137, 139, 141, 144, 145, 146–149, 152–153; recorded messages in World War II 36; relationship with son Steve 128–129; retirement 102, 104–106, 107, 112; romance with Shirley Steele 130–132; sandwich shop owner 11; script editing 33, 38–39, 40, 43, 48, 125, 133, 137, 147, 148–149, 150, 153–154; search for replacement 105–106, 108; show ratings 97, 100, 111; sixtieth anniversary at WTIC 116; social habits 124; speaker-for-hire 106–107, 112, **113**; speech and adlibbing 39, 40, 42, 43; sports predictions 34, 51, 86, 88, 94, 101, 149; stunt work 15, 160; television announcer 66–67; "Tiddly Winks" 99, 111, 149; typical day at work 125; whistling 50, 52; window-cleaning formula 128; work in WTIC studio 150–155, 157; writing talent 7–9, 11, 16, 17, 99
Steele, Shirley 33, 53, 54, 61, 75, 76, 77, 80, 117, 124, **126**, 130–132; birth 28; courtship by Bob Steele 28–29; death 120; employment at Travelers 28; home life 125, 130–132; hospitalization 80, 114; marriage **30**; romance with Bob Steele 130–132
Steele, Steven Michael 71, 76, 77, 80, 94, 100, 117, **126**, 127, 128; birth 56
Steele, Vanessa Shirley 87
Steele family lineage 3–4
Stengel, Casey 75
Sterling Salt 57
Stern, Howard 103
Stewart, Walt 43
Stillman Field (Wethersfield, CT) 162
Stirnweiss, Snuffy 144
Stock, Florence 55
Streisand, Barbra 140
Strictly Sports (radio program) 32–33, 44, 57, 61, 66, 124, 125, 144, 161
Strike It Rich (television program) 141
suffrage 12
Summer Olympic Games (1972) 88
Swanson, Herb 44
Sypek, Joe 20

Taft, William Howard 3
Taishoff, Sol 74
television technology 47, 62–63, 65
Ten Eighty Corporation 90, 95, 99, 102, 104
Thomas, Danny 79
Thomas, Lowell 1
Thompson, Fresco 144
Tiger, Dick 81
Times Farm 60
S.S. *Titanic* 21
Tracy, Spencer 15
Transportation Security Administration 81
Travelers Broadcasting Service Corporation 28, 73
The Travelers Club 33
The Travelers Insurance Company 21, 22, 60, 62, 69, 90, 93